Le Mans 2006.
July 2006
Le Mans Classic

FORD
GT
Then, and Now
VELOCE PUBLISHING
THE PUBLISHER OF FINE AUTOMOTIVE BOOKS

First published in June 2006 by Veloce Publishing Limited, 33 Trinity Street, Dorchester DT1 1TT, England. Fax 01305 268864/e-mail info@veloce.co.uk/web www.veloce.co.uk or www.velocebooks.com
ISBN: 1-84584-054-2. ISBN 13: 978-1-84584-054-9. UPC 636847-04054-3

Readers with ideas for automotive books, or books on other transport or related hobby subjects, are invited to write to the editorial director of Veloce Publishing at the above address.
British Library Cataloguing in Publication Data - A catalogue record for this book is available from the British Library. Typesetting, design and page make-up all by Veloce Publishing Ltd on Apple Mac.
Printed in Italy by Grafiche Flaminia.

Dedication

Dedication

This book is dedicated to a mad Australian and a crazy Scotsman whose great sportsmanship, professionalism, and above all else friendship, is what this book stands for.

Paul Hawkins, the mad Aussie, and Eric Liddell, the crazy Scotsman, were the very best of friends during their short, but action-packed motor racing careers.

Both drove Ford GTs. Eric drove for and against Paul Hawkins on more than one occasion, and when they weren't racing hard they were playing hard.

Paul Hawkins left this world doing what he loved; he was killed when his Lola T70 crashed at Island Bend during the 1969 Tourist Trophy race at Oulton Park. Eric Liddell survived the 1960s and went on to build himself a life. Part of that life is his son Robin, whose talent for race car driving has led to a successful professional career of his own.

Paul Hawkins and Eric Liddell are motor racing. One died and one survived, but their friendship and their legacy are part of the legend that is *The Ford GT, Then and Now.*

Eric Liddell, left, and Paul Hawkins at Le Mans in 1968. Eric was driving for the Strathaven team and Paul was driving for the J.W.A.-Gulf team. Contributor: Eric Liddell

Contents

Foreword

I felt very honoured to be invited by Adrian Streather to write the foreword to this book about the Ford GT then and now, for the Ford GT is without doubt one of the most exciting and enjoyable cars ever built, both originally in the 1960s and now in the 21st century. I remember very clearly in 1967 aged a mere nineteen years old, when my father Duncan Hamilton bought Ford GT MkI chassis number 1045 from the Girling Brake Company for £3000. The car had only 1800 miles on the clock, its exterior finished in a dark blue metallic, and was fitted with power assisted brakes and a 4-barrel Holley carburettor. Chassis no. 1045 was kept within the Hamilton family for approximately thirteen years. I remember many enjoyable drives in the car when my father was not using it as his daily drive to the office or the shops.

1045 and I became good friends, I raced her, I sprinted her, and I crashed her, albeit lightly following the filming of a new Texaco television advertisement that took place on the Croydon by-pass. I was paid £250 for the filming and did £300 worth of damage, not a good day. One very memorable drive was following a New Year's Eve party with Frank and Ginny Williams in Crowthorne, Berkshire. I looked out of the window at approximately 3.00am to discover that there had been a large snowfall and I still had to drive approximately twelve miles home in the Ford GT. We both made it home but, looking back, it was a drive that should not have been made considering my physical and mental condition, if you know what I mean?

Having bought and sold in excess of seventeen Ford GTs during my business life, I still feel the Ford GT, then and now, is ageless in design and concept. This feeling was clearly shared by the current management of the Ford Motor Co., as they've recently produced the new Ford GT which is an admirable successor to the original.

Adrian Hamilton

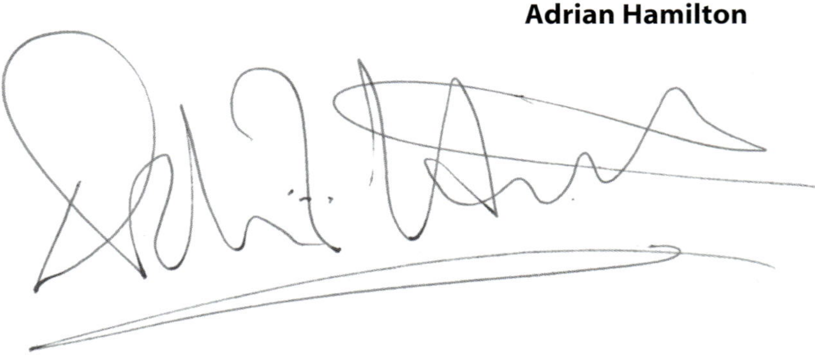

Introduction

Why this book was written

This book was inspired by my friendship with some special people, combined with what I enjoy doing the most; driving fast cars.

Eric Liddell and Sir Malcolm Guthrie are former racing drivers from the 1960s, and both spent a lot of time in the driver's seat of the Ford GT (GT40). I had always wanted to do a book about them, and their colleagues, but never had the correct angle to write something new.

Then I was contacted by my friend and freelance journalist Richard Truesdell in mid-2005. Richard, via Paul Harrison of Ford Europe and David Jones of Roush UK, invited me to join the first new Ford GT European road trip. I accepted, and the rest, as they say, is history.

I also have to say a very special thank you to Claude Nahum who opened his collection, his photographs, his knowledge, and his friendship to me. Claude's involvement took this book and its contents to a level I never thought achievable.

What is this book about?

History is the crystal ball in which we are each able to glimpse our own future. Time is one very large merry-go-round, what goes around comes around. Great ideas never fade away; they just go out of fashion until the merry-go-round of time decides to bring them back.

In the early 1960s, the first generation of low production supercars was appearing. Many of these supercars supported prototype racing car programs, but Ford was not among them. In 1963, Lee Iacocca told Henry Ford that he believed the company needed to develop a supercar and a prototype racing program to raise its profile worldwide. Ford needed something that would defeat "those fast little red cars" from Ferrari, which included the 330 P2/P3/P4 Prototypes and the 250LM series. Lee's words to Henry resulted in the creation of an enduring legend. The project may have got off to a shaky start, but by 1966 it was firing on all eight cylinders.

Grovewood Trophy race at Mallory Park in May 1966. Eric Liddell driving the rather battered Ford GT. MkI chassis no. 1022 leads the Ford GT MkI chassis no. 1021 of Richard Bond. Contributor: Eric Liddell

The 21st century Ford GT was reborn under very similar circumstances to those in the 1960s. Ford's old nemesis down in Maranello, Italy, was still churning out classic supercars. The sleek Ferrari 360 Modena and the new F430 occupied the ground once held by the revered Ford GT of the 1960s.

It was time for Ford to take on "those fast little red cars" again.

Adrian Streather

Twenty-first century Ford GT on a day out with the author and his wife Gail. Contributor: Adrian Streather

Pit stop in a small German village after a high speed Autobahn run. A preventative check is being carried out by the Ford team, Chris and Zoran, whilst Richard (back left) and Adrian (back right) look on. The photograph was taken by fellow team member Matt Malone. Contributor: Matt Malone

Acknowledgements

No book is ever complete without the enthusiastic contributions of others. I have been very lucky during the writing of this book to obtain contributions not just from official sources, but from former Ford GT drivers and private individuals with a passion for the Ford GT, old and new.

This section is designed to highlight, acknowledge, and thank, all those who have so enthusiastically contributed.

Ford GT driver contributors

Adrian Hamilton (UK).
Adrian Streather (CH/AUS).
Armin Hahne (D).
Chris Jackson (UK).
Claude Nahum (CH).
Colin Crabbe (UK).
David Piper (UK).
Derek Bell (UK).
Eric Liddell (SCO).
Matt Malone (USA).
Richard Truesdell (USA).
Sir Malcolm Guthrie (UK).
Vern Schuppan (AUS).

Factory contributors

Dr. Ing. h. c. F. Porsche AG historical archives, Jens Torner (D).
Ford Motor Co., Paul Harrison (EU).
Ford Motor Co., Steve Crosby (USA).
Ford Public Affairs (USA).
Lola Cars International, Nick Jordan, Sam Davies (UK).
Lola Heritage Archives, Glyn Jones UK).
Roush, David Jones and Chris Jackson (UK).

Club contributors

British Racing Drivers Club (B.R.D.C.) Silverstone (UK).
Greg Kolasa, GT40 Registrar, Shelby American Automobile Club (USA).
Owner contributors:
Buzz Clarke (USA).
Graham Endeacott (UK).
Geoff Hurrell (ZA).
James Holden (USA).
Joseph Feinburg (CDN).
Paul Allen (USA).
Paul Roos (ZA).
Tom Hughes (USA).

Commercial contributors

Bob Putnam, ERA Replica Automobiles (USA).
David Harvey, GT40NZ (NZ).
John Spence, Auto Futura (ZA).
Simon Farrell, Gloster Cars (UK).
Mark Sibley, M.D.A. Cars (UK).

Publication contributors

Charles Harbord, *Cars for the Connoisseur* Monthly Newsletter (UK).
Glen Smale, *Automotive Research* (UK).

Photographers

David Wendt (USA).
Douglas Anderson (USA).
Evan Selwyn-Smith (UK). Collection provided courtesy of Ted Walker (UK).
Ford Advanced Vehicles (UK).
Gail Streather (AUS).
Gérard Crombac (F). Collection provided courtesy of C. Nahum (CH).
Günther Asshauer (D).
Howard Barker (UK). Collection provided courtesy of Ted Walker (UK).
les Coyotes (F).
Manfred Förster (D).
Martin Rössler (D).
Matt Malone (USA).
Paul Sands (UK).
Peter Sands (UK).
Richard Truesdell (USA).
Udo Klinkel (D).
Veit Arenz (D).
Wolfgang Kohm (D).

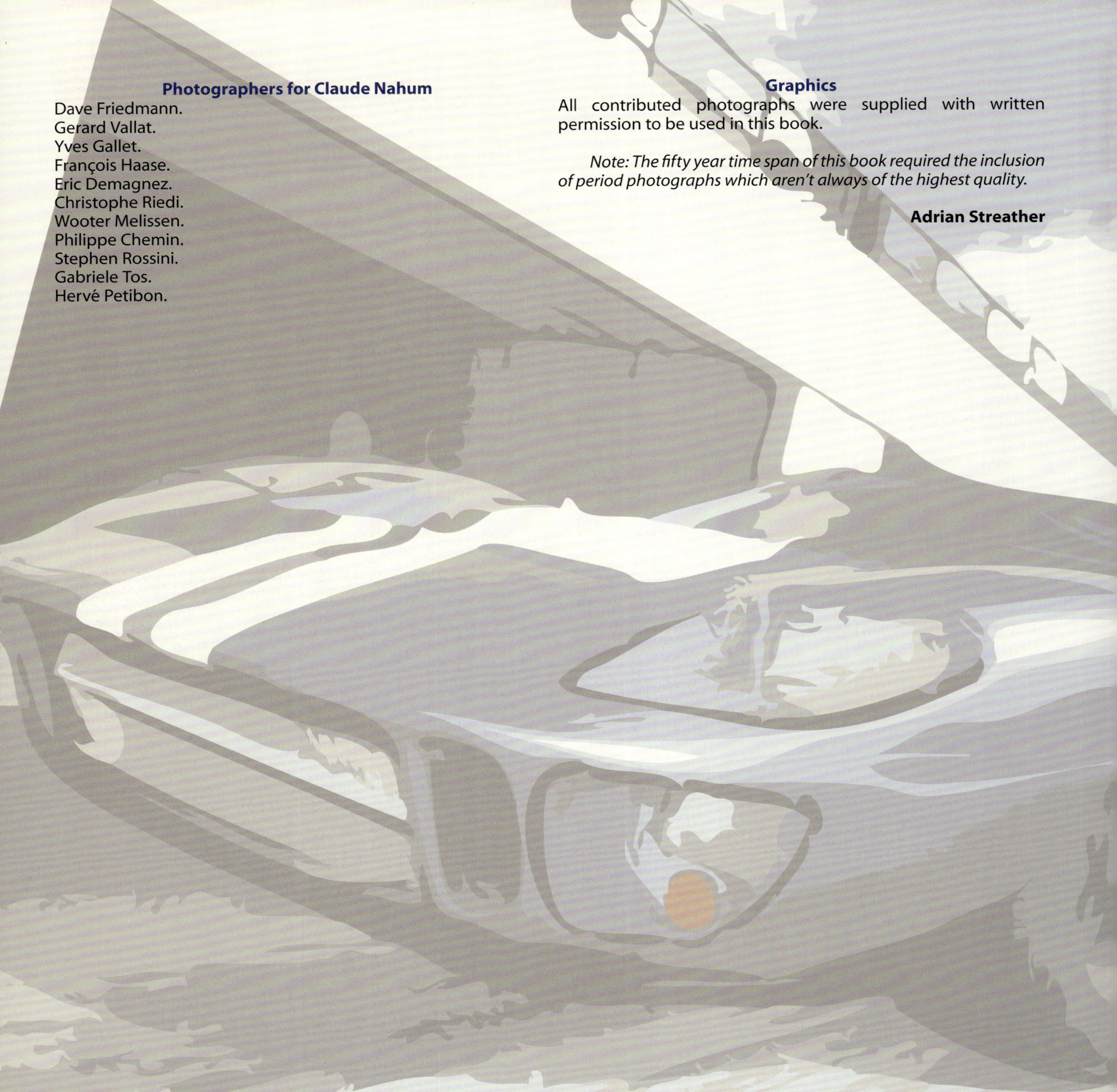

Photographers for Claude Nahum

Dave Friedmann.
Gerard Vallat.
Yves Gallet.
François Haase.
Eric Demagnez.
Christophe Riedi.
Wooter Melissen.
Philippe Chemin.
Stephen Rossini.
Gabriele Tos.
Hervé Petibon.

Graphics

All contributed photographs were supplied with written permission to be used in this book.

Note: The fifty year time span of this book required the inclusion of period photographs which aren't always of the highest quality.

Adrian Streather

One

Last in, first to glory

Last in

In 1956, Henry Ford II decided that the Ford Motor Company would develop a factory racing team to compete against the other major American car manufacturers in the domestic NASCAR stock car series created by Bill France, in 1947. Ford was the last of the major American car manufacturers to compete with an official factory team in the NASCAR series. Pete De Paolo was recruited in 1956 to set up and run the new Ford racing team and, although De Paolo's tenure at Ford was short, it was clear that Henry Ford II was going for glory.

Ford's exploits within the American racing scene, which included NASCAR, drag racing, and at Indianapolis, soon caught the attention of its competitors. The company would establish a solid relationship with Carroll Shelby, even though in 1957 he was driving a Ferrari in direct competition with Ford cars. Shelby, in association with Ford, would later go on to reach legendary status with the Ford Mustang, AC Cobra racing cars and with his involvement in the Le Mans-winning Ford GT project.

Henry Ford II was highly motivated by his burning desire to make Ford a global car manufacturer. He knew that he had to make his products relevant to the young people of the world. Ten years after the end of the Second World War the Western World's economy was well on the way to recovery, and a new phrase had entered the business vocabulary: "the consumer". Affluent younger people had become a very significant consumer group and they were now purchasing cars in ever-increasing numbers.

Henry Ford II knew he would have to win at both Indianapolis and at Le Mans to gain the real credibility the Ford brand needed to appeal to a younger age group. These races were, and still are, the greatest motor races in the world (one for endurance and the other for out-and-out bravery in an open-wheeled racing car). For Henry Ford, the battle for supremacy on the race track - and in the showrooms - was about to be stepped up a few gears. Whatever it took, he would do it ...

Pete De Paolo talking to Joe Weatherly, Ford Team driver, at the Daytona Beach Speed Weeks event in 1956. Contributor: Ford Motor Company

Ford had to wait until 1965 for its first win at the Indianapolis 500, when Scotsman – and arguably the greatest racing car driver of all time – Jim Clark, took the chequered flag. Contributor: Ford Motor Company

Henry Ford II initially tried to take the easy route to success at Le Mans. In the spring of 1963, based on an idea originally formulated by Lee Iacocca, Henry attempted to purchase the Ferrari car company, based in Maranello, Italy. Ford dispatched General Manager Donald Frey and a team of six experts to meet with Ferrari founder Enzo Ferrari. To cut a long story short, Ford was told his offer of US$10 million was an insult, and Enzo Ferrari turned it down flat. The world did not even discover this offer had been made until the end of 1965, and then the European Press, along with the massive Ferrari fanbase, was not impressed.

Only months before Henry attempted to purchase Ferrari, a small English racing car manufacturer named Lola, founded by Eric Broadley, started work on its first GT sports car. The Lola MkVI GT featured a steel monocoque chassis with the radiator and suspension supported by a front subframe. The engine and Colotti transaxle were attached to the chassis, with the gearbox and rear bulkhead supporting the rear suspension. The suspension used a double wishbone design with coilovers. The MkVI GT's wheelbase was shorter than that of the Lola single seater, but was designed to accept a large Ford V8 engine. The low drag coupé body with short front and rear overhangs was manufactured from fibreglass. The doors, which also included part of the roof, were designed to allow for quick racing driver changes. The Lola MkVI GT was one of the first racing cars with a roof-mounted air intake for the engine, while the use of commercial Ford parts, such as the rear lights from the MkI Cortina, helped reduce costs.

The first Lola MkVI GT was never fitted with an engine – it was only used as show/concept car.

The second Lola MkVI GT, featuring an aluminium monocoque chassis, was the version that Lola took racing. Fitted with a Ford V8 engine, the Lola MkVI GT had its first race at Silverstone in May 1963, followed by the 1000km race at the Nürburgring, in Germany.

Whilst the factory Lola MkVI GT chassis no. 2 was busy racing, Lola was building a third car, also with an aluminium monocoque chassis, for the 1963 Le Mans race.

Many team owners say that nothing is ever easy when preparing for Le Mans and, after its experiences in 1963, the Lola factory team would have agreed with this statement. Eric Broadley drove the Lola MkVI GT from his factory to Le Mans, but he arrived too late for official scrutineering. Luckily for Eric, despite his late arrival, the ACO officials were so impressed with the car that they decided to inspect it anyway.

Lola MkVI GT on show in 1963. Contributor: Lola Heritage Archives-Glyn Jones

The Lola MkVI GT at the Nürburgring 1000km in 1963. Contributor: Udo Klinkel

The unusual, central, roof-mounted engine air-intake immediately attracted the ACO's attention and it quickly became apparent that the ACO Officials believed it blocked the driver's rear vision. Lola removed the roof-mounted air-intake and quickly fitted redesigned engine air-intakes on each side of the car instead. The ACO officials weren't happy with the excessive fuel tank capacity either. This issue was quickly solved in a novel way: empty bottles were placed into the fuel tank to reduce its capacity. Once this work was completed, the ACO officials passed the Lola MkVI GT as eligible to race.

Unfortunately, with the all scrutineering problems, Lola had no time for track testing, resulting in some set up errors, including using the wrong set of gear ratios to allow maximum speed to be reached on the Mulsanne straight. Fifteen hours into the race, driver David Hobbs crashed due to a gearbox failure at high speed. This accident ended the very short racing career of the Lola MkVI GT, but it was the beginning of something very much bigger ...

The Lola MkVI GT is uncovered for the start of Le Mans 1963. Contributor: Lola Heritage Archives-Glyn Jones

Eric Broadley (left) and John Wyer with the Lola MkVI GT – three of the most important factors in the eventual success of the Ford GT racing program.
Contributor: Lola Heritage Archives-Glyn Jones

Note: Little did Henry Ford II realise that, by the time Ford officially quit the Ford GT program at the end of 1967, it would have spent in excess of US$250 million ... Many within the company may have questioned whether it was worth it, but the racing fans of the world know better.

By the end of 1969 the total number of Ford GTs produced worldwide was one hundred and twenty seven. This number includes the twelve (instead of ten) F.A.V.-produced prototypes. F.A.V. built all the MkI, MkII and MkIII Ford GT chassis (tub) assemblies. Kar-Kraft in the USA built eight J-car series (MkIV) chassis assemblies that were used in the Ford GT program. Alan Mann Racing used a special chassis number for the Ford GT P40, along with three exclusive X-series chassis assemblies. J.W.A. produced at least three Mirage M1 chassis assemblies which when all combined, boosted the final Ford GT series production numbers.

Note: The basic chassis (tub) assemblies for the MkI/II/IIA and IIB were essentially the same. Spare numbered chassis assemblies, and bare non-numbered chassis frame assemblies were also produced, many of which were used in rebuilding wrecked Ford GTs in the 1970s. Four spare J-car chassis assemblies were built. Two were used for the Ford G7A Spyder CamAm series car and the remaining two to create new build Ford GT MkIVs in the 1980s.

A chance to make history

Henry Ford II was very unhappy after he discovered that not only had Ferrari turned down his purchase offer, but had totally dominated Le Mans in 1963 with, not only the overall win, but also filling second through to sixth places as well. For Henry Ford II the major goal in life became simply to beat "those fast little red cars". The Ford versus Ferrari racing war was underway, but Ford needed a battle plan ... and a new racing car design.

In order to speed up its plans, Ford created a subsidiary company named "Ford Advanced Vehicles", which it established in Slough, England, under the management of John Wyer who was already well known in the motor racing world because of his association with Aston Martin.

Ron Lunn, the manager of the Ford Motor Company Advanced Concepts Division, was brought in as chief designer, and Eric Broadley was hired to assist Ron Lunn and John Wyer during the design and prototype testing of the new racing car.

Ford was so impressed with the Lola MkVI GT design that it purchased the two aluminium monocoque chassis racing cars from Lola and used them as its inspiration and design base. Project engineering work began in August 1963.

Ford Advanced Vehicles (F.A.V.) under its European Manager (his official title), John Wyer, was contracted to produce one hundred Ford GTs, consisting of ten Ford GT prototypes and ninety road and race Ford GT production models.

1964

By February 1964, Ford decided that the construction of the chassis had to be changed. Gone was the aluminium monocoque, to be replaced by a more traditional spot-welded and longitudinally stiffened steel chassis. A separate assembly attached to the back of the monocoque supported the mid-mounted engine, transmission, and rear suspension and rear bodywork.

The basis of the Ford GT monocoque was the transverse bulkhead which formed the rear of the seats, while the seat pans were designed to be an integral part of the floor. Leg room was adjusted by moving the pedals backwards or forwards.

The rear suspension layout used a widely spaced set of transverse links with long radius arms as originally designed by Eric Broadley. The front wishbone and coilover suspension system was also retained.

The chosen engine was the all aluminium, dry sump, quad cam, fuel injected Indianapolis version of the Ford Fairlane 255in^3 (4.2 litre) V8. This version of the engine provided 350bhp (261kW)

Heading home. The Ford GT prototype is loaded aboard an aircraft for the return journey. Contributor: Ford Motor Company

Ford GT MkI prototype in New York in early 1964 for an inspection by the Ford Motor Company management. Once accepted, it was flown back to England for the race test program. Contributor: Ford Motor Company

The original 289 engine.
Contributor: Ford Motor Company

at 7200rpm and maximum torque was 275lbft (372.8Nm) at 5600rpm. Only the first two Ford GT MkI prototypes were fitted with this power unit.

Power was transmitted to the rear wheels via an unsynchronised Colotti 4-speed transaxle type transmission, with ratios of:

- First gear: 2.50:1.
- Second gear: 1.70:1.
- Third gear: 1.29:1.
- Fourth gear: 1:1.
- The final drive ratio: 3.09:1.

The basic body assembly was also manufactured from steel, but many of the body panels were made from GRP material as per the original Lola MkVI design. However, while the entire body was based on a Ford Detroit Engineering Department design. Ford did incorporate the Lola pioneered canopy doors.

Unfortunately, Eric Broadley did not last long with the Ford GT team. Shortly into his one year contract he decided to leave

The Ford GT MkI prototype in its original 1964 configuration.
Contributor: Ford Motor Company

the project when he discovered that Ford planned to change his aluminium monocoque chassis (tub) to a steel one. Serious arguments had broken out between Eric Broadley and the Ford management over the Ford design team's belief that the steel chassis could be shared by both the race and road versions of the Ford GT. Eric Broadley believed that the steel chassis would impede the competitiveness of the racing car. The differences could not be bridged so Eric Broadley went back to designing and building his own racing cars.

Despite this setback, the Ford GT (now unofficially dubbed the GT40 because its roof was only 40.5in (1028mm) above the ground), was on its way towards its rollout and racing debut.

The Ford GT's first racing season

During 1964 the factory team Ford GT racing cars were entered for the 1000km race at the Nürburgring, the Le Mans 24 hours, and 12 hour endurance events at Reims and Nassau.

Testing at Le Mans in April 1964 was an abject disaster. Both the prototypes, driven by Jo Schlesser and Roy Salvadori, crashed. The accident involving Jo Schlesser on the Mulsanne straight was

The Ford GT being prepared for its first race at the Nürburgring in 1964. Contributor: Ford Motor Company

Bruce McLaren and Phil Hill discuss the Ford GT's lack of high speed stability after their first practice at the Nürburgring in 1964. Contributor: Ford Motor Company

The Ford GT MkI prototype, driven by Phil Hill, in action at the Nürburgring in 1964. Contributor: Ford Motor Company

Phil Hill flat out in the rain at the Nürburgring. Contributor: Ford Motor Company

Conditions were better for Bruce McLaren at the Nürburgring. It was dry. Contributor: Ford Motor Company

Ford GT, car no. 140, again under the control of Bruce McLaren, at the Nürburgring. Contributor: Ford Motor Company

described by the Press at the time as one of the most horrifying ever witnessed. The aerodynamics of the new Ford GT were seriously inadequate for high speed.

Both the wrecked Ford GTs had to be rebuilt and, as part of the process, modifications to the body profile and adjustments to the aerodynamic trimming devices were incorporated.

The next race on the schedule for the Ford GT factory team was the Nürburgring 1000km. Unfortunately, both the team entries failed to finish, a result the team and Ford's new racing fans would have to get used to for the rest of the 1964 racing season.

Le Mans 1964

Three Ford GT MkIs were entered for Le Mans in 1964:

- Car no. 10 driven by Phil Hill, USA, and Bruce McLaren, NZ.
- Car no. 11 driven by Richie Ginther, USA, and Masten Gregory, USA.
- Car no. 12 driven by Richard Attwood, GB, and Jo Schlesser, France.

Ford GT MkI, car no. 10, undergoes scrutineering for Le Mans 1964. Contributor: Ford Motor Company

One of two major achievements by the factory Ford GT team at Le Mans was that American driver Phil Hill broke the lap record. He lapped the Sarthe circuit in 3 minutes 49.2 seconds at an average speed of 131.37mph (211.42kph). Only the 4.0 litre Ferraris were able to match this speed.

The other major achievement was that a Ford GT MkI led for 110 laps at speeds of up to 207mph (333kph) down the Mulsanne straight, before its transmission broke. Mechanical failures, especially with the transmission, would dog the Ford GT throughout its racing life.

Car no. 11 in action in the Esses.
Contributor: Ford Motor Company

Ford GT MkI, car no. 10, driven by Bruce McLaren, in the Esses at Le Mans being chased by the Aston Martin DP 214 driven by Mike Salmon.
Contributor: Ford Motor Company

Car no. 12 in action at Le Mans 1964. Notice that there's no pit wall separating the pits from the track. It would be many years before this was finally changed. Contributor: Ford Motor Company

A rare colour picture of car no. 12 in action during Le Mans, driven by Richard Attwood, being chased by a Ferrari. The Henry Ford II plan worked, at least for a while. Contributor: Ford Motor Company

The 1964 racing season was rounded out with the factory team competing the 12 hour endurance events at Reims in France and racing in the Speed Week in the Bahamas. The results from both events were unspectacular.

At Reims all three Ford GTs were eliminated with engine and gearbox failures. Phil Hill brought a smile to the faces of the team bosses by finishing third during the 5-lap race in Nassau. This was the first podium finish for the fledgling Ford GT project.

The end of the beginning

At the end of 1964 John Wyer lost the management responsibility for the Ford factory racing program. He retained overall responsibility for the Ford GT customer racing car program and the development of the road cars. He also retained responsibility for building every chassis (tub) assembly which would be used for all models and versions of the Ford GT (except the J-car MkIV) from 1965 onwards.

Ford USA then split its factory racing program into two parts. The actual works team racing program was under the management of Carroll Shelby at American Shelby Inc., whilst Detroit-based Ford subsidiary company Kar-Kraft was charged with the design and development of the racing car program.

Note: Despite having total control over the entire Ford GT racing program, Carroll Shelby was forced to build all his racing cars for the American teams (MkI, MkII, MkIIA and MkIIB versions) around the English-built chassis (tub) assembly. He only managed to break free from the English connection with the J-car (MkIV) series.

The works team of Holman Moody entered the official Ford GT works team program in 1966 (see Chapter 2) and received its Ford GTs from Shelby American Inc. fully assembled. Upon delivery Holman Moody's in-house race mechanics would then pull the cars apart and rebuild them to its own racing specifications and install its own data plate.

Time to get serious

During the off season months of 1964 considerable effort was expended to fix the GT's gearbox problems, along with rear end instability, braking, and engine power problems.

The diversifying development work, started in 1964 and continued into 1965, resulted in three versions of the Ford GT being developed for the 1965 racing season. These were:

- MkI Coupé with a 289in^3 (4.7 litre) engine.
- MkII Coupé with a 427in^3 (7.0 litre) engine.
- Ford GT Roadster with a 289in^3 (4.7 litre) engine.

Note: Race records show a 5.3 litre engine fitted into one Ford GT in 1965.

Ford GT MkI Coupé (4.7 litre)

The original Indy all aluminium twin-cam V8 engine was replaced by the 289in^3 (4.7 litre) Ford Fairlane 500 engine. This new, cast-iron, wet-sump, V8 racing engine provided 380bhp (283.3kW) at 6500rpm with 330lbft (447.4Nm) of torque at 5500rpm. The main external difference between the production engine and the racing engine was that the racing engine was fitted with 4 Weber 48 IDA double choke carburettors.

The Ford GT's nagging gearbox problems were alleged to have been resolved by the ZF (Zahnradfabrik) gearbox company in Friedrichshafen, Germany. The ZF company designed a new 5-speed synchronised transaxle, type 5DS-25, weighing in at 127lb (57.6kg) with gear ratios of:

- First gear: 2.42:1.
- Second gear: 1.47:1.
- Third gear: 1.09:1.
- Fourth gear: 0.96:1.
- Fifth gear: 0.85:1.
- Reverse gear: 3.75:1.
- Final drive ratio: 3.33:1 (optional) or 4.22:1 (standard).

Bruce McLaren was one of the test drivers hired by Ford to help solve the GT40's stability problems. The car's rear end instability was cured by the installation of a full width rear wing.

ZF 5-speed transaxle transmission used in the Ford GT MkI from 1965 onwards. Contributor: C. Nahum Collection; photograph by Gérard Crombac

Bruce McLaren driving the Shelby American Inc. car, number 10, at the Le Mans trials in 1965. The car featured a different nose design as part of the aerodynamic trial. The car was also tested by Ken Miles and Bob Bondurant in this configuration. Contributor: C. Nahum Collection; photograph by Gérard Crombac

The Ford GT MkII driven by Ken Miles and Bruce McLaren at Le Mans in 1965 fitted with the 'droop snoot' nose. Contributor: Ford Motor Company

The final issue that had to be resolved before Le Mans 1965 was the nose shape. The requirement to carry a spare wheel in the front which, at Le Mans, had to be removed and replaced during pit stops, required some design compromises. To quote Ford directly: "an extended droop snoot will be seen on the team Ford GTs on June nineteenth 1965".

Ford Advanced Vehicles (F.A.V.) customer racing program

A ready to race, 1965 customer racing version of the Ford GT MkI cost £6900. The cars were made available for sale to the privateer teams quite early in 1965. The first purchasers included Essex Wire Corporation, Peter Sutcliffe, R.R.C. Walker Racing Team, Scuderia Filipinetti, Fred English and Colonel Hoare.

Note: Some of these teams purchased their Ford GTs via Shelby American Inc.

Parts and production for the Ford GT MkI racing car were out-sourced to a number of companies:

- The main steel body pressing was delivered to Slough as a complete assembly from Abbey Panels Ltd of Coventry.
- The nose, tail and door sections were manufactured by Fibre Glass Engineering Ltd of Farnham.
- Initial assembly took place in Slough to create a complete shell. The shell was then delivered to the well respected coach builder Harold Radford's premises where it was upholstered, trimmed and painted, and the Marchal lights (imported from France) were fitted.
- The shell was then returned to Slough for the fitting of the running gear, including front and rear suspension, the Girling disc brakes, and the steering mechanism. At the same time, the V8 engine from Dearborn, Detroit, was mated to the ZF transmission. The final job was to install the Borrani wire racing wheels imported from Italy.

Note: When Ford brought Carroll Shelby into the project he brought with him an affiliation with Halibrand. However, as more traction was needed, wider wheels were the order of the day which required yet another change of wheel manufacturer. Ford Advanced Vehicles (F.A.V.) in England first used magnesium wheels from the BRM company, and then started casting its own wheels in-house.

The specifications show, the F.A.V.-developed customer racing car was a formidable and competitive package, easily capable of going head-to-head with the Group 4 Ferraris and the pesky new Porsches from Zuffenhausen, Germany.

F.A.V. Ford GT MkI racing car specifications

Dimensions:

- Wheelbase: 95in (2413mm).
- Track – front: 55in (1397mm).
- Track – rear: 55in (1397mm).
- Length: 168in (4265mm).
- Width: 70in (1778mm).
- Height: 40.5in (1028.7mm).
- Minimum ground clearance: 4in (101.6mm).
- Weight (with oil and water, without fuel):
- Front: 920lb (414kg).
- Rear: 1080lb (486kg).
- Total: 2000lb (900kg).

Ford GT MkI, chassis number 1022, awaits delivery to its first owner, Nick Cuthbert, at the Ford Advanced Vehicles facility in Slough, England. Contributor: Eric Liddell

Body:

- The Ford GT main body assembly was constructed using a semi-monocoque from 0.024in (0.61mm) thickness steel. The doors, and front and rear sections were manufactured from reinforced fibreglass. The front and rear sections were fitted with hinges to allow easy access during pit stops.

Engine:

- Cylinders: 8.
- Bore: 4in (101.6mm).
- Stroke: 2.87in (72.9mm).
- Displacement: 289in^3 (4.7 litre).
- Compression ratio: 10:1.
- Maximum bhp (kW): 380 (283) at 6500 rpm.
- Maximum torque lbft (Nm): 330 (447) at 5500rpm.
- Carburettors: 4 Weber 48 IDA.
- Engine oil capacity: 8qt (imp) or 10qt (USA) or 9.1 litres.

Transmission:

- 5-speed ZF-5DS-25 manual transaxle.

Clutch:

- Type: Borg & Beck 3-plate.
- Clutch plate diameter: 7.25in (184.15mm).

The Ford GT MkI racing car 'office'. Contributor: Eric Liddell

Ford GT MkI chassis (tub). Contributor: Claude Nahum

289 (4.7 litre) V8 fitted to the Ford GT MkI. This is a later version with the Gurney-Eagle (Weslake) aluminium dry-deck heads. The 5-speed ZF transaxle is also fitted to the engine. Contributor: Claude Nahum

Ford GT MkI body. Contributor: Claude Nahum

Borg and Beck clutch assembly. Contributor: Claude Nahum

Brakes:

- Front type: Girling CR.
- Disc diameter: 11.5in. (292.1mm).
- Rear type: Girling BR.
- Disc diameter: 11.5in (292.1mm).

Note: The standard customer racing version of the Ford GT MkI was delivered with Girling solid rotors (discs). Ventilated rotors were offered as an option later by F.A.V. and then J.W. Automotive. Many of the privateer team owners specified the cheaper solid rotors over the protests of their contracted drivers. It took a long time for many of these team owners to retrofit their racing cars with ventilated Girling rotors.

Steering:

- Type: Rack and pinion.
- Steering ratio (overall): 14:1.
- Turns (lock to lock): 2.8.
- Turning circle diameter: 37ft (11.27m).
- Steering wheel diameter: 15in (381mm).
- Steering wheel adjustment: 2in (50.8mm).

Wheels and tyres:

- Wheels: Borrani wire-spoke, light alloy.
- Front: 6.5 x 15in.
- Rear: 8.00 x 15in.
- Tyres (Dunlop).
- Front (size): 5.5 x 15in.
- Rear (size): 7.25 x 15in.
- Tyres (Goodyear).
- Front (size): 5.5 x 15in.

- Rear (size): 7.00 x 15in.
- Optional front 15 x 8in Halibrand alloy with Goodyear or Dunlop racing tyres.
- Optional rear 15 x 9.5in Halibrand alloy with Goodyear or Dunlop racing tyres.

Fuel system:
- Fuel tanks: Goodyear fuel cells, capacity of 30.5 (imp) gallons or 37 (USA) gallons or 140 litres).
- Fuel pumps: 2 Stewart Warner 240A.

Cooling system:
- Radiator type: 3in (76.2mm) deep, Marston light alloy.
- Total area: 318.75in (2056cm).
- Oil cooler type: 2in (50.8mm) deep, Serck light alloy.
- Total area: 53.2in (343cm).

Exhaust system:
- Tuned cross-over with a pipe diameter of 1.5in (38.1mm).

Electrical system:
- 12V with a battery capacity of 57amp/hr.

Eric Liddell was contracted to drive Ford MkI chassis no. 1022 by J. Norman (Nick) Cuthbert. Eric is seen here trying out his new office at delivery. Contributor: Eric Liddell

The newly delivered Ford GT MkI, chassis no. 1022, is soon put to work. Its first race was at the Croft Autodrome circuit. Contributor: Eric Liddell

Above: Ford GT MkI chassis no. 1010 was originally delivered to the Essex Wire Corporation in August 1965. It soldiered on well into 1970 as a front line race car. Contributor: Paul Sands

Ford GT MkII Coupé (7.0 litre):

The Ford GT MkII represented a major upgrade when compared to its older MkI sibling. Out went the 289in^3 (4.7 litre) V8 engine, to be replaced by the heavier, cast-iron Ford 427in^3 (7.0 litre) V8 engine. The new engine weighed in at 550lb (249.5kg). Varying engine power output figures have been found, depending upon which magazine article, newspaper or author one reads.
Other changes incorporated included:

- 4-speed Ford (Kar-Kraft) T44 transaxle transmission. This installation required the seating position to be moved slightly forward. The engine water pump position created a bulge between the seats, therefore the ring bulkhead at the rear of the frame had to be modified.

Ford GT MkII with its huge 427 engine exposed at Le Mans in 1965. Contributor: Ford Motor Company

Kar-Kraft 4-speed transaxle transmission. Contributor: Adrian Streather

Ford GT MkII, car no. 2, driven by Chris Amon and Phil Hill at Le Mans in 1965. Contributor: Ford Motor Company

- A completely redesigned front end structure carried the wider and thicker crossflow radiator. The increased area in the front end allowed for an improved air ducting system to the new radiator.
- A new oil tank for the dry sump engine was installed in the cowl behind the spare wheel.
- The new extended nose allowed the fitting of pressure relief vents just ahead of the doors.
- Improved air-intake ducting to the carburettors.

When the MkII was finally tested by Ken Miles and Walt Hansgen, they found a racing car capable of sustaining 200mph (320kph) race speeds all day, or until something broke which, sadly for the Ford GT - of all kinds - was a common occurrence.

For the 1965 racing season the original MkII was only made available to the works team of Shelby American Inc.

Ford GT MkII-X1 Roadster

The Ford company loved its secrets, and the X1 Roadster was one of them. Deemed a special experimental version of the 427 (7.0 litre)-powered Ford GT MkII, the Ford USA-funded X1 project was secretly built around the wrecked F.A.V. MkI Roadster, chassis no. 110. The work was carried out by Gary Knutson and Howden Ganley in a sealed section of the McLaren workshops in Middlesex, England.

The X1 Roadster's first race was at the *Los Angeles Times* Grand Prix held at the Riverside International Raceway at the end of October 1965, where it was entered by Bruce McLaren's team and driven by Chris Amon. The X1 finished fifth. The car was then entered by the same team, again with Chris Amon driving, at Mosport in Canada where it failed to impress. It's believed that the X1 was fitted with a semi-automatic transmission for these races. See Chapter 2 for the MkIIA-X1 Roadster version description, a model which was, in effect, the X1 modified to 1966 MkIIA racing specifications.

Ford GT MkI Roadster

Ford Advanced Vehicles (F.A.V.) built two Ford GT MkI Roadsters. The Roadster was a 4.7 litre Ford GT MkI with the top canopy section of the doors and the roof centre support structure removed. The windows remained in the doors, and could be wound up and down as required.

The first Roadster, chassis no. 110, made its first public appearance at Le Mans testing in April 1965, driven by Sir John Whitmore. The first and last race for chassis no. 110 as a MkI Roadster was at the Nürburgring 1000km in 1965.

In May 1965, chassis no. 110 was wrecked in a testing or practice accident. The wreck was shipped to Bruce McLaren, and Sir John Whitmore had to go to Le Mans in 1965 with Ford GT MkI Coupé chassis no. 1006.

Ford GT MkI Roadster, chassis no. 110, at the Nürburgring 1000km in 1965. Contributor: Günther Asshauer-Udo Klinkel Collection

The second F.A.V.-built Ford MkI Roadster, chassis no. 112, was entered for Le Mans in 1965 by Ford France. Carrying car number 15, it was driven by Frenchmen Maurice Trintignant and Guy Ligier, but did not finish.

Note: For Le Mans 1966, the Ford GT MkI Roadster, chassis no. 112, was converted back into a Coupé by the Ford France team. Chassis no. 112 still carried car no. 15 and, like its Roadster alter ego, it failed to finish.

Note: Chassis nos. 112 (UK) and 1006 (France) still exist. See Chapter 8.

1965 racing season

In 1964, the Ford GT racing program was a full Ford factory effort with race entries under the team name of the Ford Motor Company In 1965, however, this was changed to factory supported or works teams.

Private customers who purchased the Ford GT MkI to race in

Ford GT MkI, car number 72, driven by Bob Bondurant and Richie Ginther at Daytona. Contributor: C. Nahum Collection; photograph by Gérard Crombac

Ford GT MkI, car number 73, driven by Ken Miles and Lloyd Ruby, on its way to victory at Daytona in 1965. Contributor: C. Nahum Collection; photograph by Gérard Crombac

their own teams were known as privateers. Ford didn't invent the works and privateer racing programs, in which the works team received all the official goodies and the privateers paid for and received slightly lesser equipment, but it certainly expanded it.

The 1965 racing season started out well for the Ford GT. The Shelby American Inc. Ford GT MkI won its first race, at the Daytona Continental 2000km in Florida, USA.

Note: Daytona did not become a 24 hour race until 1966.

For the Sebring 12 hour, two Ford GT MkIs were entered by the Shelby American Inc. team. Ken Miles and Bruce McLaren finished second, but the MkI driven by Richie Ginther and Phil Hill failed to finish.

The winners Lloyd Ruby (left) and Ken Miles at Daytona 1965. Contributor: C. Nahum Collection; photograph by Gérard Crombac

Shelby American Inc. Ford GT MkI, car number 11, at the Nürburgring 1000km in 1965, driven by Chris Amon. Contributor: C. Nahum Collection; photograph by Gérard Crombac

For the 1000km at Monza, Italy, Shelby American Inc. again entered its two MkIs. The Ford GT driven by Bruce McLaren and Ken Miles finished third, but the second team Ford GT, driven by Chris Amon and Umberto Maglioli, failed to finish.

The only Ford GT entered in the Targa Florio in Sicily, Italy was the Ford Advanced Vehicles MkI Roadster, driven by Sir John Whitmore and Bob Bondurant, but they failed to finish due to an accident.

Four Ford GTs were entered for the 1965 edition of the Nürburgring 1000km. Two were MkIs from the Shelby American Inc. team, one MkI was from Ford France driven by Maurice Trintignant and Guy Ligier, and the MkI Roadster from Ford Advanced Vehicles driven by Sir John Whitmore and Richard Attwood.

The Shelby American Inc. Ford GT MkI driven by Chris Amon finished eighth, whilst the other team entry, driven by Phil Hill, failed to finish. The Ford France team car and the F.A.V. team MkI Roadster also failed to finish.

Note: The fact that the 1.6 litre Ferrari 166P Dino was faster than the 4.7 litre Ford GT MkI at the Nürburgring had also not gone unnoticed by Ford management. Henry Ford II was not impressed. This was a case of a "too little and too fast red car".

All the Ford GT teams sat out the rest of the races prior to Le Mans to gather their strength for their next assault on achieving the overall race win at Le Mans in 1965.

For Le Mans, Ford USA and the Shelby American Inc. team were bringing out the big guns. The Ford GT MkII, powered by its massive $427in^3$ (7 litre) engine, was to make its European racing debut.

Two Shelby American Inc. Ford GT MkIIs, driven by Chris Amon and Phil Hill and Ken Miles and Bruce McLaren, lined up on the Le Mans starting grid with the Ford France MkI Roadster driven by Maurice Trintignant and Guy Ligier, the MkI of the R.R.C. Walker Racing Team driven by Bob Bondurant and Umberto Maglioli, the joint Shelby American Inc. Scuderia Filipinetti MkI driven by Ronnie Bucknum and Herbert Müller,

Richard Attwood in the driver's seat of the Ford GT MkI Roadster at the Nürburgring 1000km. Contributor: Martin Rössler-Udo Klinkel Collection

Carroll Shelby with one of his charges in the pits of Le Mans prior to the start in 1965. Contributor: Ford Motor Company

and the Ford Advanced Vehicles Ford GT MkI driven by Sir John Whitmore and Innes Ireland.

Twenty-four hours later the race was over and not one of the Ford GTs had made it to the finish line – not the kind of result that would make the bosses back in Dearborn very happy.

Despite the efforts of its drivers and mechanics, the entire Ford company felt the humiliation of "those fast little red cars" winning the great race again! Adding insult to injury was the fact that not only were the first three Ferrari prototypes powered by 3.3 litre engines, but the fourth and fifth places were taken by the 2.0 litre powered Porsche 904s ...

The powerful 427in3 (7.0 litre)-powered Ford GT MkIIs had been seriously beaten up by the little guys!

After Le Mans 1965, all the Ford GT teams packed up and went home. Only Ford France entered two FIA-sanctioned points scoring races with its Ford GT MkI after Le Mans, but for some reason it did not start in either.

The Essex Wire team entered a Ford GT MkI in the Bridge-

The drivers reach their cars after sprinting across the track for the start of Le Mans in 1965. Contributor: Dr. Ing. h. c. F. Porsche AG

The drivers climb in and head out on their first lap. Car number 7 is the Ford GT MkI of the R.R.C. Walker Racing Team driven by Bob Bondurant, Umberto Maglioli and Chris Amon. Contributor: C. Nahum Collection; photograph by Gérard Crombac

The Ken Miles and Bruce McLaren Ford GT MkII at Le Mans in 1965. Contributor: Ford Motor Company

The Chris Amon and Phil Hill Ford GT MkII in action at Le Mans in 1965. Contributor: Ford Motor Company

The timing gear said that Bruce McLaren was doing over 200mph (320kph) when this picture was taken during Le Mans 1965. Contributor: Ford Motor Company

A somewhat battered Scuderia Filipinetti/Shelby American Inc. Ford GT MkI, car no. 6, in action at Le Mans 1965. It was driven by Herbert Müller and Ronnie Bucknum. Contributor: Ford Motor Company

Peter Sutcliffe, one of the first customers of F.A.V., in action during the 1965 Kyalami 9hr in his Ford GT MkI, chassis no. 1009. Contributor: Glen Smale-Automotive Research

hampton 500km race in the USA, the last round of the World Sportscar Championship. The driver was to be Skip Scott, but the Ford GT did not start the race.

Minor league racing in 1965

Note: Minor league only refers to the sanctioned status of the race. The major league events were considered as FIA-sanctioned international championship, with points scoring. Minor league covers everything else, including national championships and international non-points scoring events. The actual racing in all minor league events was hard and fast, and could be just as deadly.

The only Ford GT campaigned in 1965 in the British Sportscar Championship was a MkI, owned by Fred English, and driven by Richard Attwood. The F. English team only entered two championship races with its MkI. The first was the International Trophy Meeting at the Silverstone circuit, where Richard Attwood driving car no. 32 finished third. The second was the Guards Trophy race at the Mallory Park circuit. Richard Attwood, driving car no. 14, finished second in heat one and fourth in heat two.

In the British National racing series of 1965, only the Ford GT MkI owned by Colonel R. Hoare and driven by Roy Salvadori was campaigned.

British driver John Miles was entered to drive a Ford GT in the 200 mile race at Laguna Seca, California, USA in 1965, but he did not start the race.

Chris Amon raced the prototype Ford GT MkII-X1 Roadster, chassis no. 110, at the Riverside International 200 mile race, along with Skip Scott driving a MkI for the Essex Wire Corporation team. Ken Miles was entered, but he also did not start.

Chris Amon took the MkII-X1 Roadster over the border to race at Mosport in Canada, and Skip Scott raced the 1965 200 mile Las Vegas event for the Essex Wire Corporation team in its veteran Ford GT MkI.

Note: The records suggest that Colonel Hoare purchased the Ford GT MkI driven by Richard Attwood for the F. English team in the British Sportscar Championship.

The Ford France team entered its Ford GT MkI in French non-championship races at Magny-Cours and the Grans Prix d'Albi. For both races the driver was Guy Ligier.

Pre-Springbok series

To test the possibility of creating a major South African Sportscar racing series, in late 1965 a number of sportscar teams were invited to compete in a revamped South African motor race known as the Kyalami 9 hour.

The previous Kyalami 9 hour races had never attracted much international interest. The Kyalami circuit hosted the Formula One circus once a year, but the possibility of a multiple sportscar racing series on South African soil was a major incentive to the organisers and sponsors to try and attract teams to the country. The Kyalami 9 hour was spruced up to attract the bigger sportscar teams, especially from England, and additional races were added to the pot.

Only Peter Sutcliffe took his Ford GT, chassis no. 1009, to South Africa in 1965. Peter competed in the Kyalami 9 hour race, finishing second overall. He also competed in the race at the Kumalo circuit and in the Pietermaritzburg 3 hours (Roy Hesketh) race, both of which he won.

Peter Sutcliffe stayed in South Africa to compete in the rest of the series which ran into 1966 (but was still considered part of the 1965 racing season).

The two remaining races were at East London and Killarney in Cape Town. Peter Sutcliffe finished second at East London and won Killarney: a ripping start for the Ford GT racing program in 1966!

Two
The new hunting season opens

Ford's prey

Henry Ford II decreed that the Ferrari 330 prototype series was to be the Ford GT's primary prey. Contributor: Ford Motor Company

Ford revises its hunting system

Due to the less than satisfactory performance of all versions of the Ford GT in 1965, further reorganisation was carried out in 1966. The Ford works teams were expanded to include Holman Moody Racing and Alan Mann Racing. The plan was to incorporate the expertise of these highly experienced racing organisations to create the ultimate, race winning Ford GT. Holman Moody was selected because of its extensive experience with the Ford 7.0 litre engine in NASCAR racing. Alan Mann Racing was selected for its overall racing development skills under European conditions.

Note: Alan Mann Racing had a contract with Ford USA and Holman Moody, but at no time was Alan Mann involved in any direct formal business relationship with John Wyer or F.A.V. (according to an interview given by Alan Mann in 2002).

Each of the contracted works teams accepted the responsibility of developing a race winning Ford GT. Each works

New hunting equipment for the Holman Moody team, the Ford GT MkIIA. This one was driven at Le Mans by Mario Andretti and Lucien Bianchi. Contributor: Ford Motor Company

The British works teams were also in the hunt with the new equipment. The Alan Mann Racing team had the Holman Moody prepared Ford MkIIA. This one was driven by Graham Hill and Brian Muir. Contributor: Ford Motor Company

team was to be fully supported by Kar-Kraft in Detroit and Ford USA. No stone was to be left unturned for the Ferrari hunt in 1966.

New hunting equipment – the Ford GT MkIIA

The 427in³ (7.0 litre) cast-iron V8, pushrod engine used in the MkII prototype in 1965 was revised using the Ford NASCAR racing engine as a base. Changes incorporated included:

- Aluminium heads were fitted.
- An aluminium hub was used on the vibration damper.
- The water pump was made from aluminium.
- The valve size was reduced.
- The intake guide diameter was reduced.

The new 427in³ (7.0 litre) engine provided 485bhp (361.6kW) at 6300rpm and the engine torque was increased to 475lbft (644Nm) at 4000rpm. It's said that this new 427 (7.0 litre) engine provided the driver with a much wider and more usable power band. The compression ratio was kept at 10:1.

Modifications and improvements were not restricted to the engine. Safety for the driver was improved by the installation of a purpose-built roll cage. A new shorter and lighter front end was fitted. Small rear deck scoops for additional rear brake cooling were added to the cleaned up rear end, and all tabs, fins and other aerodynamic devices were removed.

The new 427 (7 litre) engine in the pits at Le Mans 1966. Contributor: Ford Motor Company

The brakes also had to be revised to cope with the higher speeds the MkIIA was capable of reaching on the Mulsanne straight. Going super fast safely was one thing, but the driver still had to brake for the corners. It should also be noted that the gross weight of the GT had not been reduced a great deal. It was still up around 2832lb (1284.6kg). a substantial mass which required real stopping power.

New braking system of the Ford GT MkIIA in 1966. Contributor: Ford Motor Company

Phil Remington was given the responsibility of designing the brake upgrade. Not only had the brakes to be better, they also had to be easier to change during pit stops. Remington worked on the brake issue over the winter of 1965 and his solution was to fit larger, ventilated and wheel-mounted brake rotors (discs), and to change the calliper mounting. Remington developed the two-bolt calliper mounting system which is still used today.

The result of the work carried out by Ford in partnership with its racing teams was the rocket ship needed to take on "those fast little red cars".

On its very first outing for the 1966 season, the Ford GT MkIIA (chassis no. 1015) driven by Ken Miles and Lloyd Ruby won the inaugural Daytona 24hr endurance race.

Note: Not all the Ford GT MkIIAs were fitted with 4-speed manual transmissions. Chassis no. 1016 was fitted with a 2-speed automatic transmission. This particular MkIIA was entered for the Daytona 24hr race, driven by Richie Ginter and Ronnie Bucknam, and for the 1966 Sebring 12hr race driven by A.J. Foyt and Ronnie Bucknam.

Ford GT MkIIA-X1 Roadster

The original MkII X1 Roadster was brought up to MkIIA standards by the Bruce McLaren team after its last trial race at Mosport in Canada in late 1965. It was then appropriated by Carroll Shelby upon the recommendation of Ken Miles.

For some reason the X1 Roadster sat out the first Daytona 24hr endurance race in 1966 as a spare, but the Shelby American Inc. team entered the MkIIA-X1 Roadster in the 1966 Sebring 12hr race. It was driven by Ken Miles and Lloyd Ruby, and amazingly the X1 Roadster won the race.

The Ford GT MkIIA with the 2-speed automatic transmission at Sebring in 1966. Contributor: Ford Motor Company

The Ford GT MkIIA-X1 Roadster at Sebring in 1966. The only time this car ever won a race. Contributor: C. Nahum Collection; photograph by Gérard Crombac

Note: The 2-speed automatic transmission used in the MkIIA version of the X1 Roadster was replaced with a 4-speed manual Kar-Kraft transaxle for the Sebring event.

After its amazing victory at Sebring the X1 Roadster was never raced again.

Note: The remains of the original X1 Roadster developed by Bruce McLaren from the wreck of the original MkI Roadster, chassis no. 110, in 1965, have been confirmed buried under a building near to the Los Angeles International Airport. Motoring journalist Richard Truesdell is investigating further.

Alan Mann Racing

Alan Mann Racing in association with Holman Moody in the USA developed the P40, which was a lightweight Group 4 version of the Ford GT MkI. The P40 made its debut alongside the MkIIA Roadster at Sebring, USA, in March 1966.

The P40 was distinctive at the time of its debut because Alan Mann Racing used Elektron (single skin) body panels in a major weight saving effort. Alan Mann Racing created two of these lightweight Ford GTs, chassis nos. AMGT-1 and 2.

One of the two Alan Mann Racing Ford GT P40s that raced at Sebring in 1966. This one was driven by Graham Hill and Jackie Stewart. Contributor: C. Nahum Collection; photograph by Gérard Crombac

John Wyer

During this frantic period of developing the Ford GT as a

Ford GT MkI, chassis no. 1022, delivered in March 1966. Contributor: Eric Liddell

competitive force on the race track, John Wyer and his team continued to be very active in the background.

Still dedicated to the job that had been handed to them, John Wyer, David York, John Horsman, Arnold Stafford, Jack Sopp, Dickie Dean, Tony Tocock, and the rest of the Ford Advanced Vehicles division team continued production of the customer Ford GT racing car for the new price of £7200, and the racing car version was joined by the Ford GT (homologation) road car for £5900 (£6500 including taxes).

Note: John Horsman had a magnificent career in motorsport and for some of his achievements deserves to be included in this story. His career summary is courtesy of the British Racing Drivers Club (B.R.D.C.).

John Horsman was:

- Engineer in charge for Aston Martin DB 214 cars at Monza 1963 (won by Roy Salvadori).
- Engineer and assistant to John Wyer at Ford Advanced Vehicles. Working on the build and development of the Ford GT40.
- Director (with J.Wyer and J. Willment) of J.W. Automotive Engineering.
- Engineer in charge of preparation and development of the Ford GT program which won the World Sports Car Championship in 1968, and the Le Mans 24hr in 1968 and 1969. Also solved the Porsche 917 handling problems, enabling British company (J.W.A.) to win the Sports Car Championship in 1970 and 1971.
- Engineer in charge of the M1, M2 and M3 Mirage programs.
- Managing Director of Gulf Research Racing Company. Built M6, GR7 and GR8 Mirages. Won Le Mans 1975 with Jacky Ickx and Derek Bell.

Note: Jack Sopp was the most experienced team member recruited by John Wyer. Jack Sopp was a 'Bentley Boy' looking after the Le Mans team from 1928 to 1930. Before Bentley, Jack Sopp was the race mechanic to Parry Thomas.

The Ford GT road car arrives

In 1966 the Ford GT road car, based on the MkI racing car, finally made it to the market place. Hailed as the most expensive Ford ever, thirty-one road versions were built, with twenty-six being sold in the USA. According to a Ford Advanced Vehicles press release from 1967, F.A.V. made the claim that the Ford GT MkI road cars had earned the company over £100,000 in foreign currency.

Note: A number of the Ford GT racing cars were converted to road cars, even in the early days of production. These conversions differed greatly from the actual factory produced road cars (the lack of luggage capacity was one major difference). George Filipinetti of Switzerland commissioned one such conversion in 1966 with chassis no. 1033.

The changes made from the race car to produce the official road car were:

- Engine compression was reduced from 10:1 to 9:1. This, in turn, reduced the power output of the 289in^3 (4.7 litre) V8 engine to 306bhp (228kW) at 6250rpm.
- The clutch was changed from a Borg and Beck three plate to a two plate version. Diameter of the clutch plate was increased from 7.25in (184.15mm) to 8.5in (215.9mm).
- Two pairs of round headlights replaced the oblong ones of the racing car.
- A small luggage compartment box was fitted on either side of the transmission.
- Tinted door and rear glass windows.
- Deep pockets were added to the internal door trim.
- A speedometer was installed.
- The gear lever was repositioned from the right side to a centre floor position.
- Sound and heat insulation was installed.
- More comfortable, manually adjustable seats were fitted.
- A softer, more road friendly set of shock absorbers and springs was installed.
- The four IDA 48 Weber carburettor system was replaced with a single, 4-barrel Holley or Autolite carburettor.

One of the first road cars exported to the USA was for Grady Davis of the Gulf Oil Corporation (there's more on this in Chapter 3). Another early customer was the Girling company, which made the GT's brakes. This particular car was later purchased from Girling for £3000 by Duncan Hamilton.

The follow on road car version to the original MkI was the MkIII. Only seven were built. John Wyer was given one of these MkIIIs (chassis no. 1102) and it was registered in his daughter Pia's name in 1967.

Early in 1967, in order to sell off the unsold Ford GT road cars,

Doug about to take Bob for a drive around the Chaffee Ford dealership lot. Yeah right Doug, just around the lot? Contributor: Doug Anderson

Ford GT MkI chassis no. 1028 is said to have been purchased by Ford USA from a Texas rancher. It's seen here at the Chaffee Ford dealership in Hawthorne, California in March 1968. The three guys in the images are: (left) Glen the refueller, (centre) Doug Anderson, and Bob Baldwin. Contributor: Doug Anderson

Ford USA ran a promotion and disposal program. These road cars were nicknamed the Dearborn Road Coupés. Carroll Shelby at Shelby American Inc. had at least two Ford GT road cars allocated as part of the program, but these were the later MkIII road cars which had the small Ford oval behind the front wheels, not the Ford GT sill stripes.

Shelby American Inc. at one time or another owned Ford GT MkI road cars 1018 (maroon), 1020 (dark blue), and the Shell Parachute Cars 1025, 1030, 1035 and 1036, but the latter four were sent back to Ford Advanced Vehicles incomplete and, obviously, unsold. Chassis no. 1020 was sold to Ford France and competed at Le Mans in 1967. It is currently housed at the Sarthe Museum, located at the main entrance to the circuit. Chassis No. 1028 also still exists in private hands in the USA.

Chassis no. 1105, a blue, left-hand drive version was delivered to Herbert von Karajan in Austria in 1968. Being the only one of its kind (LHD) makes this particular Ford GT arguably the most unique of all because all the other road and racing cars were right-hand drive.

Note: Unused LHD MkIII chassis no. 1111 was used for the rebuild of Ford GT MkI chassis no. 1078 in 1970.

The final customer Ford GT MkIII road car, chassis no. 1103, with its exterior finished in a dark red paint and with a black interior, was delivered to Sir Max Aitken in May 1969. This particular Ford GT was fitted with the Ford 302 V8, the Gulf team style wider rear end, and wider rear wheels.

Ford GT MkIII road car. This is chassis no. 1107 which is still owned by Ford. Contributor: Richard Truesdell

Note: Not all the road cars were fitted with the Ford 289in³ (4.7 litre) V8 engine. Some were fitted with the 302in³ (5.0 litre) V8. The 289 powered Ford GT road cars delivered 306bhp (228kW). The 302 powered road cars with the dry-deck, Gurney-Weslake heads delivered approximately 335bhp (250kw).

The J-car

In the late autumn of 1965, Ford USA, with assistance from Bruce McLaren, started work on a new prototype racing car based on the Ford GT. It was dubbed the Ford J-car, but affectionately nicknamed the bread van. Why was it called the J-car? It was named after Appendix J of the FIA regulations which governed the Ford GT. Why the nickname? Just take a look at the picture.

Ford, realising that Eric Broadley was correct in his 1964 assessment, reverted to the aluminium chassis (tub) for the J-car using the aircraft industry-pioneered, honeycombed aluminium process. The honeycomb construction method provided a very light weight yet very strong assembly. The downside, however, was that when the honeycomb was damaged it was not easy to repair. Aluminium also burned easily, and a fire would usually result in the entire car being destroyed.

The first Ford J-car was road tested at the Daytona Speedway racetrack by Mario Andretti and Bruce McLaren in early 1966. The motoring Press of the time reported that the first J-car prototype tested at Daytona was fitted with a 2-speed automatic transmission.

It was whilst testing the Ford J-car at the Riverside International Raceway, USA, that motor racing great Ken Miles was killed. As reported at the time: "As his J-car slowed from approximately 175mph (281kph) to 100mph (160kph) it appeared to go out of control. It spun towards the inside of the racetrack, crashing at high speed into an embankment. The impact speed was so high that the car flew over the top of the embankment. When it hit the ground on the other side, it bounced end over end, several times before coming to rest and bursting into flames. Ken Miles was thrown from the car and sustained fatal head injuries." The J-car (chassis no. J2) was totally destroyed.

The 'bread van' nickname was apt for the J-car, seen here at the Le Mans trials. Contributor: C. Nahum Collection; photograph by Gérard Crombac

The J-car during its testing phase at Daytona in early 1966. Contributor: Ford Motor Company

The first four J-car chassis (tubs) were constructed using the two-row rivet system. After the Ken Miles tragedy, chassis nos. J3 and J4 were strengthened, and chassis nos. J5 to J8 were redesigned, then constructed using the three-row rivet system, and were fitted with the Phil Remington-designed body. Only eight Ford GT-based J-cars were constructed, and it was not until the J-car had morphed into the Ford GT MkIV in 1967 that it made its presence felt on the race track. Unfortunately, that success only lasted for one ripper of a season, and that story can be found in Chapter 3.

Note: It was Ford GT MkIV chassis no. J5 that won Le Mans in 1967.

A further four J-car chassis assemblies had been constructed. Chassis nos. J9 and J10 were used by Charlie and Kerry Agapiou to create the Ford G7A Spyder CanAm racing car in 1969. A little known fact is that chassis no. J10 completed more races in its G7A CanAm guise than all the J-car chassis in their Ford GT guise. Chassis no. J9 does not appear in any race records found, so it's assumed this chassis assembly may have been kept as a spare and not used. One source suggests that chassis no. J9 is being rebuilt into a full racing version of the Ford G7A.

The active Ford G7A Spyder CanAm racing car was built around J-car chassis no. J10. Its drivers included Sir Jack Brabham, Vic Elford, Peter Revson and John Cannon. This photograph shows Sir Jack Brabham driving the G7A in the CanAm race at Brooklyn, MI, USA in 1969. Contributor: Ford Motor Company

The other two J-car chassis assemblies were not numbered. Two new build Ford GT MkIVs were constructed around these two spare chassis assemblies many years later, and they were allocated chassis nos. J11 and J12. See Chapter 5 for more on chassis no. J11.

Note: For production number totals in this book only the eight J-car chassis assemblies used in the Ford GT racing program have been included.

Glory of the hunt is earned the hard way

The 1966 racing season started off in February with a new version of the Daytona Continental. The race had been extended to a full Le Mans style 24 hour format. A perfect testing ground for the new Ford GT MkIIA. If it could last the distance in Daytona it could last the distance at the ultimate goal of Le Mans.

Right top: Dan Gurney in car number 97 leads two Ferraris at the first Daytona 24hr race. Contributor: Ford Motor Company

Right middle: Ford GT MkIIA driven by Walt Hansgen and Mark Donohue making a night pit stop during the first Daytona 24hr in 1966. Contributor: Ford Motor Company

Right bottom: The eventual winner, the Ford GT MkIIA of Ken Miles and Lloyd Ruby making a night pit stop during the Daytona 24hr. Contributor: Ford Motor Company

Ken Miles at Sebring in 1966. Tragically, Ken was to lose his life later that year. Contributor: C. Nahum Collection; photograph by Gérard Crombac

The Ford GT MkIIA-X1 Roadster makes a night pit stop on its way to victory. Contributor: Ford Motor Company

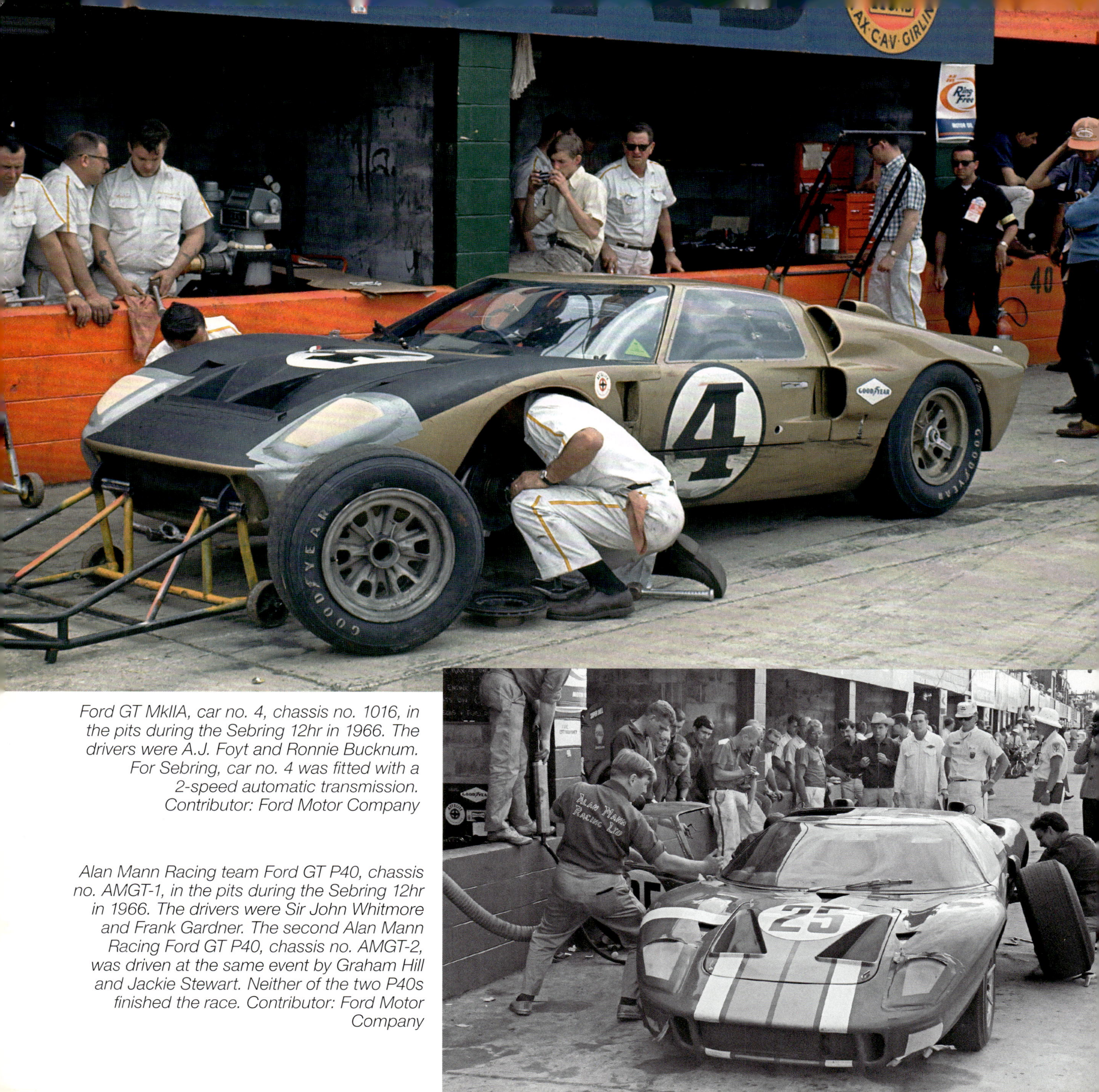

Ford GT MkIIA, car no. 4, chassis no. 1016, in the pits during the Sebring 12hr in 1966. The drivers were A.J. Foyt and Ronnie Bucknum. For Sebring, car no. 4 was fitted with a 2-speed automatic transmission. Contributor: Ford Motor Company

Alan Mann Racing team Ford GT P40, chassis no. AMGT-1, in the pits during the Sebring 12hr in 1966. The drivers were Sir John Whitmore and Frank Gardner. The second Alan Mann Racing Ford GT P40, chassis no. AMGT-2, was driven at the same event by Graham Hill and Jackie Stewart. Neither of the two P40s finished the race. Contributor: Ford Motor Company

Shelby American Inc. entered three MkIIAs, driven by Ken Miles, Lloyd Ruby, Dan Gurney, Jerry Grant, Chris Amon and Bruce McLaren. Holman Moody entered two MkIIAs, driven by Walt Hansgen, Mark Donohue, Richie Ginther and Ronnie Bucknum.

These MkIIAs were joined on the starting grid by four privateer team Ford GT MkIs. Two Ford GTs were entered by the Essex Wire Corporation, driven by Richard Thompson, Skip Scott, Peter Revson and Masten Gregory. Peter Sutcliffe drove the Ford Advanced Vehicles Ford GT, with Bob Grossman sharing the driving, and Ray Wonder entered his own car and shared the driving with Herbert Wetanson.

When the race at the Daytona International Speedway had reached its conclusion after twenty-four gruelling hours, Ford GT MkIIAs occupied the top three podium places, Bruce McLaren and Chris Amon were in fifth place. The Ford Advanced Vehicles' Ford MkI finished in fourteenth place, and one of the Essex Wire Corporation Ford GT MkIs finished in seventeenth place.

Things were looking good for the Ford GT in 1966. However, the achievement was slightly overshadowed by the fact that the Ferrari factory team did not turn up for the race.

Nevertheless, the important issue was that an American car, raced by an American team, with one American driver (Lloyd Ruby) and one honorary American driver (Ken Miles) had won the longest racing event ever held on US soil.

The second round of the World Sportscar Championship was the Sebring 12hr. No less than thirteen Ford GTs were lined up on the grid. Shelby American Inc. had two MkIIAs and the MkIIA-X1 Roadster entered using the same drivers as at Daytona. Ken Miles and Lloyd Ruby had the honour of driving the Roadster. Why not? It was Ken Miles' idea in the first place for Shelby American Inc. to race it.

Holman Moody entered two Ford GT MkIIAs with the same drivers as in the Daytona 24hr race. The Essex Wire Corporation team used three of the same drivers as at Daytona, with Augie Pabst replacing Richard Thompson.

William Wonder entered his own Ford GT MkI, with Bobby Brown, while Peter Sutcliffe also entered his own Ford GT MkI, with Innes Ireland sharing the driving.

New Ford GT teams showed up for Sebring. Alan Mann Racing entered its two equally new Ford GT P40s, with drivers Frank Gardner, Sir John Whitmore, Graham Hill and Jackie Stewart.

The Scuderia Bear team entered a single Ford GT MkI driven by Bruce Jennings and Richard Holquist. The Canadian Comstock Racing team entered two Ford GT MkIs driven by Eppie Wietzes, Craig Fisher, Bob McLean and Jean Oulette.

When the twelve hours were up at Sebring, the Shelby American Inc. Ford MkIIA-X1 Roadster had won, with a Holman Moody MkIIA in second place and an Essex Wire Corporation MkI in third place. A total of seven Ford GTs finished the race.

The 2-speed automatic version of the Holman Moody Ford GT MkIIA, car no. 4 driven by A.J.Foyt and Ronnie Bucknum, finished twelfth overall.

April third and fourth 1966 were the days set aside by the ACO for the Le Mans testing period. Ford was there in force, with two MkIIAs and the Ford J-car prototype.

The reported team budget allocated by Ford for the 1966 effort was in excess of US$4.5 million, and on the test days of April 1966 it showed. The list of test drivers was equally impressive:

- Ronnie Bucknum (USA).
- Frank Gardner (AUS).
- Bruce McLaren (NZ).
- Chris Amon (NZ).
- Ken Miles (GB).
- Lucien Bianchi (I/B).
- Graham Hill (GB).
- Jackie Stewart (GB).
- Walt Hansgen (USA).

Testing started on Saturday the second of April, but disaster struck the Ford camp almost immediately. Walt Hansgen took the Holman Moody MkIIA out onto a wet Sarthe circuit. On his second fast lap as he passed the pit lane, he appeared to aquaplane, lost control and crashed heavily at the Dunlop bend. Lack of emergency equipment and trained personnel resulted in Hansgen being trapped in the wreckage. After much heated discussion between the Ford team and the ACO officials, the team members finally freed Hansgen and he was rushed to Le Mans hospital. Walt Hansgen succumbed to his injuries on the seventh of April 1966.

Note: A memorial plaque honouring Hansgen's memory is located at the site of his crash.

Ken Miles also had an off at Indianapolis (Sarthe circuit) during Saturday testing, resulting in Ford losing both its MkIIAs very quickly. A lack of spares also meant a long delay before either of the cars could be repaired and returned to the track. Enter George Filipinetti, the Swiss-based Ford GT team owner. He had the parts Ford needed, though they were at the team's home base in Geneva, Switzerland.

Whilst Ken Miles was waiting for the repairs to be carried out, he took the prototype J-car out for a drive and crashed that as well. Suddenly, Ford had no cars to test and the day's work came to an abrupt halt. The MkIIA driven by Ken Miles and the J-car were repaired overnight, thanks to George Filipinetti, but the Walt Hansgen MkIIA was totally destroyed.

When Sunday dawned, Ford had only two cars to take out for testing, so Ken Miles went back out in the J-car, whilst the rest of the team shared driving stints in the lone MkIIA. Ken found to

The J-car in the pits at the Le Mans trials of 1966. Contributor: C. Nahum Collection; photograph by Gérard Crombac

his astonishment that the Ford computer predictions were totally wrong. At high speed the J-car had serious handling problems. It quickly became apparent that the J-car was far too dangerous to drive over 220mph (354kph).

Bruce McLaren tested the J-car on the Sunday (third of April) and came to the same conclusion as Ken Miles, that the J-car needed a lot more aerodynamic development.

The rest of the drivers testing in the remaining MkIIA also faired badly and their lap times did not impress anyone. The Ford challenge for Le Mans 1966 looked decidedly shaky.

The works teams and their Ford GT MkIIAs missed the next two major Italian endurance races at Monza and the Targa Florio. Alan Mann Racing took its works Ford GT MkIIA to Spa in Belgium

The J-car driven by Bruce McLaren in the rain at the Le Mans trials in 1966. Contributor: Ford Motor Company

Car no. 46 of the Essex Wire Corporation team at the Nürburgring in 1966. Contributor: Udo Klinkel

Ford GT MkI, car no. 49, chassis no. 1021, driven by Richard Bond and Mike Spence doing battle with the Chaparral 2D, car no. 7, driven by Jo Bonnier and Phil Hill during the Nürburgring 1000km in 1966. Contributor: Veit Arenz

Ford GT MkI, car no. 50, chassis no. 1009, driven by Peter Sutcliffe and John Taylor at the Nürburgring 1000km in 1966. Contributor: Veit Arenz

where it was driven into second place by Sir John Whitmore and Frank Gardner. After a promising start to the season, then the tragedy at Le Mans testing and missing races, things had once again started to look up for Ford in its European campaign, despite being beaten by a Ferrari 330P3 at Spa. At least it was only one Ferrari this time.

The works teams decided to the 1966 Nürburgring 1000km a miss, but the privateer teams attended. Two Essex Wire Corporation Ford GT MkIs were entered. Car no. 46 driven by Peter Revson and Skip Scott, and car no. 47 driven by Sir John Whitmore and Jochen Neerspasch.

The Essex boys were joined by the Ford France MkI driven by Jo Schlesser and Guy Ligier. Peter Sutcliffe shared his own entry with John M. Taylor. Richard Bond entered Nick Cussons' MkI, and shared with Mike Spence. Last, but not least, there was the F. English team entry MkI driven by Innes Ireland and Mike Salmon. The Ford GT MkIs of Ford France, Peter Sutcliffe and Richard Bond all finished the race.

The works teams of Shelby, Holman, J.W.A. and Alan Mann Racing decided they needed a period of time to gather their thoughts, recharge their batteries, and to prepare for the big hunt, because it was to be all or nothing at Le Mans in 1966.

Le Mans 1966

At 4pm on Saturday the 18th of June 1966, six Ford GT MkIs and eight Ford GT MkIIAs were lined up along the Le Mans starting grid.

Note: There should have been seven MkIs on the starting grid, but the Scuderia Bear entry crashed during practice and wasn't able to start.

The teams were:

- Shelby American Inc. (USA).
- Holman Moody (USA).
- Essex Wire Corporation (USA).
- Ford France (F).
- Alan Mann Racing (GB).
- Scuderia Filipinetti (CH).
- F. English Racing Ltd. (GB).

The Ford GTs lined up for the start of Le Mans 1966. Contributor: Ford Motor Company

The Ford GT drivers list for Le Mans read as a Who's Who *of motor racing.*

Bruce McLaren (NZ).
Chris Amon (NZ).
Denis Hulme (NZ).
Dan Gurney (USA).
Guy Ligier (F).
Graham Hill (GB).
Brian Muir (AUS).
Mario Andretti (USA).
Jochen Rindt (A).
Ken Miles (GB).
A.J. Foyt (USA).
Ronnie Bucknam (USA).
Lloyd Ruby (USA).
Richard (Dick) Thompson (USA).
Lucien Bianchi (I).
Jackie Stewart (GB).
Richard (Dick) Hutcherson (USA).
Fred Lorenzen (USA).
Robert Grossman (USA).
Peter Arundell (GB).
Jerry Grant (USA).
Sir John Whitmore (GB).
Frank Gardner (AUS).
Mark Donohue (USA).
Paul Hawkins (AUS).
Peter Sutcliffe (GB).
Dieter Spörry (CH).
Herbert Müller (CH).
Willy Mairesse (B).
Innes Ireland (GB).
Mario Casoni (I).
Peter Revson (USA).
Skip Scott (USA).
Henri Greder (F).
Jean-Michel Giorgi (CH).
Jochen Neerpasch (D).
Jacky Ickx (B).
Masten Gregory (USA).
Richie Ginther (USA).
Mike Salmon (GB).
Jack Sears (GB).
Eppie Wietzes (CDN).
Craig Fisher (CDN).
Richard Holquist (USA).
M.R.J. Wyllie (GB).
Bruce Jennings (USA).

Bruce McLaren. Contributor: Ford Motor Company

The Mario Andretti and Lucien Bianchi driven MkIIA was a non-finisher at Le Mans in 1966. Contributor: Ford Motor Company

Opposite: Mark Donohue (left) and Paul Hawkins with their Ford GT MkIIA at Le Mans in 1966. They failed to finish the race. Contributor: Ford Motor Company

Henry Ford II drops the flag for the start of Le Mans 1966. Contributor: Ford Motor Company

The lead driver for the Ford France team enters his Ford GT. This is the former Roadster, chassis no. 112. Contributor: C. Nahum Collection; photograph by Gérard Crombac

Dan Gurney and Jerry Grant's Ford GT MkIIA did not finish. Contributor: Ford Motor Company

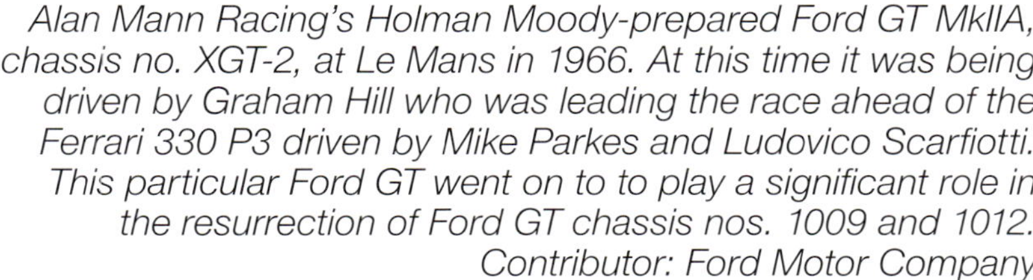
Alan Mann Racing's Holman Moody-prepared Ford GT MkIIA, chassis no. XGT-2, at Le Mans in 1966. At this time it was being driven by Graham Hill who was leading the race ahead of the Ferrari 330 P3 driven by Mike Parkes and Ludovico Scarfiotti. This particular Ford GT went on to to play a significant role in the resurrection of Ford GT chassis nos. 1009 and 1012. Contributor: Ford Motor Company

Note: The long list of drivers was due to the practice at the time of having multiple drivers nominated across multiple cars within many teams. This was to ensure that the top drivers were able to keep on racing even if their primary racing car had failed. It was always good for company publicity to have the top drivers on the podium. This practice is no longer permitted.

The Alan Mann Racing team of Sir John Whitmore and Frank Gardner in the Holman Moody prepared Ford GT MkIIA failed to finish. Contributor: Ford Motor Company

Henry Ford II had been invited by the ACO to start the race, so the Ford GTs and the teams running them were under more than normal pressure to perform for the big boss this time around.

When the great race finished at 4pm on Sunday the 19th June there were only three Ford GT MkIIAs left. The five other MkIIAs and the entire Ford GT MkI contingent had fallen victim to accidents and mechanical failures, resulting in the dreaded acronym 'DNF' (did not finish) being added alongside their names in the race record. The difference for the Ford Motor Company in this race was that the three Ford GT MkIIAs classified as finishers occupied the three top steps on the podium for both the overall and class race categories.

Bruce McLaren and Chris Amon's Ford GT MkIIA, chassis no. 1046. Contributor: Ford Motor Company

• First: Shelby American Inc. car no. 2, driven by Bruce McLaren and Chris Amon.
• Second: Shelby American Inc. car no.1, driven by Ken Miles and Denis Hulme.
• Third: Holman Moody car no. 5, driven by Ronnie Bucknum and Richard (Dick) Hutcherson.

Ken Miles and Denis Hulme's Ford GT MkIIA, chassis no. 1015. Contributor: Ford Motor Company

At last! Henry Ford II and his works Ford GT teams had finally succeeded in their quest for glory ... the one-two-three finish, an historic first for Ford, was something that could only have been dreamed about previously. However due to a miscalculation (Ford didn't take into consideration the race rules) the eventual winning Ford GT team was not the one that Henry had ordered.

Henry Ford II decided to stage a publicity generating photo finish between the Ford GT MkIIAs of Ken Miles and Denis Hulme and Bruce McLaren and Chris Amon. Following team orders, Bruce McLaren allowed Ken Miles to stay in front by what he thought was a comfortable winning margin, but without spoiling the photo finish publicity shot.

Note: Bruce McLaren stated afterwards that he clearly felt the gap between his car and Ken Miles' car would be sufficient.

Ronnie Bucknam and Richard Hutcherson's Ford GT MkIIA, chassis no 1016. Contributor: Ford Motor Company

The famous one-two-three team-ordered photo finish. Contributor: Ford Motor Company

However, according to the race Stewards, the gap Bruce McLaren allowed was not enough to show a clear winner crossing the finish line. The two cars were so close that the Stewards decided to calculate the total race distance covered, which was the intent of the race regulations. They soon declared Bruce McLaren and Chris Amon the race winners, because they had actually covered a longer race distance over the 24 hours. Bruce McLaren and Chris Amon had started the race behind Ken Miles and Denis Hulme on the grid (ninth place). The race Stewards had calculated the difference between the starting grid positions minus the gap at the finish to be 26ft (8m) in favour of Bruce McLaren and Chris Amon. This ruling was a terrible disappointment for Ken Miles who wanted to win the triple crown of endurance racing, the Daytona 24hr, Sebring 12hr and the Le Mans 24hr. Unfortunately,

Ford should have kept a closer eye on Porsche KG. This is what happens when too much focus is given to just one car manufacturer and competitor; you lose. Contributor: Dr. Ing. h. c. F. Porsche AG

all the people, except Chris Amon, who were directly involved in this disappointing end to a great race, have passed away and their comments and feelings from 39 years ago passed with them.

Ken Miles died whilst testing the Ford J-car in August 1966. Bruce McLaren died whilst testing his own CanAm car in June 1970. Henry Ford II died in September 1987. Denis Hulme died of a heart attack whilst competing in the Bathurst 1000km endurance race (Australia) in October 1992.

Note: Chris Amon could not be reached for comment.

Internal team disputes aside, this was not just a victory for Ford, this was a victory for the United States of America. For the very first time, an American-owned brand had won the great race outright. With the Le Mans victory, Ford also won the International Manufacturer's Championship by the slender margin of only two points more than Ferrari.

As for Ford factory involvement or the works teams racing after Le Mans, it just didn't happen.

Ford, like Ferrari, just wasn't interested in racing anymore during 1966. The great Le Mans race was done and dusted and car development time and finances were required for the 1967 racing season.

This left the door open for the Porsche KG sports car manufacturing company from Zuffenhausen, Germany to ply its trade almost unopposed. This would be a mistake, but it would take some years to realise how much of a mistake it really was.

Minor league motor racing

The 1965 season had sown the seeds for the development of a strong and vibrant minor league of motor racing, with Ford GTs competing in the British Sports Car Championship, British National Racing series, American National Racing series, and

Grovewood Trophy race at Mallory Park in April 1966. Car no. 17 is an Attila Chevrolet. Contributor: Eric Liddell

other non-points scoring international races such as the Kyalami 9hr event.

As more and more Ford GTs were sold by F.A.V., so their use in international non-championship racing increased. Jean-Michel Giorgi of Switzerland drove his Ford GT MkI in the Trophée d'Auvergne Clermond Ferrand at the Circuit de la Charade in France in June 1966.

Peter Sutcliffe had his Ford GT MkI, chassis no. 1009, shipped to Surfers Paradise in Queensland, Australia for the 12 hour race

Henry Ford II holds court alongside car number 15 at Le Mans in 1966. This Ford GT MkI was chassis number 112 converted back to a Coupé from its 1965 Roadster configuration. This was the Ford GT purchased by Peter Sutcliffe. Contributor: C. Nahum Collection; photograph by Gérard Crombac

in August 1966. Peter Sutcliffe and his Australian co-driver Frank Mattich drove a hard race and won it, or so they thought. David McKay, owner of the Ferrari 250LM which came in second, driven by Jackie Stewart and New Zealander Andy Buchanan, protested the result. The stewards upheld the McKay protest and Jackie Stewart and his team-mate were elevated to first place and Peter Sutcliffe and Frank Mattich relegated to second.

It was some time before the protest results reached Peter Sutcliffe. After he thought he had won the Surfers Paradise 12hr, he took all his friends out for dinner to celebrate: the dinner funded out of his 'winnings'. When the stewards of the race eventually found against him and ruled in favour of the Ferrari team, Peter Sutcliffe suddenly discovered he was a little short when it was time to pay for the dinner. He had to go around to all his guests and ask them to contribute to his "Save me from debtors prison fund".

Peter Sutcliffe purchased one of the Ford France MkIs (chassis no. 112) after he had raised enough money by selling chassis no. 1009 (whilst still in Surfers Paradise) to Ed Nelson. Alan Mann Racing replaced the 4.7 litre engine with the 1965 Le Mans 5.3 litre V8 engine, and the car was shipped to South Africa for the first official Springbok series.

September 1966 was a busy month for motor racing. Jo Schlesser stoked the French interest in the Ford brand when he raced the Ford GT MkI at the ACIF Circuit de Montlhéry where he won the race. A week later, Belgian driver Jean 'Beurlys' Blaton raced his Ford GT MkI in the Coupes de l'Avenir at Zolder in Holland.

Five privateer Ford GT MkIs were entered in the exclusive Group 4 Austrian GP at the Zeltweg airfield circuit. This race was the last round of the FIA International Sportscar Championship. Ford GTs finished fourth, seventh, ninth and tenth. Home town hero Jochen Rindt was driving the Ford GT that came ninth.

Note: Jochen Rindt went on to greater glory when he won the 1970 Formula One Driver's Championship. Sadly, he was awarded the championship posthumously. He was killed during training at Monza in September 1970. He had amassed sufficient points from the previous races to be awarded the Formula One World Championship.

The first race in the 1966 American National racing series to attract the Ford GT was the SCCA National Championship Race held at the Virginia International Raceway. The sole Ford GT MkI entry was driven by Richard Thompson, and he won. Dr. Al Whatley was entered in his own Ford GT MkI chassis no. 1024 in the 26th Santa Barbara Road Races.

The 1966 edition of the Road America 500 mile endurance race was held in September at the Elkhart Lake race track. A number of privateer team Ford GTs were entered. The drivers included: Doctor Al Whatley, Richard (Dick) Thompson and William Wonder, but none finished.

Al Whatley's Ford GT with tow bar at Riverside International circuit in October 1966. Notice the centre stripe design is different in this photograph as compared to the photograph showing car no. 44. Contributor: Doug Anderson

Al Whatley in Ford GT MkI racing car chassis no. 1024 in preparation for his practice session on the track. His race was a support event for the 1966 CanAm series Times Grand Prix. Contributor: Doug Anderson

Forgotten American racer

Al Whatley was a successful dentist from Las Vegas, Nevada, with a passion for motor racing and, for a while, the Ford GT MkI. He liked the car so much he purchased two. One road car and one racing car. The racing car was chassis no. 1024.

It's known that chassis no. 1024 was delivered new to Whatley by Shelby American Inc. The origin of the car isn't known.

During practice Al Whatley spun at turn one on the Riverside circuit. His speed was estimated to be approximately 100mph (160kph). The result was that the Ford GT MkI was wrecked. Whatley was not injured, and he is seen on the far right of the image. Contributor: Doug Anderson

Whatley had a small modification done to his registered road Ford GT; it was fitted with a tow bar, and he would turn up to race meetings driving one Ford GT, whilst towing a trailer with another Ford GT parked on it!

Whatley was quite active, if not that successful, with his Ford GT, racing primarily on the road racing circuit on the west coast of the USA. His luck on the race track with his Ford GT MkI, chassis no. 1024, ran out on the twenty-ninth of October 1966 during practice for a support race to the 1966 CanAm Series Times Grand Prix at the Riverside International raceway.

Note: 1966 was the first year of the Canadian-American Challenge series, or CanAm.

Note: In 1966, Riverside International was a road racing circuit. It was later dug up and converted into the better known oval type circuit for NASCAR and other uniquely American racing formulas.

This accident at Riverside ended the racing career of Ford GT MkI chassis no. 1024. The story goes that the bill from Shelby American Inc. for straightening and repairing the chassis amounted to almost as much as the original purchase price.

Whatley sold the Ford GT after it was repaired, and it doesn't appear again on any official race records, so its life between then and more recent owners is not totally clear.

Chassis no 1024 returned to the historic racing circuit in the USA during the 1980s. It is believed that it was crashed at the Portland International Raceway in the USA during this decade, but has been rebuilt and is once again back on the race track.

Note: Only the 1966 racing season records provide information on Al Whatley's racing career with the Ford GT.

Back to the racing

At the end of September 1966, Innes Ireland and Jean-Michel Giorgi, both driving for Ford France, competed in the Coupes de Paris. Innes Ireland won the race, but Jean-Michel Giorgi failed to finish.

Jo Schlesser drove the Ford France Ford GT in the 1966 Coupes du Salon at Montlhéry in October, and he drove for Ford France in the last race in Europe in 1966 that involved the Ford GT, the Paris 1000km. Three teams each entered a single Ford GT MkI: Scuderia Filipinetti, driven by Willy Mairesse and Jean 'Beurlys' Blaton; Ford France, driven by Jo Schlesser and Richard Attwood; Scuderia San Ambroeus , driven by Nino Vaccarella and Mario Casoni.

The cars of Ford France and Filipinetti were involved in a first lap accident and were taken out of the race. The remaining Ford GT team also failed to finish.

In December 1966, David Hobbs and Mike Hailwood travelled to Rhodesia for the Rhodesian Grand Prix at the Kumalo circuit. They drove the Ford GT MkI owned by Bernard White, and won the race.

There were four events that made up the Canadian Sports Car Championship in 1966 in which the Canadian Comstock team raced a Ford GT MkI driven by Eppie Wietzes. For the 1966 Players 200 at Mosport, the Canadian Comstock team was joined on the grid by William Wonder and his Ford GT MkI.

British home events in 1966

The various British national series provided fertile ground for lower budget privateer racing teams to gain vital experience before moving into the big league. These racing events also allowed major league drivers, such as Australian Paul Hawkins, to develop their own teams.

Paul Hawkins purchased one Ford GT MkI (1019) and the ex-Alan Mann P40 (AMGT-2) and hired young guns to drive them for him. A major contributor to this book, Eric Liddell, was one of these drivers. Eric Liddell also drove chassis no. 1022 under contract to J. Norman (Nick) Cuthbert, as well as chassis no. 1009 for Ed Nelson.

Another privateer Ford GT purchaser was Nick Cussons. He purchased 1021 from F.A.V., did some driving himself, and later hired other drivers to race it for him. Alan Mann Racing purchased 1023 to be used for the British-based events in the racing season of 1966.

Note: Nick Cussons sold his car, chassis no. 1021, to Ed Nelson and Colin Crabbe in November 1966, so providing them with a car to take to South Africa to compete in the Springbok series.

Eric Liddell in car no. 110 trails Mike Salmon in car no. 108 (owned by Lord Downe) and the Ferrari 250LM of David Piper at the British Eagle Trophy race at Brands Hatch in August 1966. Contributor: Eric Liddell

On the twenty-ninth of August 1966, five privateer Ford GT MkIs lined up on the starting grid for the British Eagle Trophy at Brands Hatch, UK. Two of them were former Essex Wire Corporation Le Mans machines. The Ford drivers were Innes Ireland, Mike Salmon, Bernard White, Eric Liddell and Nick Cussons. Ford GTs finished second, fourth and fifth.

It was during the non-FIA championship Group 4 race, the Ilford Films 500 at Brands Hatch in May 1966, that a Ford GT set the world record for the "Most number of pit stops in a race and still be classified a finisher". The record set was 35 pit stops and it is believed that this record still stands today.

Eric Liddell, one of the drivers involved in the record breaking effort said "Our engine heads were cracked and were leaking water. Everytime the engine temperature reached a certain point we had to make a pit stop to fill up with water. It took 35 pit stops, but we finished and were classified".

Springbok series 1966

Through their efforts in 1965, South African race officials and organisers saw an enormous increase in sportscar racing interest with the official start of the Springbok series in 1966.

Peter Sutcliffe entered the 1966 Kyalami 9hr race with the former Ford France Ford GT MkI powered by the 5.3 litre engine from Alan Mann Racing. Sharing the driving duties with Peter Sutcliffe was John Love.

Peter Sutcliffe's Ford GT was joined on the grid by the former Essex Wire Corporation (now owned by Bernard White) Ford GT chassis no. 1010, driven by Mike Spence and David Hobbs. Ed Nelson and Colin Crabbe were also there, driving the converted MkI road car, chassis no. 1021, which they had quickly purchased from Nick Cussons so that Ed Nelson could honour his racing contract with Alex Blignaut of SAMRAC (see Chapter 5 for more on this story). None of the Ford GTs finished the race.

The first Ford GT MkI in South Africa was Peter Sutcliffe's, chassis no. 1009, which he purchased from F.A.V. in November 1965. Contributor: Glen Smale-Automotive Research

Only the teams of Mike Spence and David Hobbs and Ed Nelson and Colin Crabbe competed at the next race in Cape Town, and both Ford GTs failed to finish. A Ferrari 365 driven by David Piper and Richard Attwood won the race.

All three Ford GT teams competed in the Laurenço Marques 3hr race, and this time they all finished ... but behind the Lola T70 of Roy Pierpoint and Doug Serrurier. At the Pietmaritzburg 3hr the Ford GT MkI driven by Mike Hailwood and David Hobbs won the race, with Ed Nelson and Colin Crabbe finishing in seventh place.

The last two South African races were held early in January 1967. The first was a sportscar support race for the 1st Grand Prix of South Africa at the Kyalami circuit. All three Ford GT teams started and Peter Sutcliffe finished second behind David Prophet driving the McLaren Elva-Ford.

Peter Sutcliffe repeated his second place, with Colin Crabbe coming in fourth in the last race of the 1966 Springbok series at the Killarney circuit.

Decision time

At the end of 1966, Henry Ford II shut down the F.A.V. operation in Slough, England, and had the entire endurance racing program transferred back to the USA. The plan for 1967, despite all the setbacks in 1966, was for Ford to solely develop the Ford J-car into a race winning prototype.

Just three short years after it started, the Ford factory backed works Ford GT racing program appeared to be over, or was it?

Three
Storm clouds gather

All American

After Le Mans 1966, Henry Ford II had made it clear to anyone who would listen that he was only interested in funding and developing the Ford J-car racing car program which had been started in 1965. The Ford GT MkIIA was to have been the last international Ford GT racing car project as Ford had won Le Mans and the Manufacturers' championship, achieving all set goals.

Henry's decision to shut down Ford Advanced Vehicles in England had created a situation which made things look grim for John Wyer and his team. John Wyer was also cut out of the American decision to convert their existing Ford GT MkIIAs to MkIIB specification. John Wyer also learned that he was not to play a role in the building of the new Ford HT MkIV chassis assemblies which had morphed out of the disappointing J-car program.

Ford USA also cut Alan Mann Racing from the Ford GT works team program, though Alan Mann still retained his works Ford Mustang team and the relationship with Holman Moody.

The man in charge of the entire All American Ford GT racing program would be Carroll Shelby. He's seen here with the new Ford GT MkIV, which morphed out of the J-car project. Contributor: Ford Motor Company

The last official Alan Mann team entry with a Ford GT was at Le Mans in 1966. Graham Hill is in there somewhere, running across the track. Contributor: Ford Motor Company

However, to Henry's credit he encouraged John Wyer to purchase the assets in England, under very favourable terms as Wyer was still very enthusiastic about continuing with the Ford GT MkI customer racing program.

In order to get the deal with Ford done, John Wyer recruited his long time friend John Willment to join him as a business partner. They co-founded a new company, J.W. Automotive (J.W.A.) and completed the purchase of the now defunct Ford Advanced Vehicles company.

J.W. Automotive builds its own

The core business for J.W. Automotive would be based around the in-house Ford MkI GT road and racing car programs. John Wyer had lost some ground in the customer racing car program because both the American works teams of Shelby and Holman had supplied their MkIIAs to other teams. The MkI road cars were not selling well in the USA, and a MkIII road car was developed for the American market. MkIs sold into the USA were being returned to the new company. Shelby American Inc. shipped back at least four new unassembled cars in 1967.

Despite this slow start in 1967, John Wyer would recover much of the customer racing program market in 1968 and 1969, whilst retaining a healthy, if not official, working relationship with the Ford Motor Company.

The saviour for J.W.A. was that the Ford GT was still a competitive force in motor racing, with new privateer teams still wanting to purchase the racing cars, and existing teams needing their racing cars refurbished, especially after accidents. J.W. Automotive was a robust company in early 1967, but it was about to become even more robust thanks to an American named Grady Davis.

Davis was the Vice President of the Gulf Oil Corporation and he had purchased one of the first Ford GT MkI road cars (chassis no. 1049). Not only was he very impressed with car itself, he also felt that supporting a racing team would be perfect for his desire to market and promote his company's products worldwide. He knew that a racing car, driven by household name drivers, painted in Gulf Oil Corporation colours, and winning major endurance race events would achieve this goal admirably. Davis also knew that motorsport on television was the future and, with the introduction of colour TV, the spectacles that were the major endurance races would provide plenty of 'free' advertising.

Davis remained an ardent and enthusiastic supporter of motor racing for many years, in partnership with John Wyer. Even when the glory days of the Ford GT were over, Davis moved with J.W.A., first to the Porsche 917 and, later, to a new series of J.W.A. Mirage racing cars which produced another Le Mans win for the team in 1975. However, back in 1967, John Wyer and Grady Davis knew that they would have to do something with the Ford GT to remain competitive in the 1968 racing season.

Secret American racing program?

Henry Ford II and his company were not very good at keeping secrets. The worst kept secret of 1966 was what Ford was really going to do in 1967. John Wyer was fully aware that Ford was developing an interim racing car, known as the MkIIB, and that the J-car had morphed into the Ford GT MkIV.

The Ford GT MkIIB was supposed to be a lighter and more powerful version of the MkIIA. It was certainly more powerful, with its new 520bhp (388kW) 16-valve, 427in^3 (7.0 litre) engine.

However, in reality, the MkIIB was not significantly lighter than the MkIIA. It weighed in at 2650lb (1202kg) dry, and over 3000lb (1361kg) with fuel and driver.

The basic problem for the MkIIBs was that they were all converted MkIIAs so, in effect, they were really just an upgrade, and as the race results show, nothing could really help the MkIIB. It was soundly thrashed by Ferrari in the first race of the season, the Daytona 24hr.

The major differences between the versions were:

• The engine's aluminium cylinder heads were replaced with steel versions.
• The single Le Mans style 4-barrel Holley carburettor was replaced with two 4-barrel downdraught Holley carburettors installed inside a pressurised box.
• A new profile camshaft was installed.
• New, 1.25in (31.75mm) thick, Kelsey-Hayes-designed ventilated brake rotors (discs) were installed. The new rotors were mounted on the wheel studs, as originally developed for the MkIIA, to allow for quick rotor and pad changes. The new, thicker ventilated rotors reduced brake temperatures dramatically, which resulted in reduced brake fade and a 30 per cent increase in brake pad wear life. No direct change in actual stopping power was recorded.
• New brake callipers, redesigned for the thicker rotors, were installed.
• A new rear torsion bar design was created in an effort to stop the MkIIB bottoming out on race track banking.
• Body panels were manufactured using a single skin fibreglass construction process.
• The passenger door was modified to remove the roof section from the door which became fixed as part of the roof.
• The front end was widened.
• The rear end was lightened and widened.

Holman Moody made some additional changes:
• The radiator to engine plumbing was re-routed through the passenger compartment instead of through the "fake propshaft".
• The entire interior was changed to resemble that of its NASCAR racing cars.

Shelby American Inc. Ford MkIIB driven by Paul Hawkins and Ronnie Bucknum.Contributor: Ford Motor Company

The new carburettor setup for the MkIIB. Contributor: Adrian Streather

Revised MkIIB rear suspension. Contributor: Adrian Streather

The Holman Moody MkIIB interior. Contributor: Adrian Streather

The Holman Moody MkIIB interior.
Contributor: Adrian Streather

Note: The Shelby American Inc. MkIIBs retained both the radiator to engine plumbing running through the "fake propshaft", and the standard Ford GT interior.

Improving access to the office

Anyone that has ever tried to get into a Ford GT with its canopy doors understands that it is not easy. For the tall driver the first impression when finally seated is that the door is going to chop off your head when it is shut. The natural reaction is to duck whilst pulling the door closed.

In the racing cars, the taller drivers had to have a bubble installed in the roof section of the driver's door. This is often called the "Gurney bubble".

The Colin Crabbe special extra tall person's bubble fitted to car no. 67, chassis no. 1021, (which Colin part owned with Ed Nelson) at the Nürburgring in 1967.
Contributor: Veit Arenz

For English driver Colin Crabbe who, at six foot six inches was one of the tallest Ford GT drivers, the Gurney bubble was not good enough, so he had a special bubble designed and installed in August 1966.

Note: Colin Crabbe told the author that, when he arrived in South Africa in November 1966 for the Springbok series, the Rand-Daily Mail *newspaper ran a front page article about the 'giant' of motor racing who had arrived.*

For first time passengers in the old and the new Ford GT, the fear was that they'd got into a car with a built in guillotine. If the passenger was 'height challenged' there was no problem, but if they were tall they could take some convincing when it was explained that they wouldn't lose their heads to the guillotine mounted to the top of the door.

At the race track mechanics were supposed to help the drivers in and out. The canopy doors made this extremely difficult. The doors had to be fully opened on both sides to allow the driver and mechanic to work as a team. It was not until 1967 that this problem was partially rectified.

Both the Ford GT MkIIB and MkIV were fitted with the normal driver's side canopy door, but the canopy section of the passenger side door was cut off and fixed to the body section of the roof. This allowed the mechanic to enter the GT easily to help the driver and also did not make the car so wide in the pits because the door did not need to be fully open.

Another office issue with the original Ford GTs was choosing the right kind of trousers to go driving in. The gearstick location and its size was perfect for hooking trouser legs. There is not an

The "Gurney bubble" in the driver's door of a Ford GT MkIIB.
Contributor: Adrian Streather

Access problem with the passenger door finally solved. Contributor: Adrian Streather

Life in the pits was then much easier for all concerned. Contributor: Ford Motor Company

The gearstick issue was never resolved on the first generation of Ford GT racers. It was not until the 21st century, second generation Ford GT (inset) was designed that the gearstick was moved into the centre of the car. Contributor: Adrian Streather

original Ford GT driver alive who has not felt the embrace of the gearstick as it travelled up their trouser leg.

The Ford GT MkIV

The MkIV was planned to be even lighter than the MkIIB, weighing in at 2250lb (1021kg), but fitted with the same 427in^3 (7 litre) engine. In fact, the official prime use for the MkIIB was to test and debug the new engine under the stress of a major race.

Most of the details on the MkIV are contained in Chapter 2 under the "J-car" heading. The fundamental differences between the MkIV and the MkIIB were the chassis (tub) assembly and the body shape. The MkIV chassis (tub) was constructed from 'honeycomb' aluminium. This form of construction had previously only used been used in the aircraft industry. The engine, transmission, running gear, and interior used for the MkIV were, essentially, identical to the MkIIB.

Ford GT MkIV 427 (7 litre) engine. Contributor: Ford Motor Company

Ford GT MkIV driven by Bruce McLaren and Mark Donohue in the heat of battle. Contributor: Ford Motor Company

The J-car gets its day of glory on the starting grid at Le Mans in 1967, as the Ford GT MkIV. Contributor: Ford Motor Company

The body was a completely new design, with much smoother lines, and was more efficient aerodynamically. The MkIV also had the modification carried out to the passenger side door to allow easier access for the mechanics in the pit stops.

A total of twelve MkIV numbered chassis (tub) assemblies were manufactured and they were only raced by the Shelby American Inc. and Holman Moody works teams. The MkIV would only last one season, but what a season that would turn out to be!

What else was the Ford GT up against?

For the 1967 racing season the Ford GT had to compete against:

- A new Jim Hall-designed Chapparal-Chevrolet 2F with its 427 (7.0 litre) 560bhp (418kW) V8 engine.
- A revised prototype Ferrari 330, known as the P3/P4.
- The return of Eric Broadley and his Lola team with the Lola-Aston Martin Mk3 T70 V8, and the Lola-Chevrolet T70 V8 customer racing cars.
- An ever stronger Porsche KG racing team with its Porsche 906, 907 long tail and 910.

Note: The Porsches might have had much smaller engines, at 2 litres as compared to the Ford GT 4.7 and 7.0 litre and the Ferrari with its 4 litre V12, but they started to get among the top place finishers at the end of many races.

Ford GT MkI, car no. 54, driven by Eric Liddell, versus Porsche 906, car no. 71, driven by Tony Dean, at the 1967 Guards International (Evening News Sports Car Race) at Brands Hatch. Contributor: Eric Liddell

Enter the J.W.A.-Gulf Ford Mirage M1

Whilst for most of its short life in the limelight, the J.W.A.-Gulf Mirage M1 carried the name Ford in its full title; it was never recognised as a Ford by the governing bodies of motorsport. Ford argued that the Mirage was 100% Ford and, included in the submission, was the claim that the Mirage M1 was based on the Ford GT design. Despite the effort and the claims, Ford still lost the argument and manufacturers points won in any race were awarded to the Mirage brand.

The Mirage M1 was built exclusively for J.W.A. and none were manufactured for other teams. The surviving Mirage M1 was sold off to a privateer team owner in November 1968.

The Mirage M1 may have looked like an updated Ford GT, but was, in fact, supposed to be giant leap forward in motor racing engineering. Former drivers of the Mirage M1 had a different perspective, and the race results of the M1 during the 1967 racing season were nothing to write home about.

The Mirage M1 design included:

- A lightweight steel chassis assembly.
- A modified cockpit area to produce a narrower and more aerodynamic shape. The A-pillars were completely redesigned and, as a result, the space inside the car for the driver was significantly reduced.
- The side-mounted engine air-intakes were removed to improve the aerodynamics.

J.W.A.-Gulf Mirage M1 as it is today in its original trim complete with front fins. Contributor: Chris Clarke-Blackhawk Collection

• Factory images show that the body parts made from fibreglass were thinner than before.
• The main body structure was manufactured from aluminium; further evidence of the 'lightweight' tag applied to the M1.
• For some race tracks, front side fins were added. However, they were not used in every race. Images exist of Jackie Icxk's Mirage M1 with, and without, fins fitted.
• Extra large ventilated brake discs had been designed for the Mirage M1. The front brakes were fitted with large flexible air hoses leading to aluminium muffs installed over the brake rotor (disc) surface.
• Compared to the MkIIA, the M1 had a significantly more sophisticated suspension system. During practice on the Mirage M1's competition debut at Monza, driven by Jacky Ickx, a rear suspension mounting collapsed. The suspension mounts were reinforced and new springs fitted before the start of the actual race.
• The spare wheel (required to be carried) was mounted between the radiator and the front suspension.
• The 5-speed ZF transaxle was retained.

Initially, the Mirage M1 was fitted with the 289in³ (4.7 litre) V8 engine used in the standard Ford GT MkI, but by the time the M1 was ready for its first race at Monza in Italy, at the end of April 1967, the engine had been replaced with the Gurney-Weslake 302 (5.1 litre) V8 unit.

The Gurney-Weslake 302 engine was soon replaced by the brand new Ford 351in³ (5.7 litre) V8 racing engine. John Wyer wasn't satisfied with the standard Ford 351 (5.7 litre) racing engine, so he set to improving it before it was used in anger in the M1. The Ford factory C6FE racing cylinder heads were modified to feature a dropped combustion chamber. This provided a lower valve seat area which allowed for substantially larger and straighter intake and exhaust port runners. These modifications increased the airflow into the engine by approximately 15 per cent.

Note: One of the two M1s entered for the Spa 1000km (600 mile) race in Belgium used the J.W. Automotive version of the 351in³ (5.7 litre) V8 racing engine for the first time.

Mirage versus Ford GT? Not yet

The 1967 racing season started with the second Daytona 24hr race. The Ford GT MkIV was still not raceworthy, which meant Ford was represented by the Shelby American Inc. and Holman Moody works teams, racing six of the interim MkIIBs between them, but Ford was still serious about winning. The J.W.A.-Gulf Mirage was not yet ready for competition.

During practice it was reported by the Press that the Holman Moody cars were handling well, but the Shelby American Inc. machines were handling like pigs.

The J.W.A.-Gulf team entered two standard Group 4 Ford GT MkIs, car no. 11 driven by Jacky Ickx and Dick Thompson, and car no. 20 driven by William (Bill) Wonder and Raymond Caldwell.

Car no. 11 was painted in a shade of dark blue which, at the time, was the official colour of the Gulf Oil Corporation.

Note: The much more famous light (powder/pale) blue with marigold (orange) stripe which epitomised the Gulf Oil-sponsored racing car era were originally the colours of the Californian-based Wiltshire Oil Company, purchased by Gulf. The actual paint codes used to create the original J.W.A.-Gulf team colours were British

In 1968, the Gurney-Weslake engine was replaced with the Gurney-Eagle engine of the same capacity. M10001 was usually raced with the 351 engine during the 1968 season. Contributor: Chris Clarke-Blackhawk Collection

The start of the 1967 edition of the Sebring 12hr. Contributor: Ford Motor Company

Leyland colours, originally used for its Triumph line of sportscars:
Light or Powder blue – colour code P030-8013.
Marigold – colour code P030-3393.

When the race was over, Ford's old nemesis Ferrari occupied the top three podium places, and the Porsche KG team from Zuffenhausen, Germany, occupied fourth and fifth.

Jacky Ickx and Richard Thompson finished sixth overall and first in Group 4, with Wonder and Caldwell in eighth overall and second in Group 4. Sandwiched between them, in seventh place, was the lone works MkIIB still in the race, driven by Bruce McLaren, Lucien Bianchi and Dan Gurney.

The Sebring 12hr, on the first of April 1967, saw the long awaited debut of the Ford GT MkIV, but still no J.W.A.-Gulf team Mirage M1s.

Several Ford MkIV, MkIIB and MkIs contested the race start. Twelve hours and 268 Sebring laps later, the MkIV driven by Bruce McLaren and Mario Andretti took the chequered flag.

In second place was the crippled Ford GT MkIIB of A.J. Foyt and Lloyd Ruby. They were very lucky to hold onto second place after suffering a camshaft failure with only thirty minutes of the race remaining. As they waited anxiously in the pits, the Porsche Carrera 10 of Gerhard Mitter and Scooter Patrick continued to circulate. When the chequered flag came down it was judged that Foyt and Ruby had covered a marginally longer race distance than Mitter and Patrick after 226 laps, compared to the winner's record breaking 268 laps.

In fifth place, and the Group 4 winner, was the MkI of Umberto Maglioli and Nino Vaccarella, with the other MkI of Bill McNamara and Bob Grossmann coming home in eighth place and second in

Bruce McLaren (left) and Mario Andretti pose with their 1967 Sebring 12hr winning Ford GT MkIV.
Contributor: Ford Motor Company

Group 4. Not a bad day's work for the Ford GT. First and second overall, first and second in the Group 6 class, and first and second in the Group 4 class.

Note: In the USA all the Ford GT teams used Firestone tyres.

The Mirage M1 debuts

Testing for Le Mans 1967 took place on the eighth and ninth of April. J.W.A.-Gulf Mirage M1s attended, albeit powered by standard Ford 289 (4.7 litre) V8 racing engines. Joining the Ford product testing battleground, were the works teams with their MkIVs and MkIIBs, and the privateer teams with the Group 4, MkIs.

When the results were compiled they showed that Richard Attwood driving the Mirage M1 with its 4.7 litre V8 was six seconds a lap slower than the best of the works teams' MkIIBs driven by Mark Donohue, but only two seconds a lap slower than the fastest of the works teams' MkIVs, the one driven by Bruce McLaren. The Ferrari 330 P3/P4 driven by Lorenzo Bandini recorded the fastest lap, seven seconds quicker than Mark Donohue.

The Ford works teams did not show up at Monza on the twenty-fifth of April 1967, but the J.W.A.-Gulf Mirage M1s did, and this time they were both running the brand new 302 (5.0 litre) Gurney-Weslake Ford V8 racing engine.

Note: The Gurney-Weslake heads were made from aluminium and incorporated the steeply downdraughted inlet ports. They were dry-decked, which meant no water was flowing through them for cooling purposes. The idea of removing the water passages from the heads was to improve the reliability of the head gaskets which were constantly blowing on the older, water-cooled steel heads.

These 302 (5.0 litre) engines were not driver friendly. All the power was in a narrow band at the top end of the rpm range. This made the engine suitable for some tracks but not for others. The Press at the time reported that on some race tracks, the drivers had to play 'tunes' with the gearbox to keep the revs up in the power band.

Holman Moody Ford GT MkIIB, car no. 2, finished in second place at Sebring in 1967 after an anxious wait in the pits for its drivers.
Contributor: Ford Motor Company

Eric Liddell and Ed Nelson drove Ford GT MkI, car no. 36 (chassis no. 1009) at Monza, Italy in 1967. They finished eleventh overall and second in class. Contributor: Eric Liddell

The M1 drivers for Monza were the usual suspects: Jacky Ickx, Alan Rees, David Piper and Richard Thompson. Monza was not to be the most impressive of debuts for the Mirage. Jacky Ickx was forced out with ignition problems. David Piper had a very eventful race. First he spun in the Parabolica when a loose manifold stud caused water to spray onto the rear wheel and he lost two laps having this repaired in the pits. Later, a shock absorber collapsed resulting in another lengthy pit stop, but David Piper and Richard Thompson managed to nurse their Mirage M1 into ninth place overall.

An interesting semi-works entry at Monza was the Ford France MkI. Ford France was the only team running the new, 1967 4-bolt version of the 289 (4.7 litre) V8 engine. This engine was also fitted with the dry-deck Gurney-Weslake heads. The new engine was installed in the equally new, single panel, lightweight GT40. The Ford France GT finished first in Group 4 and 6th overall.

Note: The 4-bolt engines had 4-bolt main caps supporting the crankshaft instead of the original 2-bolt main cap system.

In May 1967, Spa in Belgium hosted the 1000km endurance race in which the J.W.A.-Gulf Mirage M1 would show its true metal, driven by home town hero, Jacky Ickx. The Ford works teams were absent again as most of their drivers were racing in the Indianapolis 500, which just happened to be scheduled on the same day. Other teams also lost some star drivers to Indy.

Two Mirage M1s were entered by the J.W.A.-Gulf team. One was fitted with the new 351 (5.7 litre) Gurney-Weslake V8 engine, the other with the 302 (5.0 litre) Gurney-Weslake V8.

The original driver pairings were to be Jacky Ickx with Alan Rees crewing the 351-powered M1, and David Piper with Richard Thompson in the 302-powered M1. However, when David Piper spun off during the seventh lap, Dick Thompson was immediately transferred to the Jacky Ickx M1. Thompson took over the driving of the lone M1 left in the race when Jacky Ickx finally pitted for a driver change, 3 hours and ten minutes after the start.

Note: The maximum time per driver per stint under FIA rules in 1967 was three hours. Going over by ten minutes in Jacky's first stint,

J.W.A.-Gulf Mirage M1 driven by Jacky Ickx and Richard Thompson at the Spa 1000km fitted with the 351 (5.7 litre) engine. Contributor: Ford Motor Company

The Jacky Ickx and Richard Attwood Gulf team Mirage M1 at the Nürburgring in 1967. Contributor: Veit Arenz

Jacky Ickx and Richard Thompson in the Mirage M1 enjoy their debut win at the Spa 1000km. Contributor: Ford Motor Company

resulted in a post race protest. The protest was dismissed.

1000km after setting off from second spot on the grid, Jacky Ickx brought the J.W.A.-Gulf Ford Mirage M1 over the finish line in first place. Peter Sutcliffe and Brian Redman finished 6th overall, with Mike Salmon and Jackie Oliver finishing in 8th overall in their Group 4 privateer MkIs.

The Mirage M1 was back in action for the 1967 Nürburgring 1000km. Jacky Ickx driving with Richard Attwood had the Spa winning 351 (5.7 litre) powered M1. David Piper and Richard Thompson had the M1 fitted with the 302 (5.0 litre) engine, which was known not to be suited to the Nürburgring.

Ford France was back with its Group 4 MkIs – one older version, with the standard Ford 289 V8 racing engine, and the new lightweight GT fitted with the Gurney-Weslake-Ford V8 engine. Two other privateer teams from the UK also entered their MkIs in the Group 4 class. Ferrari 330P4s, Lola-Aston Martins and Chaparrals were also well represented.

Practice for the race started with a disaster for car no. 5, the Mirage M1 driven David Piper and Richard Thompson. Driving first was Richard Thompson and he managed to take off at the 13.2km track marker. As he spun down the road he slammed into John Markey's Climax-powered Ginetti which was still parked on the side of the track where it had crashed three hours earlier.

Ford GT MkI, car no. 57, chassis no. 1021, driven by Colin Crabbe and Roy Pierpoint being followed by MkI car, no. 62, chassis no. 1009, driven by Ed Nelson and Peter de Klerk. Contributor: Veit Arenz

The Udo Schütz and Joe Buzzetta's 2-litre Porsche 910 at the Nürburgring 1000km in 1967. Contributor: Dr. Ing. h. c. F. Porsche AG

Richard Thompson suffered only minor injuries, but the Mirage M1 looked decidedly second-hand and would never race again. The chassis (no. M10002) was written off and scrapped.

The race itself was a disaster for all the Group 6 prototypes. One by one they fell by the wayside. The Jacky Ickx and Richard Attwood Gulf team Mirage M1 did make a race of it only to be thwarted 14 laps from the end. Their car was lying in third place overall when Richard Attwood ran over a brick at the Adenau crossing which resulted in both right-hand side tyres blowing out. Which car won? A 2.0 litre Porsche 910 ...

The old Ford France GT MkI won the Group 4 class, finishing seventh overall. Eighth place went to one of the privateer Ford GTs, ninth to the Chevron-BMW, tenth to the other Ford France Ford GT, and eleventh to thirteenth to three of the 2.0 litre Porsche 911S teams, placing them first, second and third in the GT class.

The Shelby American Inc. Ford GT MkIV, car no. 2, of Bruce McLaren and Mark Donohue on pole for the start at Le Mans. Their car is surrounded by grid girls dressed in the latest 1967 fashions. Grid girl fashion has changed a lot since then ...
Contributor: Ford Motor Company

Old rivalries re-ignited

The Ford works teams missed all the European endurance races leading up to Le Mans, and the Ferrari teams didn't attend the American endurance races at Daytona or Sebring. The motoring press was having a field day with the rivalry issue. Even the PR teams from both companies were firing broadsides at each other. A real head-to-head confrontation was looming ...

Many people, including the race organisers and the other manufacturers, complained that too much attention was being paid to Ferrari and Ford, and that the other teams were being ignored. In the end, though, it didn't matter, because as the race progressed it became a Ferrari versus Ford contest for the podium places, as expected. Everyone else was just there to make up the numbers and to fight for the minor class wins.

The J.W.A.-Gulf Mirage M1 of Jacky Ickx and Brain Muir.
Contributor: Ford Motor Company

Le Mans 1967

The mood for Le Mans 1967 was tinged with sadness. The great Ferrari driver Lorenzo Bandini had been badly burned in a crash at the Monaco Grand Prix in his Ferrari F1 car. He succumbed to his injuries on the tenth of May. He would eventually be replaced in the Ferrari team by privateer Ford GT driver Peter Sutcliffe.

Le Mans 1967 was to provide a spectacular stage for Ford's commitment to promoting its products via motorsport. The race was full of drama, excitement, mistakes and records broken.

Most of the teams had been worried about the dull and overcast skies, but as the starting time approached, their nerves improved as the weather changed and the sky began to clear.

The entire complement of works Shelby American Inc. and Holman Moody teams, with their Ford GT MkIIB and MkIVs, made it to the starting grid for Le Mans. Bruce McLaren and Mark Donohue with their MkIV were on pole.

The full starting line-up for Le Mans 1967.
Contributor: Ford Motor Company

And they're off! Bruce McLaren in car no. 2 and the Chapparal, car no. 7, seem to be very slow off the line. Contributor: Ford Motor Company

Ford GT MkIVs shared both the second row grid positions. Ford GT MkIIBs shared both the third row grid positions, and the Mirage M1s shared both the eighth row grid positions.

There were eleven Ford-powered cars in the first twenty places on the grid. These cars were joined by seven Ferrari 330 P3/P4s, a lone Chaparral 2AF (second on the grid), and a singleton Lola-Aston Martin T70 MkIII (fourteenth on the grid). The eventual winners of the race started from grid position nine.

The French tricolour fell at exactly 4pm and 54 drivers sprinted to their cars parked on the other side of the track. When the confusion was over, the MkIIB of Shelby American Inc. driver Paul Hawkins was in the lead, closely followed by fellow Australian Frank Gardner, driving a MkIIB for the Holman Moody team.

Mario Andretti, driving the Holman Moody MkIV, had been left stranded on the starting grid. He did get going eventually and, by lap 33, had clawed his way back up to third place.

For the J.W.A.-Gulf Mirage M1s, Le Mans 1967 was to be a most forgettable event. On the first night practice both 351 (5.7 litre) engines self-destructed beyond pit garage repair. For some strange reason, J.W.A.-Gulf had no replacement engines.

The smaller, lower-powered, but more reliable 289 (4.7 litre) V8s couldn't be installed because the Mirage M1 was using fuel tanks sized for over 5.0 litre engines. There was only one possible solution – J.W.A. had to install the 302 (5.0 litre) Gurney-Weslake V8 engines. These engines weren't race proven past the three hour mark, and they required playing music with the gearbox.

Not unexpectedly, both engines expired during the early hours of the race. One failed after three hours and the other after

The Mirage M1 of David Piper and Richard Thompson during the early part of the race. Contributor: Ford Motor Company

four hours. The latter seized solid as the Mirage M1 driven by David Piper rolled into the pit lane. The problem with this engine was later diagnosed as a broken inlet valve.

For the Mirage M1 it was not only the first but also the last appearance at Le Mans.

Unfortunately for Mario Andretti and two others driving for the Holman Moody team, their race was over around 4am on Sunday morning when the team won the 'biggest mistake' award of the race, and possibly the motor racing goof of the century.

Mario Andretti was at the front of a trio of Holman Moody team cars. As Andretti passed under the Dunlop Bridge and headed down the hill, he appeared to misjudge his approach to the Esses. The end result was Andretti playing passenger as his MkIV spun off the circuit into the wall. Jo Schlesser and Roger McCluskey, both driving MkIIBs behind Andretti, took evasive action but both ended up in the wall as well. Amazingly, none of the three cars touched each other. Only Mario Andretti suffered any injury, and he was taken to hospital for X-rays. The other two drivers just suffered from damaged pride.

Earlier in the race, Mario Andretti and Denis Hulme, each driving Ford GT MkIVs for the Holman Moody team, set an equal fastest lap. According to the race records it was on the same lap, lap forty-one.

They achieved an identical fastest and record lap time of 3 minutes 23.6 seconds, covering the 1967 version of the Sarthe circuit at an average speed of 148.7mph (239.3kph).

Note: The Sarthe circuit has been modified in shape and length a number of times. In 1967 the track length was 7.27 miles (13.469km).

Another view of the David Piper and Richard Thompson Mirage M1. Contributor: Ford Motor Company

A happier moment for Mario Andretti as he leads Lloyd Ruby through the Esses. Contributor: Ford Motor Company

Mario Andretti and Lucien Bianchi shared the drive of the Holman Moody Ford GT MkIV. Contributor: Ford Motor Company

The Shelby American Inc. Ford GT MkIV of Dan Gurney and A.J. Foyt as night begins to fall. Contributor: Ford Motor Company

The Shelby American Inc. pits, with the Bruce McLaren and Mark Donohue MkIV pitted at the same time as the MkIIB of Ron Bucknam and Paul Hawkins. Contributor: Ford Motor Company

Le Mans 1967 was a race of attrition, and Ford was playing the numbers game: the more cars in the race, the better the chance of a podium finish. However, the drop out rate for the Ford GTs during the race became alarmingly high. Apart from the three Holman Moody team cars parked in the wall in full public view at the Dunlop Bridge, the following teams were also eliminated:

- Viscount Downe Ford GT MkI, two hours into the race after it caught fire.
- Holman Moody Ford GT MkIV, eight hours into the race after an accident.
- Scuderia-Filipinetti Ford GT MkI, nine hours into the race after a cylinder head failure.
- Ford France Ford GT MkI, fourteen hours into the race after a cylinder head failure.

Note: Ford France was a co-sponsor, with Holman Moody, of the MkIIB driven by Jo Schlesser and Guy Ligier. This car was caught up in the altercation initiated by Mario Andretti in the Esses.

- Shelby American Inc. Ford GT MkIIB, eighteen hours into the race after an engine valve failure.

All-American victors Dan Gurney and A.J. Foyt take the chequered flag to win Le Mans 1967. Contributor: Ford Motor Company

Ford GT MkIIB belonging to the Ford France team driven by Jo Schlesser and Guy Ligier. Contributor: Ford Motor Company

Celebrations for the drivers and mechanics of car no. 1, Le Mans winner 1967. Contributor: Ford Motor Company

Bruce McLaren and Mark Donohue, driving their Shelby American Inc. MkIV, came in fourth. Contributor: Ford Motor Company

By the end of the race only two Ford GT MkIVs were still running. The Shelby American Inc. team of Dan Gurney and Anthony Joseph (A.J.) Foyt in car no. 1 finished in first place. They started from grid position nine and covered a record race distance of 3250 miles (5230km).

The Ferrari 330 P3/P4 of the S.P.A. Ferrari SEFAC, Italy team came in second, driven by Italian Ludovico Scarfiotti, partnered by Englishman Mike Parkes.

Third place was also taken by a Ferrari 330 P3/P4 from the Equipe National Belgium team.

The Shelby American Inc. team of Bruce McLaren and Mark Donohue finished in fourth place, with fifth to eighth positions occupied by Porsche factory team types 907/6, 910/6, 906/6 and 906/6 respectively, all with 2.0 litre engines.

Of the 54 starters at Le Mans 1967 only 16 were classified as finishers. Unfortunately, as events unfolded after the race, it would be the last time racing fans would see the factory-supported Ford GT works teams, such as Shelby American Inc. and Holman Moody, in action in Europe. Collective Ford and Ferrari dummies were about to be spit out onto the ground ...

Storm upgraded to a Hurricane

Ford's race director Jacques Passino complained bitterly about the safety of the Sarthe (Le Mans) circuit after the tragic death of American driver Walt Hansgen in April 1966. However, when Ford returned to Le Mans in 1967, little had been improved at the track.

Straw bales were the only protection afforded to drivers who went off line at high speed on the Le Mans Sarthe circuit. Contributor: C. Nahum Collection; photograph by Gérard Crombac

Note: The list of drivers killed in racing related accidents from 1963 to 1967 numbered thirty five. Most were burned to death. Along with the driver fatalities, five course marshals and nine spectators also lost their lives as a direct result of a race track incidents over the same time span.

Reports from the time indicate that Ford believed itself to have been deceived by both the Federation Internationale De L'Automobile (FIA) and the Automobile Club De L'Ouest (ACO). However, many believe the real argument was between Ford and the Commission Sportive Internationale (CSI) over its refusal to homologate the J.W.A.-Gulf Mirage M1 as a Ford product which would then count towards Ford's total points in the Manufacturers' championship.

The CSI's argument was that the Mirage had nothing directly to do with Ford. Ford had sold its entire UK-based assets to J.W. Automotive, and J.W.A. had constructed its own racing car. The chassis was constructed from scratch and the body was made from aluminium, it just happened to look like a Ford GT.

The argument became so intense that, at Le Mans in 1967, John Cowley, Roy Lunn and Jacques Passino of Ford advised both the FIA and ACO that if they did not accept the J.W.A.-Gulf Mirage M1 as a Ford and fix the major safety concerns they had for the Sarthe (Le Mans) circuit, they would leave the sportscar racing scene in Europe and never come back.

Ford warned both the FIA and the ACO that they would never see such a Ford line-up in Europe again, if they didn't back down. Neither side budged. Contributor: Ford Motor Company

Hurricane force controversy

Prior to Le Mans 1967, the ACO was in a complete panic over the threats being made by Ford. They made direct contact with Prince Metternich-Winnenburg, Vice-President of the CSI, and advised him they (the ACO) could not afford to make major safety improvements to the Sarthe circuit. The ACO asked the Prince to intervene and to try and convince Ford to stay, without agreeing to major financial burdens being placed upon their organisation. Ford refused to negotiate.

An emergency meeting of the CSI was hastily organised by Prince Metternich-Winnenburg for the Monday after the race, at the Automobile Club De France in Paris. Only the Prince and the delegates from France, Italy, Germany, USA and Great Britain attended the meeting. Eight hours later they had made their decision.

The Commission Sportive Internationale (CSI) decided, as of the first of January 1968, to reduce the Group 6 prototype engine size from 7 litres to 3 litres, and to allow Group 4 cars to have up to a 5 litre engine, as long as fifty of the type were built.

Note: Fifty cars did not need to have been built prior to acceptance, but 50 must have been proven to be planned to be built. Both Ford and Lola were on the low side of fifty but were never stopped from competing in Group 4.

It took ten days for the decision to get out to all those concerned. The reaction from Enzo Ferrari, Eric Broadley, Bill France Sr. and the other racing car barons was nothing short of outrage. Many simply scoffed at the idea that reducing engine capacity would slow the prototypes. Ford GT fans around the world joined the argument claiming the French were trying to legislate their favourite American-made racing car out of existence. The story was quickly blown up into another 'France doing the dirty on the USA' situation. The belief that the French legislated against the American Ford to protect the European companies like Ferrari, Matra and Renault became a legend, which 40 years later is still as strong as ever. Reality, however, is somewhat different.

Who lost what?

- Ford lost the ability to use the 427 (7.0 litre) V8 engine and the ability to race the GT in the prototype Group 6 class. The GT40 was already homologated as a Group 4 and so was allowed to use the 5.0 litre engines, which Ford already had in its arsenal. Ford also had the 3 litre Cosworth V8 engine available, but chose not to install this into the MkIV to create a new prototype. Two spare MkIV chassis assemblies were used for the 1969 Ford G7A CanAm car project.

Note: With the exception of one MkIIB loaned to Ford France after Le Mans 1967, all the Ford works teams which had the MkIIB and MkIVs cars returned them to Ford. These GT40s were all retired and would not be seen racing again until the Historic racing series started in the 1970s.

- Lola filled in some paperwork and the 5.0 litre version of the T70 was homologated in Group 4.
- Jim Hall's Chaparral 2F prototype with its 7.0 litre V8 engine

Ford lost only the 427 (7 litre) engines fitted to the MkIIB and MkIV Ford GTs. Could it have created a 3-litre group 6 prototype from the MkIVs? Contributor: Ford Motor Company

Jim Hall's 7.0 litre Chaparral 2F was consigned to the garage of history by the new regulations. Contributor: les Coyotes

and distinctive rear wing that reached for the stars was gone. The C2F was a pure Group 6 prototype and it could not be homologated in Group 4.

• The J.W.A.-Gulf Mirage M1 was gone. J.W.A.-Gulf had the Gurney-Weslake 302 (5.0 litre) V8 engine, but again the Mirage M1 could not be homologated in Group 4 due to the fact that only three had been built for the 1967 racing season, and the M1 had not been approved by the FIA as a Ford product so Ford wasn't interested in pursuing (read financing) such an homologation program. By the time the Mirage M1 was accepted as a Ford in 1968, the game was over.

• The Ferrari 330 was gone. Being a pure Group 6 prototype, using a 4 litre V12 engine, it could not be homologated into Group 4.

• The French Matra M630-Ford Group 6 prototype was in trouble, though Matra was developing a 3.0 litre V12 engine which it used in 1968.

• Alan Mann Racing immediately started plans to build its own Len Bailey-designed Group 6 prototype using the new 3-litre Ford-Cosworth V8 engine, which would allow it back into top class of the World Sportscar Championship. Remember, Alan Mann Racing had been dumped at the end of 1966 as a Ford works team.

Many commentators and historians look back at the efforts of Alan Mann Racing and others who made a quick return to racing under the new rules of the World Sportscar Championship. Many wonder why Ford didn't take its lightweight honeycomb aluminium Ford GT MkIV chassis and use it as a base for a new Ford 3 litre prototype. The company had the engine and the in-house talent but, clearly, decided not to go down that route.

Ferrari lost the 330 P3/P4 to the new 3.0 litre regulations. Contributor: Ford Motor Company

Alan Mann Racing Len Bailey-designed Ford F3l P68 powered by a 3-litre Ford-Cosworth V8. Contributor: Udo Klinkel

Both Ferrari and Ford stuck to their positions and continued to argue that they could not afford to build 50 Group 4 versions of their cars. Nonetheless, a meeting of the outraged took place in early August 1967. The group produced a list of demands for the CSI, including a delay of twelve months for the engine capacity and Group homologation changes. Their demands were rejected, and the new rules stood as of the first of January 1968.

Ferrari and Ford were full of huff and puff, but they did not blow the motor racing house down.

1967 racing season conclusion

After Le Mans, four major long distance races still remained to be fought over. These were:

- Reims 12hr.
- Surfers Paradise 12hr in Australia.
- Paris 1000km.
- Kyalami 9hr in South Africa (described in the Springbok series section).

Ford USA loaned a GT MkIIB to Ford France and, with drivers Jo Schlesser and Guy Ligier, the car was entered in both the Reims 12hr and the Paris 1000km. They won the Reims race, and the J.W.A.-Gulf Mirage M1 driven by Jacky Ickx and Paul Hawkins won the Paris 1000km.

When the 1967 season finished, the over 2-litre Group 6 Manufacturers' Championship had been won by Ferrari, with Porsche KG second and Ford third. The under 2-litre championship was won by Porsche KG.

Minor league racing expands

Whilst 1966 had been a topsy-turvy racing year for the Ford GT, there was no stopping the numbers being entered into international and national events around the world.

During the 1967 racing season, Ford GT MkIs driven by privateer teams and, occasionally, the J.W.A.-Gulf team Mirage M1s thrilled the fans at The Grand National at Zolder in Holland; the GP of Paris at Montlhéry; and the Trophée Auvergne 300km, which was won by Paul Hawkins in his own Ford GT, chassis no. AMGT-2. The Ford GT of Peter Sutcliffe came in second, and Jo Schlesser was third for Ford France. The Reims 12hr, the ADAC Norisring-Rennen International, the 200 Meilen von Nürnberg and the Criterium de Vitesse at Magny-Cours had Ford GT entries also.

The Swedish GP at the Karlskoga circuit had a star line-up, with the race eventually being won by Jacky Ickx driving the Gulf team Mirage M1. In second place was the second Gulf team Mirage M1, driven by Jo Bonnier and Paul Hawkins. Ed Nelson and Colin Crabbe drove the other Ford GT MkI entries.

Only Jo Schlesser raced in the Coupes de Paris at Montlhéry in the Ford France Ford GT MkI, chassis no. 1012, which is now housed in the Sarthe museum at Le Mans. Mike Spence raced at Zeltweg in the Colin Crabbe-owned Ford GT MkI, chassis no. 1021, once owned by Nick Cussons.

The two Gulf team Mirage M1s attended the Skarpnack race in Stockholm, Sweden. The winner was Jo Bonnier, in one of the Gulf team Mirage M1s. Second was Paul Hawkins driving in the other Gulf team Mirage M1.

Ed Nelson also competed at the 1967 AvD Hockenheimring-Rennen at Hockenheim in Germany. Umberto Maglioli entered and drove his Ford GT MkI for the Donaupokalrennen at the Wien-Aspern circuit in Austria.

Ford GT MkIs from Ford France, Scuderia Brescia Corse, and privateer Neil Corner, joined the J.W.A.-Gulf team Mirage M1 for the Paris 1000km. The race was won by Jacky Ickx and Paul Hawkins driving the Mirage M1. None of the Ford GT MkIs finished the race. The last race of the international season was the Rhodesian GP. David Prophet entered and drove his own Ford GT MkI in this race. He finished third.

For 1967, the Canadian Sports Car Championship was expanded to ten events. As in 1966 the main Ford GT campaigner was Eppie Wietzes driving the Canadian Comstock team Ford GT MkI. Records showed that only the Comstock team raced the Ford GT in this series.

British home events in 1967

The Ford GT and Mirage M1 were also thrilling fans in the UK. The RAC British Sportscar Championship series consisted of seven races. The Ford GT drivers for this series read again like a who's

Ford GT MkI, chassis no. 1022, driven by Eric Liddell, versus Ferrari at the Wills Trophy race at Silverstone in 1967. The Ferrari is believed to be the 250LM of David Piper who eventually won the race, with Denis Hulme, Paul Hawkins and Eric Liddell, all in Ford GTs, coming in second, third and fourth respectively. Contributor: Eric Liddell

A rare photograph of the Kyalami 9hr. The J.W.A.-Gulf team Mirage M1 can be seen on the left rejoining the race after a pit stop. Contributor: David Harvey

who of motor racing. Paul Hawkins, Frank Gardner, Denis Hulme, Mike Salmon, John Harris, Ed Nelson, Eric Liddell, Terry Drury, Ron Fry, Colin Crabbe, Peter Sutcliffe, Peter Gethin, Keith Holland, Richard Bond, Julian Sutton, Pedro Rodriguez and Richard Thompson (driving the Mirage M1), Charles Lucas, Roy Pike, Dave Charlton, David Prophet, David Hobbs, George Humble and Neil Corner.

The British National race calendar consisted of twenty-one events, and privately entered MkIs were campaigned by Terry Drury, Charles Lucas and Neil Corner in a number of these races.

Springbok series 1967

The first race in the 1967 Springbok series was again the Kyalami 9hr. This time the race was won by the 5.7-litre powered J.W.A.-Gulf Mirage M1 driven by Jacky Ickx and Brian Redman.

Two Ford GT MkIs were also in the race. One was owned by Ed Nelson, who shared the driving with Mike Hailwood, and the other was owned by David Prophet, who shared driving stints with Peter de Klerk. Both the Ford GT MkIs finished and both scored valuable points towards the overall Springbok series championship.

The second race was the Cape 3hr with the Ed Nelson and David Prophet Ford GTs flying the flag. The Mirage M1 was shipped home.

These two Ford GTs and their drivers continued to compete in the other races in the series, which included the Mozambique 3hr, Dickie Dale 3hr and, in early 1968, the Kyalami F1 support race and the South Eastern Meeting in Cape Town.

Ed Nelson won his class in the 1967 Springbok and was third overall. He said in a recent article that this should have been the highlight of his racing career, but because he only raced for fun, it didn't really matter.

*Opposite: Ford GT MkI, car no. 54, driven by Eric Liddell, versus Ford GT P40 driven by Paul Hawkins at the 1967 Guards International (*Evening News *Sports Car Race) at Brands Hatch. Contributor: Eric Liddell*

Four

The show must go on

Cleaning up after the storm

With Ford and Ferrari spitting their respective dummies to the dirt in 1967, the pessimists were having a field day. The traditional first race of the sportscar championship was the Daytona 24hr, who and what would turn up in 1968? Would the pessimists be right?

John Wyer, John Willment and Grady Davis were not put off by the banning of the big bangers. They still had the Gurney-Weslake 289 (4.7 litre) and Gurney-Weslake 302 (5.0 litre) engines, so they did some lateral thinking:

- Mirage M1 chassis no. 0001 was retained for non-championship races.
- Mirage M1 chassis no. 0002 had been totally destroyed by Richard Thompson so that was out of the loop because J.W.A. scrapped it.
- Mirage M1 chassis no. 0003 was converted to components. J.W.A. took the chassis from 0003, re-identified it as chassis no. 1074. Then fitted a new, wider aluminium GT MkI styled body assembly, the size of the fuel tanks were reduced, six spoke magnesium alloy racing wheels were fitted and, *voila!*, the Ford GT MkI had been re-invented.
- J.W.A. built three more Group 4 Ford GT MkIs from scratch: chassis nos. 1075, 1076 and 1084. The J.W.A.-Gulf team was ready to race again.

Note: In 1970, 1074 had its roof cut off and was used as a camera car (Solar Productions) for Steve McQueen's famous movie Le Mans. *Chassis no. 1074 was later restored from camera car form back to its Monza 1000km winning configuration. It is currently in the USA as part of a private collection.*

Note: Dan Gurney severed his business relations with the Weslake engine company of Sussex, England. Whilst many Gurney-Weslake aluminium heads remained in circulation, from 1968 onwards, the aluminium heads would be produced with the name Gurney-Eagle on them instead of Gurney-Weslake.

Alan Mann Racing also decided to get back into the fray, but with its Ford-based 3-litre prototype named the Ford F3L P68.

Daytona opens the 1968 racing season

The J.W.A.-Gulf team entered Ford GT MkIs, chassis nos. 1074 and 1075, for the 1968 Daytona Continental 24hr. Two privateer Ford GT teams from England led by Ed Nelson also entered so, despite all the huffing and puffing, the Ford GT was still in the big league.

Car no. 9 was the Gulf team Ford GT MkI driven by Paul Hawkins and David Hobbs at the Daytona 24hr race in 1968. Contributor: C. Nahum Collection; photograph by Gérard Crombac

The winner of the Daytona 24hr in 1968 was Porsche 907LH, car no. 54, driven by Vic Elford and Jochen Neerspasch. Contributor: Dr. Ing. h. c. F. Porsche AG

Ed Nelson and his Ford GT MkI, chassis no. 1009, failed to finish at Daytona in 1968. Contributor: C. Nahum Collection; photograph by Gérard Crombac

One-two-three finish for the Porsche KG team at the Daytona 24hr. Contributor: Dr. Ing. h. c. F. Porsche AG

Top: Gulf team Ford GT, car no. 29, was driven by Paul Hawkins and David Hobbs at the Sebring 12hr race in 1968. Contributor: C. Nahum Collection; photograph by Gérard Crombac

Middle: Ed Nelson did better at Sebring in 1968 with the same Ford GT MkI he raced at Daytona. Contributor: C. Nahum Collection; photograph by Gérard Crombac

Bottom: Porsche 907, car no. 51, driven by Vic Elford and Jochen Neerspasch, came second at the Sebring 12hr in 1968. Contributor: Dr. Ing. h. c. F. Porsche AG

Ferrari was represented by privateer teams driving the 250LM and 275GTB. Ford, on the other hand, did not abandon anything. It just switched to the Ford Mustang of the Shelby American Inc. team.

Porsche KG arrived with a large entry list of 907s and 911s. The Sunray DX Oil Company entered three Chevrolet Corvettes. Chevrolet entered its Camaro, joining Alfa Romeo, Lancia, Dodge, Jaguar, TVR, Triumph, Mercury, Volvo and MGB on the starting grid.

None of the Ford GTs finished the race and the top three positions were taken by Porsche 907s.

As usual, the next race on the calendar was the Sebring 12hr. The Gulf team entered two Ford GT MkIs, and privateer Ed Nelson entered as well.

Porsche KG dominated Sebring with its 907s. Porsches occupied first and second places, with the Chevrolet Camaros of Penske-Hilton taking third and fourth. Ed Nelson and David Piper finished sixteenth. Of the two Gulf team cars, car no. 29 wasn't classified and the other did not finish. Shelby American Inc. came fifth with its Ford Mustang, so maybe those rule changes were not such a bad idea after all?

Back to Europe

The combatants headed to Europe for the BOAC 500 mile race, held at Brands Hatch, England. Did the American Ford and Chevrolet factory car teams follow? Sadly, the answer was no.

However, the BOAC 500 did see the return of Alan Mann Racing with its brand new Ford F3L P68.

Note: The F3L P68 was often found in the hands of Frank Gardner right through until the end of the 1969 racing season.

Five Ford GT MkIs were entered in the BOAC 500 along with the Porsche KG teams with their 906, 907 and 910s.

Jacky Ickx and Brian Redman won the race driving the J.W.A.-Gulf team car no. 4.

Left: Bruce McLaren and Mike Spence drove the Alan Mann F3L P68 prototype at the BOAC 500. Contributor: Ford Motor Company

Porsche 906, car no. 28, driven by Martin Hone and John Harris, leads the Jacky Ickx and Brian Redman J.W.A.-Gulf Ford GT MkI, car no.4, at the BOAC 500. Contributor: Dr. Ing. h. c. F. Porsche AG

The Strathaven team Ford GT MkI driven by David Piper and Mike Salmon at the BOAC 500. Contributor: Ford Motor Company

The next event on the 1968 European racing season calendar was Le Mans testing.

The ACO started much belated Sarthe circuit safety changes before the scheduled Le Mans testing in 1968. When the drivers turned up for testing in March, they found a very slow left-right chicane, called the "Ford Chicane", had been built just before the pits. The point of the chicane was to slow the cars down before driving past the pits. Unbelievably, the installation of a pit wall was not considered. Nothing separated cars entering and leaving the pits from those hurtling down the start-finish straight, apart from due diligence by drivers.

Up until Le Mans 1969, the only protection against hitting a tree, telephone pole or entering somebody's house on the public sections of track were the straw bales placed in front of each such obstacle.

Both Eric Liddell (Le Mans 1968) and Sir Malcolm Guthrie (Le Mans 1969) commented that driving a Ford GT MkI at 216mph (348kph) with only a straw bale for protection kept them on their

Jacky Ickx and Brian Redman in the J.W.A.-Gulf team Ford GT MkI win the 1968 BOAC 500. Contributor: Ford Motor Company

The new Ford chicane leads on to the start finish straight at Le Mans. The pits are directly to the right. It would be some time before this issue was dealt with. Contributor: Eric Liddell

Straw bales were all that stood between the driver and the local police at Le Mans in 1968. Contributor: C. Nahum Collection; photograph by Gérard Crombac

toes: their concentration level high. They also went on to say that all the drivers knew the risk, and their job was to race, not to complain.

Note: It was not until 1969 that the ACO started installing Armco barriers on one side of the track to protect drivers from hitting the trees, telephone poles or even entering people's houses! Tragically, the implementation of these safety modifications was still not enough to save 1968 Le Mans winner Lucien Bianchi. He was killed when his Alfa Romeo T33 spun into a telegraph pole nearing the end of the Mulsanne straight during Le Mans testing in March 1969.

Note: Vic Elford said in a commentary he did for a Le Mans 1969 video with Peter Sadler that it took 300 metres to slow and get around this corner after flying down the Mulsanne straight flat out.

None of the factory American teams attended the Le Mans' testing session, but privateer American teams using the Ferrari 250LM, 275GTB, Dino 206S and the Lola T70 MkIII did attend. The Ford GT was also well represented, led by the two car J.W.A.-Gulf team and the privateer teams of:

- Strathaven Ltd. Racing.
- Claude Dubois Racing.
- Terry J. Dury Racing.
- Ecurie Intersport SA.
- Alain de Cadenet Racing.

Also present for testing at Le Mans was the new Matra 3.0-litre V12 prototype. Matra, founded in 1964, launched its first major assault on sportscar racing in 1967 with the Matra M620-Ford, using the same 289 (4.7 litre) engine as the original Ford GT MkI.

As the 1968 racing season progressed so did the J.W.A.-Gulf team successes. Paul Hawkins and David Hobbs won the Monza 1000km in April.

The next race on the European stage was the Nürburgring 1000km race in May 1968 at which the Ford GT brigade was well

Paul Hawkins driving the J.W.A.-Gulf team Ford GT MkI at the 1968 Nürburgring 1000km. Contributor: Ford Motor Company

The Strathaven Ltd. team Ford MkI driven by Mike Salmon and David Piper at the Nürburgring in 1968. Contributor: Veit Arenz

represented with a total of eight Ford GT MkIs entered. Alan Mann Racing also brought along its Ford F3L P68 for another run.

Alongside the two J.W.A.-Gulf team cars were the Strathaven

Ford GT MkI, car no. 67, driven by Terry Drury and Terry Sanger at the Nürburgring in 1968. Contributor: Veit Arenz

Ford GT MkI, car no. 71, chassis no 1010, driven by Peter Sadler and Willie Green at the Nürburgring in 1968. Contributor: Veit Arenz

Ford GT MkI, car no. 74, driven by Nicholas Granville-Smith and John Raeburn at the Nürburgring in 1968. Contributor: Veit Arenz

Frank Gardner and Richard Attwood drove the Alan Mann Racing team Cosworth Ford F3L P68 at the Nürburgring in 1968. Contributor: Ford Motor Company

Jacky Ickx (second right) and Paul Hawkins (second left) on the rostrum at the Nürburgring in 1968. Contributor: Ford Motor Company

Ltd. team, and the private entries of Nicholas Granville-Smith, Peter Sadler, Terry Drury, Ed Nelson and David Prophet.

Gulf team drivers Jacky Ickx and Paul Hawkins came in third, and their team-mates David Hobbs and Brian Redman finished sixth.

Jacky Ickx teamed up with Brian Redman and the pair won the next race, the Spa 1000km, with Gulf team-mates Paul Hawkins and David Hobbs coming home in fourth.

Note: Paul Hawkins owned his own team of two Ford GTs. The ex-Alan Mann Racing AMGT-2 and his original MkI, chassis no. 1019. Hawkins tended to enter these cars in non-championship events in the UK, whilst driving for major teams in the World championship events. AMGT-2 was sold to a Spanish team after Hawkins' death in 1969.

Note: Le Mans usually followed Spa in June. Unfortunately for the ACO, in June 1968, serious rioting broke out across France, and Le Mans 24hr was postponed until September.

The J.W.A.-Gulf team travelled to the USA for the Watkins Glen 6hr in July 1968 where it finished first and second. Jacky Ickx and Lucien Biancho taking the top spot on the podium, with Paul Hawkins and David Hobbs in second.

J.W.A.-Gulf decided to sit out the ninth round in Zeltweg, Austria, but Paul Hawkins took his own Ford GT and finished third.

Note: For 1968, Zeltweg was designated a non-championship event.

Le Mans 1968

Le Mans is traditionally run on the second weekend in June, with the race starting on the dot at 4pm. In 1968, the race was delayed until September, and started at 3pm. Not a good sign for those with a superstitious nature. The weather was unusually warm, but during the night the temperature dropped quickly and it rained cats and dogs.

Eric Liddell and Grady Davis

Eric Liddell told me this story during my stay with him in Scotland during the research stage of this book. "My co-driver, Mike Salmon, and I were staying at the Hotel de France, in the village of La Chartre Sur Le Loir for Le Mans 1968. I was sitting at the bar when this gravel-toned American voice boomed in my ear, "You're a Scotsman aren't you?" I turned and immediately recognised Grady Davis, and replied, "Yes I am". Grady then asked me what I was doing there. When I told him that I was driving a Ford GT MkI (chassis no. 1078) with Mike Salmon for the Strathaven team,

The Hotel De France in La Chartre Sur Le Loir as photographed by Eric Liddell during his stay there for Le Mans 1968. Contributor: Eric Liddell

Grady Davis immediately offered us a J.W.A.-Gulf works engine as opposed to our customer version.

"Our team owner accepted the offer, and the J.W.A.-Gulf works engine was delivered to our garage. As it turned out this was very lucky for us because we had blown our engine in practice.

"Our team became the unofficial fourth J.W.A.-Gulf team entry in the race. I believe that Grady Davis was trying to even up the odds of a Ford GT finishing and beating the emerging powerhouse factory Porsche team. There were no works Ferrari or Ford teams to worry about in 1968. Sadly, our car was defeated by a transmission failure during the race and did not finish."

Eric finished the story with, "Grady Davis was not just the man with the cheques. He was a genuinely honest person, with a

A Gulf works engine with Gurney Eagle heads, as opposed to the original J.W.A. customer engine with Gurney Weslake heads. Contributor: C. Nahum Collection; photograph by Gérard Crombac

The engine change. Contributor: C. Nahum Collection; photograph by Gérard Crombac

heart of gold who was not averse to helping people out, whether they thought they needed it or not."

Note: A BBC One documentary crew accompanied the Strathaven Ltd. racing team for the entire week of Le Mans in 1968. Some of their footage is believed to have been used in the 1971 Steve McQueen movie, Le Mans.

Both Jacky Ickx and Derek Bell appeared in the Le Mans entry list as drivers for the J.W.A.-Gulf team in 1968, but neither actually drove in the race.

When Derek Bell was asked why he didn't drive? He replied, "I drove the Ford GT40 at Thruxton earlier in 1968 and John Wyer asked me to drive with Pedro Rodriguez, but as I'd joined Ferrari two months earlier, they would not release me for Ford at Le Mans, which was in September that year. That's my only experience, apart from the fact Pedro Rodriguez won. I drove a GT40 at Monterrey Historics last year, wonderful."

Strathaven team Ford GT MkI, chassis no. 1078, about to enter the Gulf garage to have its engine replaced courtesy of Grady Davis. Contributor: Eric Liddell

Five Ford GTs lined up on the starting grid. Three 5.0-litre Ford GT MkIBs were entered by the J.W.A.-Gulf team, while the privateer teams of Strathaven Ltd. and Claude Dubois Racing used the more standard 4.7-litre-powered Ford GT MkIs. The Strathaven Ltd. team was using chassis no. 1078, and the Claude Dubois team chassis no. 1079. Both cars were J.W.A. tweaked, built to 1968 specifications, but not quite up to the Gulf team car specifications.

The Claude Dubois team drivers were Belgians Willy Mairesse, Jean 'Beurlys' Blaton, and Hughes de Fierlandt. Sadly, their Ford GT lasted less than one lap with Willy Mairesse in the driver's seat.

After Willy Mairesse had run across the track, jumped into his

Ford GT MkI, car no.12, in the pits before the start at Le Mans in 1968. Contributor: Eric Liddell

car, shut the door, started the engine, got his seat belts sorted out, and was off and running, everything should have been fine. Unfortunately for Willy Mairesse, who was not unaccustomed to freak accidents, all was not fine. As he roared down the Mulsanne straight at an estimated speed of 186mph (300kph) the driver's side door flipped open. The change in aerodynamics caused control to be lost and Willy Mairesse crashed heavily.

The Ford GT MkI, chassis no. 1079, was totally destroyed and its driver seriously injured. Willy Mairesse did recover physically from his injuries, but his racing career in the topflight was over. Tragically, twelve months after his accident, Willy Mairesse took his own life, and thus ended a magnificent racing career.

Eric Liddell also provided an interesting account of driving the Strathaven Ford GT MkI, no. 12, in the wet at Le Mans. "I felt like I had drawn the short straw. Mike Salmon handed the car over to me and a short time later the heavens opened. I had to pit to put on wet weather tyres. Unfortunately, there were two

The two of the three J.W.A.-Gulf team Ford GT MkIs running together at Le Mans. Contributor: Ford Motor Company

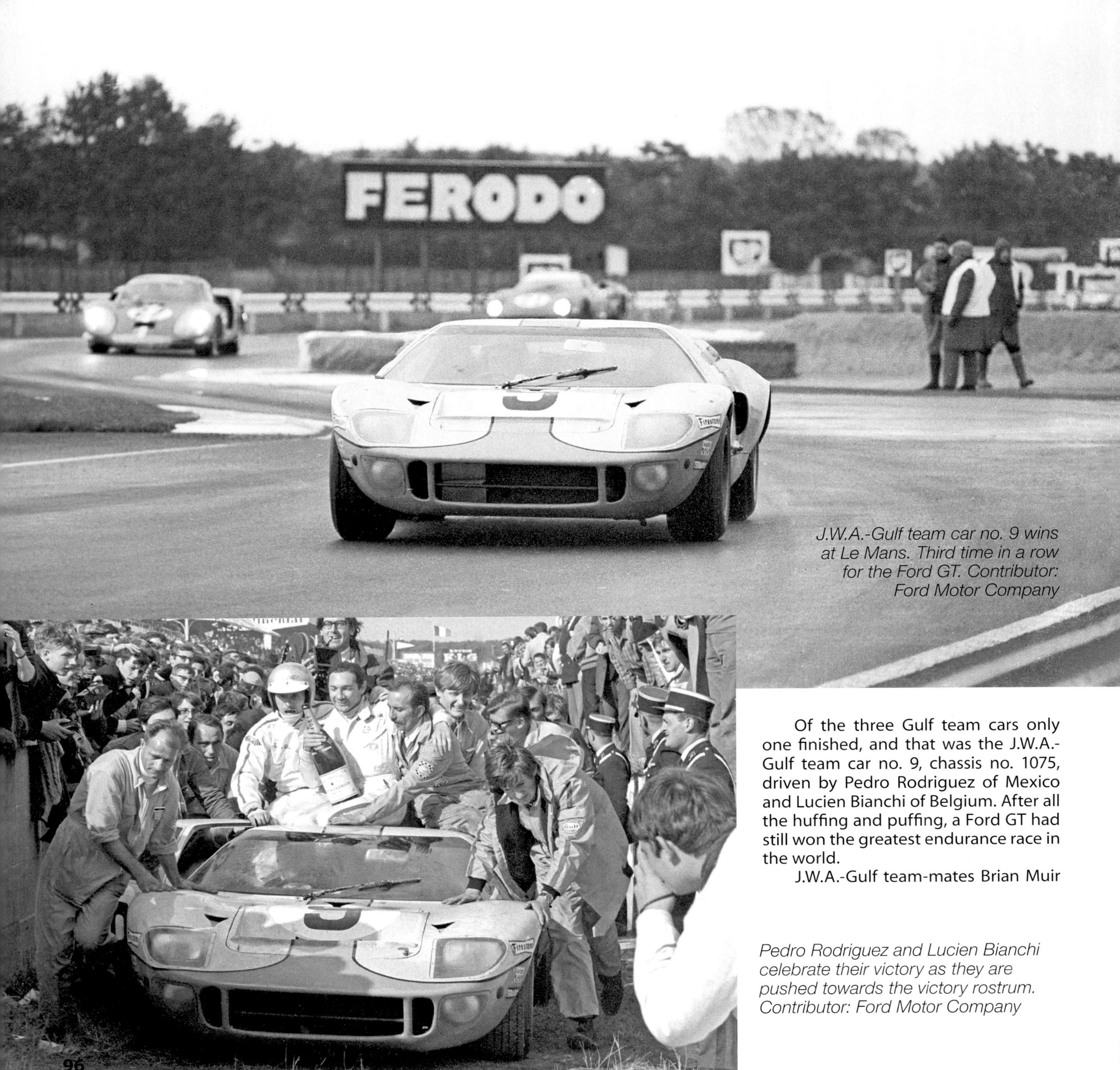

J.W.A.-Gulf team car no. 9 wins at Le Mans. Third time in a row for the Ford GT. Contributor: Ford Motor Company

Of the three Gulf team cars only one finished, and that was the J.W.A.-Gulf team car no. 9, chassis no. 1075, driven by Pedro Rodriguez of Mexico and Lucien Bianchi of Belgium. After all the huffing and puffing, a Ford GT had still won the greatest endurance race in the world.

J.W.A.-Gulf team-mates Brian Muir

Pedro Rodriguez and Lucien Bianchi celebrate their victory as they are pushed towards the victory rostrum. Contributor: Ford Motor Company

and Jackie Oliver in car no. 11 crashed out after five hours, and Paul Hawkins and David Hobbs in car no. 10 broke their engine after ten hours.

Minor league racing in 1968

The international racing scene in 1968 outside of the major FIA sanctioned championships continued to attract quality drivers and teams, including the privateer Ford GT teams.

A new race for 1968 was the Barcelona 6hr: it was won by Australian Brian Muir and Spaniard Francisco Godia-Sales driving the team Escuderia Montjuic Ford GT MkI, Peter Sadler and Willie Green came in fifth.

In May 1968, Paul Hawkins, driving his own Ford GT MkI (P40), chassis no. AMGT-2, won the Trophy of the Dunes at Zandvoort in Holland. His team-mate, Eric Liddell, driving chassis no. 1019, came in third. Australian driver, John Raeburn, driving Andy Cox's Ford GT MkI, failed to finish the race.

Only David Prophet drove a Ford GT at the GP of Paris, and he failed to finish. The next race in which the Ford GTs featured was the Anderstorp 1 Hour, at the Scandinavian Raceway. Paul Hawkins finished second, Eric Liddell fourth, Peter Sadler fifth, and David Prophet eighth. Peter Sadler entered his Ford GT in the 1968 edition of the 200 Meilen von Nürnberg, ADAC Norisring-Rennen International in Germany, but failed to qualify.

The Ford GTs were back in action for the Grande Premio de Vila Real at Vila Real in Portugal. Paul Hawkins finished third, with Portuguese driver Carlos Gaspar coming in fourth, Eric Liddell fifth, and John Raeburn tenth. Ed Nelson failed to finish. The lone Ford GT in the Grande Premio do Portugal at the Montes Claros circuit in Portugal was Carlos Gaspar, and he won the event.

In July 1968 there was a big Ford GT turnout for the International Solitude-Rennen at the Hockenheimring. Paul Hawkins, David Prophet and John Raeburn finished ninth to eleventh respectively. Eric Liddell and Ed Nelson failed to finish. For the Swedish GP support race in August 1968 Paul Hawkins and Ed Nelson were the only Ford GT drivers to turn up. Hawkins finished third and Nelson fifth.

Only Paul Hawkins raced in the Preis der Nationen race at Hockenheimring where he finished third. Paul stayed in Germany for the Eifelpokal race on the Nürburgring Südschleife, which he won. Ed Nelson came in second and Peter Sadler ninth.

Jean-Michel Giorgi in the Ford France Ford GT MkI took on the rest at the Coupes de Paris at the Montlhéry circuit and won. Three Ford GTs turned up for the Paris 1000km, with Peter Sadler and Willie Green finishing third. The other Ford GT driver teams were Belgians Jean "Beurlys" Blaton and Hughes de Fierlant, and Spaniards José Juncadella and Francisco Godia-Sales.

Portuguese driver, and Ford GT owner, Carlos Gaspar competed with Ford MkI chassis no. 1022 in the last two races in Portugal. He finished his season by winning the Vila do Conde.

British home events in 1968

With so many Ford GT teams now competing in the various international races around the world, it could have been expected that the number of Ford GT teams and drivers racing in England would be reduced in number compared to the 1967 season. This was not the case at all. The eight events which made up the British Sportscar Championship attracted the Gulf team with its new versions of the Ford GT MkI, and drivers Jacky Ickx and Brian Muir.

Paul Hawkins was there with his own team, including driver David Hobbs. The Strathaven team, with primary drivers Mike Salmon and David Piper, did battle with Terry Drury's Ford GT team. David Prophet also entered his own Ford GT team, and Alan Mann Racing entered its new Ford F3L P68 driven by Bruce McLaren, Mike Spence and Jochen Rindt.

Other Ford GT teams owned by George Humble and Ron Fry entered the fray later, and Paul Hawkins started entering his second car, driven by Eric Liddell when available.

Robin Darlington entered his own Ford GT team late in the series, with drivers Tony Lanfranchi and Maurice Charles. Even Ed Nelson made an appearance in a couple of the races. All in all, this was a very successful series.

Unfortunately, there were only so many Ford GTs to go around, so the British National racing series of events did suffer somewhat. Only four races at Oulton Park, Silverstone, Crystal Palace and Croft saw entries from the Ford GT brigade.

Another British series, started in 1967 but not attracting Ford GT teams until 1968, was the *Motoring News* Special GT series. This series consisted of seventeen rounds at various circuits around England. At different rounds of the series Ford GTs entered by privateers Peter Sadler, Bob Vincent, Ron Fry, Maurice Charles, Tony Lanfranchi and John Jordan competed.

1968 Springbok series

The first race of the Springbok series was the Kyalami 9hr. The J.W.A.-Gulf team decided to give its last remaining Mirage M1 with the 351 (5.7 litre) V8 engine fitted a run.

The Gulf team was joined by Team Malcolm Guthrie with its Ford GT MkI, chassis no. 1009, the former Peter Sutcliffe and Ed Nelson Ford GT. The Mirage M1 was driven to victory by Jacky Ickx and David Hobbs. Life was not quite so grand for Malcolm Guthrie and Mike Hailwood. Guthrie crashed his GT into the rock face and it was destroyed. Immediately after the race he spoke to John Wyer and negotiated the purchase of the Mirage M1.

Under Team Malcolm Guthrie ownership, drivers Malcolm Guthrie, Mike Hailwood and David Hobbs raced the Mirage M1 for the rest of the Springbok series and took one win and two seconds. Team Malcolm Guthrie, with the Mirage M1, also competed in the 25 lap race as part of the Rhodesian Grand Prix at Bulawayo. Malcolm Guthrie drove the M1 into third place.

Note: Ed Nelson retired from professional competitive motor racing in 1968. Ed said that he had his fun, he was getting married and now was the time to concentrate on his business interests. However, that did not stop him doing the odd race, as will be seen in the 1969 racing season.

The pendulum swings in 1969

Enzo Ferrari finally came to grips with the fact that his dummy spitting exercise in 1967 had done his company no good at all. A new prototype racing car project was publicly launched in December 1968, the Ferrari 312P Spyder. Development and race testing was carried out over the winter of 1968 and into January of 1969.

As fate would have it, the Ferrari 312P would not be ready for the Daytona 24hr race, but at the 1969 Sebring 12hr, Chris Amon and Mario Andretti put the Ferrari factory team 312P Spyder into pole position. They finished the race in second place overall, and first in class.

For the rest of the 1969 racing season the Ferrari 312P racing results were good, but with no wins in major events. Enzo Ferrari

Ford GT MkI versus Porsche 917. Contributor: Dr. Ing. h. c. F. Porsche AG

hoped that by 1970 FIAT would have completed its takeover of his Ferrari company, and he would finally have the budget to get things moving in the right direction again.

Unfortunately for Enzo Ferrari, others had the same idea. Quietly working away behind the scenes were the race engineers from Porsche Weissach, Germany. Porsche KG publicly launched the brand new Porsche 917 prototype in 1969.

John Wyer hedges his bets

John Wyer knew that the glory days of the Ford GT project were over and 1969 would be its last season. During 1969, the last of the road cars were delivered and the small production line shut down. J.W.A.-Gulf never backed away from competing against the GT, but John Wyer knew he had to find something new for the next decade.

John Wyer decided to have another go at making his own Group 6 prototype: enter the J.W.A.-Gulf Mirage M2 and M3. The Mirage M2 was the coupé version fitted with the F1, BRM 24 valve, 4-overhead cam, 3 litre V12, putting out around 450bhp (336kW). Apparently, the transmissions used went from the original Ford GT style ZF 5-speed, to the notoriously unreliable DFV 5-speed to, eventually, the more race reliable Hewland.

The Mirage M2 body design and the running gear were all clearly influenced by the original Mirage M1. The Mirage M2 was a resounding failure on the race track thanks in part to terrible aerodynamics, but also the unreliable BRM engine. The M2 was eventually fitted with a Ford Cosworth engine, but it was still not very good.

First and third Gulf team Mirage GR8s together on the track at Le Mans in 1975. Contributor: Ford Motor Company

The Mirage M3 was the open top or Roadster version, but fitted with a 9-series Cosworth-DFV V8 engine. This car was also a resounding failure. Despite Jacky Ickx's best efforts at Zeltweg in Austria, the Mirage project was sent back to the drawing board.

John Wyer never abandoned his Mirage project. A new series of Ford-powered Mirages would return for the 1974, 1975 and 1976 seasons. The J.W.A.-Gulf team Mirage-Ford GR8, car no. 10, driven by Jacky Ickx and Derek Bell won at Le Mans in 1975. Vern Schuppan and Jean-Pierre Jaussaud finished third in car no. 11, the sister J.W.A.-Gulf team Mirage GR8.

J.W. Automotive-designed and built Mirage M2/300. This is the Ford Cosworth V8 version. Contributor: Udo Klinkel

Pre-Le Mans

The Daytona 24hr as usual was the first endurance race of the racing season. The only Ford GTs that made it to the starting grid were those of the J.W.A.-Gulf team, chassis nos. 1075 and 1076. David Hobbs and Mike Hailwood driving 1075 didn't finish, and 1076, driven by Jacky Ickx and Jackie Oliver, was classified twenty-sixth overall.

The big winners at Daytona in 1969 were the

Roger Penske and American International Lola T70 Mk3s which finished first and second respectively. There were five Porsche 911s in the top ten.

Florida sunshine and the Sebring 12hr brought the J.W.A.-Gulf Ford GT back to the top step of the podium. The race was won by Jacky Ickx and Jackie Oliver driving the Le Mans 1968 winning chassis no. 1075. Sebring was a great psychological win for the tired old J.W.A.-Gulf Ford GT because it beat into second place the new Group 6 prototype Ferrari 312P factory team of Chris Amon and Mario Andretti. The only other Ford GTs in the race were the second J.W.A.-Gulf car and the Auto Enterprises team from the USA whose Ford GT was driven by Francis Grant and Dieter Oest.

The BOAC 500 at Brands Hatch boasted the largest entry list of Ford GTs so far in the season. For the first time in the history of the Ford GT, a German team was entered, the IGFA German Racing Team, with drivers Helmut Kelleners and Reinhold Jöst.

They were joined on the starting grid by one J.W.A.-Gulf Ford GT driven by David Hobbs and Mike Hailwood, the Peter Sadler team, with drivers Peter Sadler and Paul Vestey, and the Escuderia Montjuich team, with drivers José Juncadella and Gordon Spice.

Note: Jacky Ickx and Jackie Oliver were driving the BRM-powered J.W.A.-Gulf Mirage M2 Coupé in the Group 6 prototype class, but it broke down and failed to finish.

David Hobbs and Mike Hailwood drove their Ford GT into fifth place, with Porsche 908/02s occupying first, second and third, and one of "those fast little red cars", the Ferrari 312P, in fourth place.

The Alan Mann Racing Ford F3L P68 driven by Denis Hulme and Frank Gardner was also entered in the BOAC 500, but it failed to finish.

The Monza 1000km endurance race in Italy was a successful

The Porsche 917 made its debut at the 1969 Spa 1000km. Only Gerhard Mitter drove it this day because the new flat-twelve cylinder engine expired on lap one. Contributor: Dr. Ing. h. c. F. Porsche AG

outing for the IGFA Racing Team and drivers Helmut Kelleners and Reinhold Jöst. They finished fourth overall behind three Porsches.

Another new Ford GT team, Zitro Racing, with drivers Jean-Pierre Hanrioud and Dominique Martin, finished fifteenth overall. The Peter Sadler team blew an engine and did not finish, and for some reason the Ford France entry did not start the race. No Ford GT teams attended the Targa Florio in May 1969.

For the Spa 1000km the Gulf team only entered its BRM-powered Mirage M2s, one driven by David Hobbs and Mike Hailwood who finished seventh, and the other, driven by Jacky Ickx and Jackie Oliver, failed to finish.

Privateers Peter Sadler and the German IGFA team finished ninth and tenth respectively. A Porsche 908 long tail (LH) finished first, the Ferrari 312P Spyder and a Porsche 908 long tail third.

Only the IGFA team entered a Ford GT for the Nürburgring

German IGFA Racing Team Ford GT MkI driven by Helmut Kelleners and Reinhold Jöst are behind David Piper in the Lola T70 during the Monza 1000km in 1969. Contributor: Lola Heritage Archives-Glyn Jones

The Porsche 917, car no. 61, of Frank Gardner and David Piper, being hunted down by the Ford GT MkI, car no. 56, of the IGFA team driven by Helmut Kelleners and Reinhold Jöst at the Nürburgring. Contributor: Dr. Ing. h. c. F. Porsche AG

The two J.W.A.-Gulf team Mirages at the Nürburgring in 1969. Car no. 9 is Cosworth powered M2/300; car no. 5 is the BRM powered M2/200. Contributor: Udo Klinkel

1000km in Germany. It was the team's home race, and it came in fifth overall behind four Porsche 908/02s. J.W.A.-Gulf entered its two Mirage M2s and both failed to finish. The Porsche 917 entered by the Porsche KG factory team and driven by Frank Gardner and David Piper finished eighth.

Note: For the Nürburgring race, J.W.A.-Gulf entered one BRM-powered Mirage M2/200 Coupé and the M2/300 Coupé which was powered by the new 9-series Cosworth engine.

Le Mans 1969

With full Ford factory support the 427 (7.0 litre) Ford GTs had won Le Mans in 1966 and 1967. Abandoned by its creator at the end of 1967, the Ford GT won Le Mans again in 1968, albeit without having to go up against "those fast little red cars". However, the five GTs sitting on the starting grid for Le Mans in June 1969 were now the tired underdogs. The Gulf team had even entered the same Ford GT MkI that had won Le Mans the previous year, albeit built to 1969 J.W.A. specifications.

How well could the J.W.A.-Gulf team, along with the privateer team entries of Malcolm Guthrie, Peter Sadler and *Deutsche Auto Zeitung*, perform against the new kids on the block?

Who were the new kids on the block?

- Matra-Simca with its MS630 Coupé and MS650 Spyder.
- Porsche System Engineering with its flat-twelve powered Porsche 917 long tail.
- S.P.A. Ferrari and its 312P 3 litre prototype Coupé.

Porsche 917, car no. 12, at Le Mans in 1969 driven by Vic Elford and Richard Attwood. Contributor: Dr. Ing. h. c. F. Porsche AG

The old school was also present, with the greatest danger being from the Porsche System Engineering 908s and 910s.

Note: John Wolfe, driving his privately entered Porsche 917 long tail, died when he crashed on the first lap of Le Mans 1969. This 917 was to have been taken over and raced by former Ford GT driver Eric Liddell on the Monday after Le Mans. John Wolfe had approached Eric Liddell asking him if he was interested in the drive and Eric Liddell said he was, but after seeing his next drive go up in flames with its driver, and after just burying his long time friend Paul Hawkins, Eric Liddell decided enough was enough and he stopped racing.

The Ford versus Porsche battle raged on throughout the whole race. Contributor: Dr. Ing. h. c. F. Porsche AG

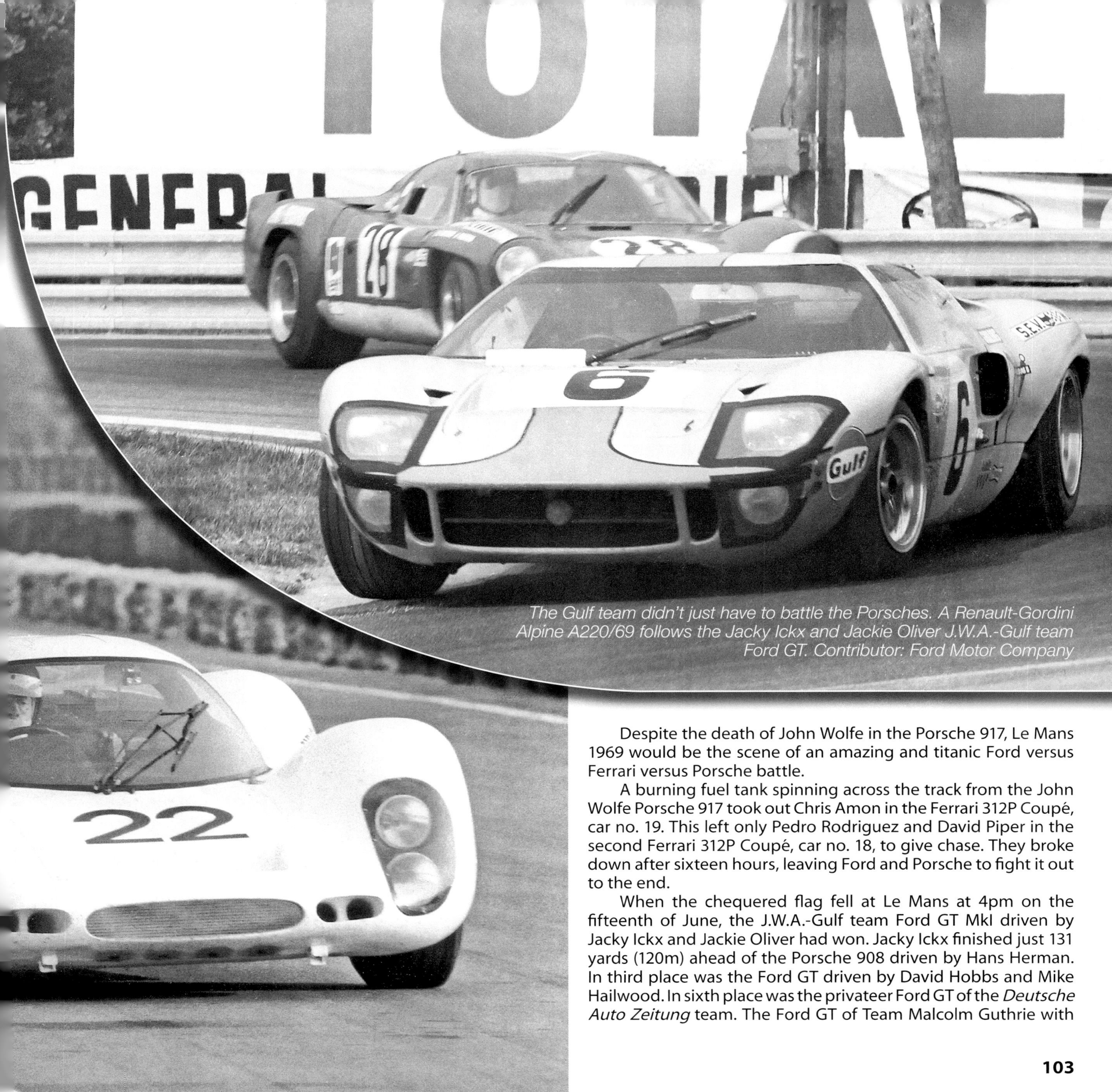

The Gulf team didn't just have to battle the Porsches. A Renault-Gordini Alpine A220/69 follows the Jacky Ickx and Jackie Oliver J.W.A.-Gulf team Ford GT. Contributor: Ford Motor Company

Despite the death of John Wolfe in the Porsche 917, Le Mans 1969 would be the scene of an amazing and titanic Ford versus Ferrari versus Porsche battle.

A burning fuel tank spinning across the track from the John Wolfe Porsche 917 took out Chris Amon in the Ferrari 312P Coupé, car no. 19. This left only Pedro Rodriguez and David Piper in the second Ferrari 312P Coupé, car no. 18, to give chase. They broke down after sixteen hours, leaving Ford and Porsche to fight it out to the end.

When the chequered flag fell at Le Mans at 4pm on the fifteenth of June, the J.W.A.-Gulf team Ford GT MkI driven by Jacky Ickx and Jackie Oliver had won. Jacky Ickx finished just 131 yards (120m) ahead of the Porsche 908 driven by Hans Herman. In third place was the Ford GT driven by David Hobbs and Mike Hailwood. In sixth place was the privateer Ford GT of the *Deutsche Auto Zeitung* team. The Ford GT of Team Malcolm Guthrie with

Ford versus Ferrari for the last time. The drivers of the Ferrari 312P Coupé, car no. 18, following the Gulf team car, no. 6, are Pedro Rodriguez and David Piper. Contributor: Ford Motor Company

Above: Following the Gulf team Ford GT MkI is the Racing Team VDS Alfa Romeo T33B/2. Contributor: Ford Motor Company

Old timers versus the new kids on the block. David Hobbs in his old timer Ford GT leads an equally old timer in the shape of car no. 17, the Ferrari 250LM of Teodoro Zeccoli and Sam Posey. Both are being hunted down by car no. 14, the new Porsche 917 long tail driven by Rolf Stommelen and Kurt Ahrens Jr. Only the old timers finished the race. Contributor: Ford Motor Company

With just one lap to go the J.W.A.-Gulf team Ford GT MkI was not far ahead of the Porsche 908. Contributor: Ford Motor Company

Jacky Ickx takes the chequered flag for the J.W.A.-Gulf team just ahead of the Porsche 908. What a battle. This was the Ford GT's fourth win in a row at Le Mans, second for chassis no. 1075, and the last ever for a Ford GT. Contributor: Ford Motor Company

Fletcher appeared on the scene, and Ford France entered some French races, such as Dijon, with driver Michel Martin.

Team Malcolm Guthrie entered the bigger races of the non-championship international series, like 200 Meilen von Nürnberg, International ADAC-Norisring-Race-Meeting at Nürnberg in Germany with his Mirage M1, driven by Mike Hailwood, and his Ford GT MkI which he drove himself.

For the Norisring race Team Malcolm Guthrie was joined by the Brescia Corse team Ford GT, driven by German Willy König.

For the 6 Horas de Vila Real race, Willie Green and John Blades were entered in the Willie Green Ford GT MkI, chassis no. 1013. They had other Ford GT company in the form of Team Evergreen, with American driver David Weir in chassis no. 1078, and Team Palma, with Portuguese drivers Luís Fernandes and Carlos Santos.

Note: According to Willie Green, chassis no. 1013 started life as a road car which he purchased for his road needs. He then said that he had it converted into a racing car. In 1982 chassis no. 1013 was undergoing a full restoration by Bryan Wingfield as reported in the July edition of the Classic and Sports Car *magazine.*

For the 1969 edition of the International Solitude-Rennen at the Hockenheimring, Team Malcolm Guthrie employed Ed Nelson to drive the Mirage M1 whilst Malcolm Guthrie drove the Ford GT MkI himself. John Jordan raced his own Ford GT MkI in the Swedish GP support race at Karlskoga. The sole Ford GT in the race.

Jacky Ickx took the Gulf team Mirage M3/300 Ford to the 500km di Imola held at the Autodromo Dino Ferrari. He won the race after it was stopped following the accident that befell German driver Hans Herrmann in the Porsche Salzburg Porsche 908.

Willie Green and Ford France both entered their Ford GTs in the 1969 edition of the Tour de France (car race not the cycle race!), but both failed to finish.

Michel Martin drove again for Ford France at the Coupe de Salon at the Montlhéry circuit in October 1969. Team Escuderia Montjuich entered two Ford GTs, driven by José Juncadella, Gordon Spice, Willie Green and Félix Serra, for the Barcelona 6hr race, but again both Ford GTs failed to finish.

Willie Green (left) and John Davenport with their Ford GT MkI, chassis no. 1010, at the 1969 Tour De France. Willie Green had just purchased this Ford GT from its previous, long-time owner, Peter Sadler. Contributor: Charles Harbord – Cars for the Connoisseur

October 1969 also saw the running of the Paris 1000km at the Montlhéry circuit. The Ford GT was well represented. Ford France with drivers Michel Martin and Jean-François Piot were there, along with Team Willie Green, with driver Clive Baker sharing with Willie Green. Team Escuderia Montjuich entered with drivers José Juncadella and Gordon Spice. A new team, E.S.C.A. Zitro, with drivers Dominique Martin (Swiss) and Pierre Maublanc (French) also entered.

Willie Green entered the Grand Prix de Casablanca and engaged Jean-Pierre Rouget to drive, but he crashed and did not finish. Willie Green entered and drove himself at the 300 mile race at the Hockenheimring, where he was joined by team E.S.C.A. Zitro and its driver Dominique Martin. Both finished the race.

The last race for the Ford GT in 1969 in the international series was at Montlhéry at the end of October 1969. Ford France entered the race with its trusty long time driver Michel Martin, but sadly it was another Ford GT DNF.

South America had its own sportscar series in 1969, and a Ford GT MkI, chassis no. 1083, had found its way to Brazil. It was

David Hobbs and Mike Hailwood take third place in their J.W.A.-Gulf team Ford GT. Contributor: Ford Motor Company

Frank Gardner, and the other Ford GT of Peter Sadler failed to finish.

Why was this the greatest victory for the Ford GT? Because the old Ford GT was not expected to be competitive let alone have any chance at winning.

Sadly, all good things must come to an end, and Le Mans 1969 was the end of an era for the Ford GT, for it was the last time:

to his car rather than running to it. He was always concerned that drivers would forget to do up their seat belts or not shut the door (which happened at Le Mans in 1968) before roaring off to do battle. Jacky Ickx still won the race and so proved his point that running across the track for the start was just for show.

campaigned by the Equipe Colégio Arte e Instruçao racing team and driven by Brazilian driver Sidney Cardoso.

British home events in 1969

The British Sportscar Championship consisted of eight events for 1969. In the first event, the *Daily Express* race at Silverstone, only three Ford GT MkIs were entered. Peter Sadler drove his own car, Andrew Fletcher drove the Scottish Privateers entry, and José Juncadella drove the Escuderia Montjuich entry. Dennis Leech had his own Ford GT, and joined the fray after the first couple of races.

The J.W.A.-Gulf team Mirage M2s made an appearance at the 6hr race at Brands Hatch with David Hobbs teamed with Mike Hailwood and Jacky Ickx teamed with Jackie Oliver. This race was the debut for the new IGFA-German Racing Team, with drivers Helmut Kelleners and Reinhold Jöst.

For the Martini Trophy 300 at Silverstone another new team, Malaya Garage, with driver Mac Daghorn, tried to boost the Ford GT numbers. Unfortunately, no other Ford GT teams entered the race. This was also the case at the Tourist Trophy race at Oulton Park (the race in which Paul Hawkins was killed).

Ian William, driving for Malaya Garage, joined Ford GT stalwart Peter Sadler for the W. D. & H. O. Wills International Trophy Race at the Croft racing circuit. Only two Ford GTs were entered for the Kodak Super 8 Trophy at the Thruxton Park circuit. Mac Daghorn, driving for Malaya Garage, and the Piers Forrester entry driven by himself and Andrew Hedges (Ford GT MkI, chassis no. 1071). The Kodak Super 8 Trophy was the last of the championship series. It was also the very last for the Ford GT in the British Sportscar Championship.

No Ford GT was entered for the seven races that made up the 1969 British National racing series.

The *Motoring News* Special GT series continued in racing season 1969. There were only nine events making up the series, down from seventeen the previous year. How many Ford GTs teams competed in the series, if any, is not known.

Springbok series 1969

Only one team using Ford GTs turned up for the Springbok series in 1969. Team Malcolm Guthrie Racing campaigned the Mirage M1 with its 351 (5.7 litre) engine, and one Ford GT MkI (the new chassis no. 1009, ex-chassis no. XGT-2).

Results of the series for the team were mixed with three podium places and a fourth place. The team's last race was in Pietermaritzburg on the twenty-seventh of December. The very last time a Mirage M1 and a Ford GT40 would grace a race track together in a major competition.

Waning of the Ford GT star

J.W. Automotive and the Gulf Oil Company abandoned the Ford GT and moved to Porsche KG to campaign the Porsche 917K prototypes. On the surface this may have appeared to have dealt a body blow to the Ford GT, but there was life in the old girl yet.

Note: The relationship between Porsche KG and J.W.A.-Gulf was very good in the beginning, but Porsche KG co-founder Louise Piëch and her son, Porsche 917 designer Ferdinand Piëch, were never happy with what they considered the English/American invaders. They formed their own 917 racing team, Porsche KG Salzburg, Austria, which would morph into the world famous Porsche-Martini Racing team in 1974.

A review of the records of the 1970 racing season shows a new batch of privateer teams purchased Ford GTs and raced

The J.W.A.-Gulf team Mirage M2/200, car no. 51, driven by Jacky Ickx, is following the Paul Hawkins Racing Ltd. Lola T70, car no 1, driven by Paul Hawkins at the Brands Hatch 6hr in 1969. Neither car finished. Contributor: Lola Heritage Archives-Glyn Jones

them in selected rounds of the Sportscar World Championship. The rules for the British Sportscar Championship were changed in 1970, limiting the entrants to 2-litre engines, which disqualified the Ford GT from this competition.

For the Daytona 24hr race in early 1970, Trevor Graham Racing engaged Piers Forrester and Andrew Hedges to drive its Ford GT MkI.

The Ford GT they were to drive was one of the former Essex Wire Corporation machines, chassis no. 1010. Suspension failure robbed the team of a finish.

Note: Chassis no. 1010 is currently owned by Formula One racing car designer Adrian Newey. See Chapter 5.

Trevor Graham Racing also engaged Piers Forrester and Andrew Hedges to drive the Daytona mount in the Sebring 12hr race. Engine failure struck early in the race taking them out of contention.

Note: Andrew Hedges passed away in October 2005. A giant of the racing world, he will be sorely missed.

Note: At the Sebring 12hr in 1970, Hollywood film legend Steve McQueen shared the driving with Paul Revson of the Solar Productions team Porsche 908/02 and they finished second.

Ford GTs also competed in the Nürburgring 1000km and at Zeltweg in Austria.

The Trevor Graham/Peter Sands owned ex-Essex Wire Corporation Ford GT MkI, chassis no 1010, driven by Andrew Hedges and Piers Forrester at the 1970 Daytona 24hr. The photograph was taken by Peter Sands. Contributor: Paul Sands

John Jordan competed with his Ford GT in the thirteenth event of the *Motoring News* Special GT series of 1970 in England.

Unfortunately for the Ford GT teams, the dialled in Porsche 917K run by J.W.A.-Gulf and Porsche-Audi USA works teams, along with the factory Ferrari 312P and 512S teams were simply overwhelming everything else on the tracks. The Martini team with its Porsche 908s were providing excellent backup to the Porsche 917K.

Race records show that by the end of the 1971 racing season the Ford GT had effectively disappeared from all the official FIA points scoring sportscar championships around the world, just leaving the non-championship international series and some national series for the Ford GT to ply its trade.

Some of the last official races which included a Ford GT MkI on the grid were:

- Interlagos-Preliminar da Formula 3, Interlagos, Brazil, held in January 1971. The Equipe Colégio Arte e Instruçao team entered its Ford GT MkI, chassis no. 1083, driven by Sidney Cardoso.
- Campeonato Sudamericano de SP, Tournoi de Sao-Paulo, Interlagos, Brazil, held in December 1971. The Equipe Greco-Ford-entered Ford MkI, chassis no. 1083, driven by Brazilian Wilson Fittipaldi.
- Interlagos 500km, Brazil, held in September 1972. The Equipe Greco-Ford team entered with driver Brazilian Paulo Gomes. The same team and driver were entered into the

Ecurie Evergreen team Ford GT MkI, chassis no. 1078, racing in the 1970 Nürburgring 1000km. The drivers were Piers Forrester and Alain De Cadenet. Contributor: Manfred Förster

Taruma 1hr and the Festival de Roncos at Interlagos.
• Luanda 2hr, Angola, held in July 1973, driven by Emilio Marta.
• Moçamedes, Angola, held in late 1973, driven by Emilio Marta.
• 6 Horas de Nova Lisboa, Angola, held in July 1974, by Emilio Marta.
• Benguela, Angola, held in August 1974, driven by Emilio Marta.
• Moçamedes, Angola, held in 1975, driven by Emilio Marta.
• Brighton Speed Trials, held in Brighton, England in 1975, driven by Adrian Hamilton.

Adrian Hamilton driving a Ford GT MkI, chassis no. 1045, at the Brighton Speed Trials in 1975. Contributor: Adrian Hamilton

What really finished off the Ford GT? It wasn't the French aristocrats often accused of trying to protect Ferrari, nor was it the regulations which cost Ford the 427 (7.0 litre) engine, but the reason for the Ford GT in the first place. The Ford GT was created to beat "those fast little red cars" from Ferrari. Other manufacturers created cars to beat "those fast, not so little, variously coloured Ford GTs".

Even the J.W.A.-Gulf Mirage team was eventually sold off. In early 1976, the Pittsburgh based Gulf team was purchased by Grand Touring Cars, Inc. owned by Harley E. Cluxton III. John Wyer was hired as a team consultant.

Time and technology overtook the Ford GT, in other words, the continuing evolution of motorsport. The Ford GT passed from the present into the past, and became a legend.

Some Ford GTs survived the racing. Undamaged originals were purchased by private collectors and museums. The wrecks were purchased by people who saw potential in the old Ford GT in the future. Many of the wrecked Ford GTs would, like a phoenix, rise out of the ashes and take their place alongside their original surviving brethren.

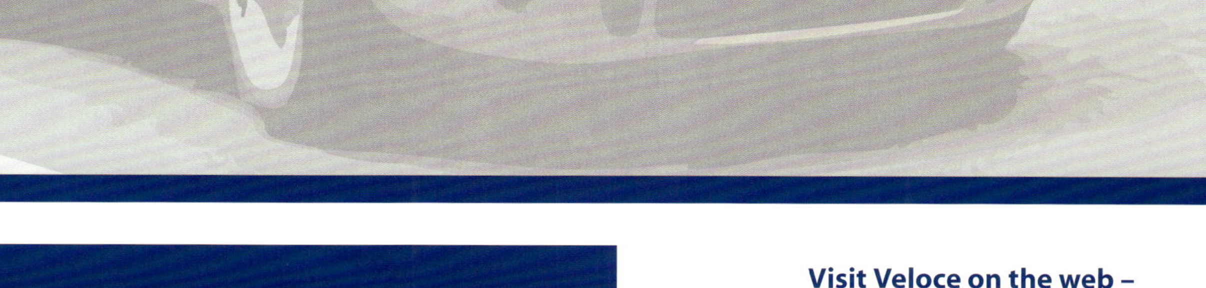

The end result, a brand new, super powerful engine to be installed in a new supercar.
Contributor: Ford Motor Company

Production Ford GT engine.
Contributor: Adrian Streather

The dimension differences are much clearer when an original Ford GT MkIIB (left) and a new Ford GT are viewed from above.
Contributor: Claude Nahum

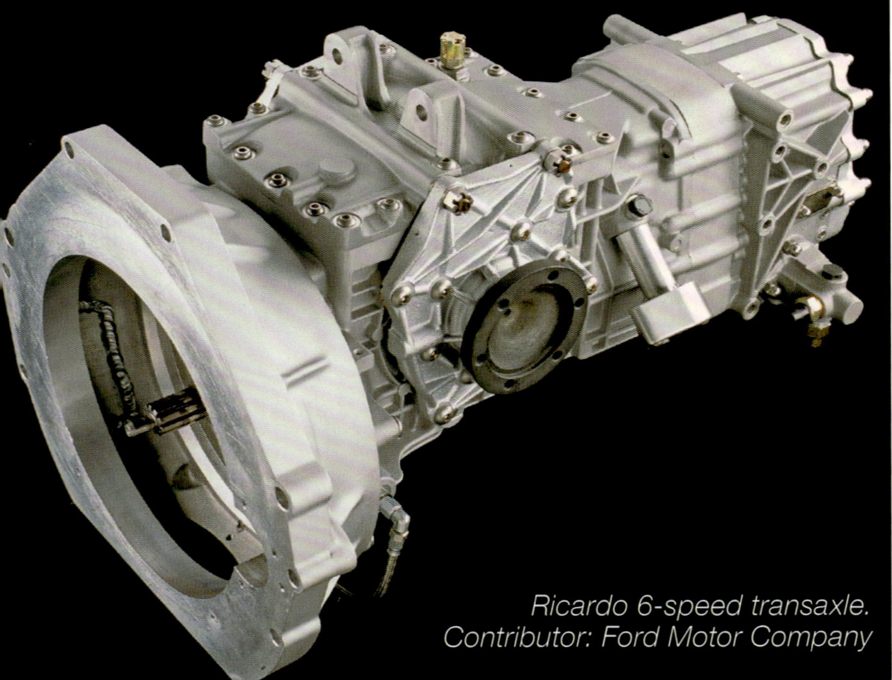

Ricardo 6-speed transaxle.
Contributor: Ford Motor Company

whilst providing the required strength to handle the massive 500lbft (678Nm) torque output.

Selected to be mated to the new engine was the Ricardo (RCT) six-speed manual transaxle featuring a helical limited-slip differential. This transmission was selected because it was able to handle the projected engine power output.

New dimensions

The roof of the original Ford GT MkI stood only 40.5in (1028.7mm) above the ground, hence its nickname, "GT40". The new Ford GT dimensions were adjusted for the reality of owner requirements in the twenty-first century. The Ford GT concept car was designed to be 3in (76.2mm) taller, 6.8in (172.7mm) wider, 12.6in (320mm) longer, and the wheelbase was stretched by 11.4in (289.6mm).

Note: For the Ford GT production car the ride height and roof height depends on the suspension system settings and compliance with various national ride height regulations which differ around the world.

Note: Various reports, articles and books may offer slightly different values in the dimension comparisons between the new Ford GT and the original Ford GT. These differences will only be slight, but are caused by different versions of the original Ford GT being selected for the comparison.

Jeremy Clarkson, Colin Crabbe and Dan Gurney require no bubble in the canopy roof to get in and out of the new Ford GT.

New chassis design

The original Ford GT chassis (tub) was built around an all steel monocoque or honeycomb aluminium design (MkIVs only).

The Ford design team knew its version of the Ford GT would require a stiff and rugged structure. Whilst the new Ford GT was to look and handle as much like a racing car as possible, the design team recognised that its new car would be driven regularly on ordinary roads. These roads vary dramatically in quality, and an

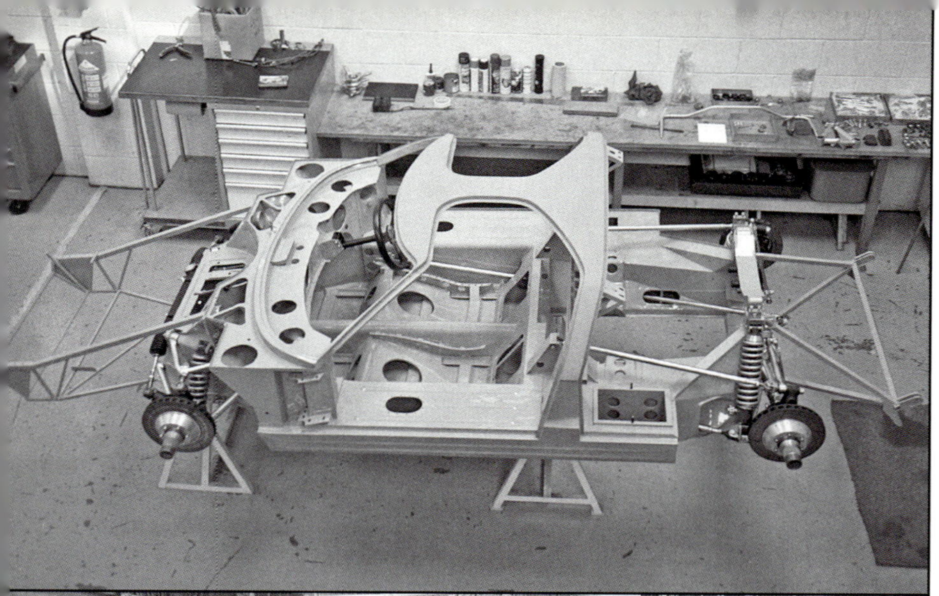

Original Ford GT MkI chassis (tub) design.
Contributor: Claude Nahum

The Ford GT MkIIA chassis (tub) design from 1966.
Contributor: Ford Motor Company

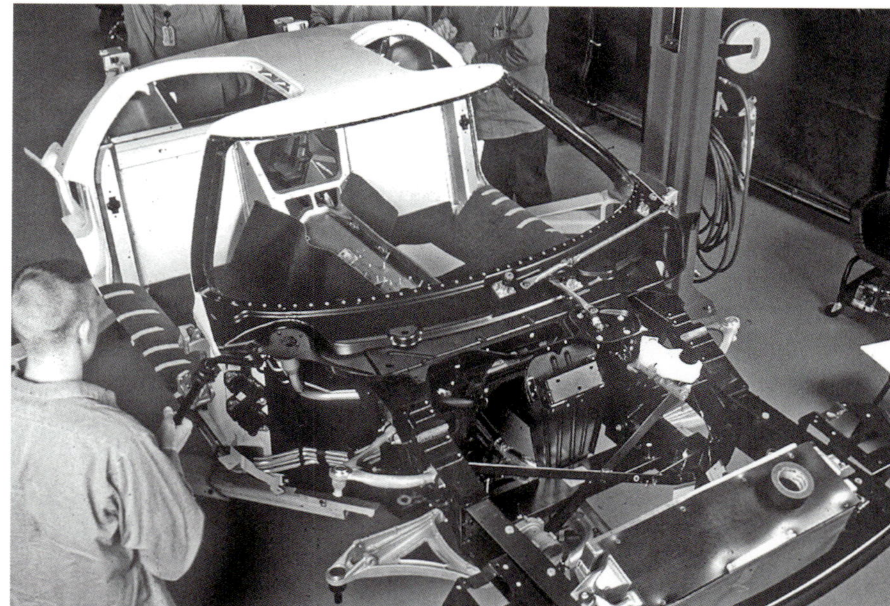

The new Ford GT chassis (tub) design.
Contributor: Ford Motor Company

owner in New York had to be as comfortable driving as the owner in Germany using the fastest and some of the best kept roads in the world.

The engineers were determined to fix the high speed aerodynamic front end lift inherent in the original Ford GT's design. This was a major priority because the new Ford GT was going to have to travel at speeds in excess of 200mph (320kph) to classify it as a true supercar.

The engineers at Ford FVT developed an all-aluminium space frame design. This hybrid aluminium space frame chassis structure is based on the efficient use of thirty five extrusions, seven complex castings, two semi-solid formed castings, and various stamped aluminium panels. The chassis also features unequal length control arms and coil-over spring-damper units to allow for its low profile.

Is the new Ford GT body much different to the original?

The new Ford GT features many new and unique technologies, including super-plastic-formed aluminium body panels, roll-bonded floor panels, a friction-stir welded centre tunnel, a 'ship-in-a-bottle' fuel tank, a capless fuel filler system, one-piece door panels, and an aluminium engine cover with a one-piece carbon-fibre inner panel.

The new Ford GT has cooling scoops fitted to the leading edge of the rear quarter panel to direct fresh air to the engine. The shape of the rear wheel wells ensures the car maintains its distinctive original look, which is complimented by the accent line from the front cowl to the integrated ducktail-style spoiler

On the left is the new Ford GT and right is Ford GT MkI chassis no. 1078 manufactured in 1968. The photograph shows the difference in ride height between the original and the new. New ride height (bumper height, 5mph rule) regulations have been introduced in the USA since the first Ford GTs hit the street. The old MkI is clearly smaller and more compact. Contributor: Claude Nahum

Ford GT MkIIA brake rotors (discs) being measured in the Ford garage during Le Mans 1966. Contributor: Ford Motor Company

Much bigger brakes

In 1966, when the brake system for the upgraded Ford GT MkIIA was revised, the vented brake rotors (discs) fitted were the largest known to mankind at the time. Unfortunately, the brakes used on the original 427 (7 litre) powered Ford GT MkIIAs and Bs from 1966 onwards were far too small for the new Ford GT. Seriously large 'Monster' brakes are required for a car designed to exceed 200mph (320kph) on the open road.

Stopping power is provided by four-piston aluminium Brembo monoblock callipers, each clamping down on internally vented and cross-drilled rotors (discs) mounted at each wheel.

The front rotors are 14in (355.6mm) and the rear rotors are 13.2 in (335.3mm) in diameter.

Note: Be aware that the cross-drilled rotors (discs) are prone to cracking.

Power assistance to the driver when operating the brake pedal is provided by a vacuum brake boost system. The entire brake system works well and is more than capable of stopping

Ford GT in the Austrian mountains near Innsbruck. Brakes are very important up here because, sadly, the time will come when the Ford GT has to go back down the mountain. Contributor: Adrian Streather

the Ford GT from extremely high speed. The deceleration rate is extremely good with little fade.

Wheels and tyres

The original Ford GT was fitted with 15 inch diameter wheels of varying widths depending on the version and the bodywork fitted. The four main wheel suppliers were:

- Borrani of Italy for the wire-spoke, light alloy wheels.
- Halibrand of the USA, light alloy wheels.
- BRM of England, light alloy wheels.
- J.W. Automotive in-house cast light alloy wheels.

The main tyre suppliers for the original Ford GT were:

- Goodyear.
- Dunlop.
- Firestone.

The new Ford GT has substantially different wheels. The only thing they have in common with the original Ford GT is that they are round.

The new Ford GT is fitted as standard with BBS painted cast aluminium wheels in sizes:

- Front: 9 x 18in.
- Rear: 11.5 x 19in.

Ford also offers the optional BBS painted forged lightweight aluminium wheels for the new Ford GT in sizes:

New Ford GT fitted with the optional BBS lightweight wheels compared to the J.W. Automotive cast versions from 1968 fitted to the Ford GT MkI. Contributor: Claude Nahum

New Ford GT fitted with the standard BBS wheels compared to the Halibrand alloy wheel design from 1966 fitted to the Ford GT MkIIB. Contributor: Adrian Streather

- Front: 9 x 18in.
- Rear: 11.5 x 19in.

The standard tyres fitted to both the standard and optional wheels are:

- Front: Goodyear Eagle F1 Supercar – 235/45 ZR18.
- Rear: Goodyear Eagle F1 Supercar – 315/40 ZR19.

Recommend tyre pressure front and rear is 2.2 bar (32psi).

Note: The Ford GT owner's manual clearly states that these tyres are for use in dry and wet conditions. They are not be used in the snow and ice, nor can they be fitted with snow chains.

Interior design

The most significant visual differences between the original and new Ford GT interiors are the position of the steering wheel and gearstick. In the good old days of the original the driver sat on the right side of the car. The new Ford GT has the steering wheel on the left side, regardless of the market the car is sold into. Sadly, this means that, for some countries like Australia, the Ford GT cannot be imported because right-hand drive is mandated by law in all the nation's States.

The original Ford GT design had a long throw gearstick installed on the right side of the steering wheel next to the driver's door. The new Ford GT also has the gearstick to the right of the driving position, but it's located in the centre of the car instead of next to the door.

The actual driving position and the level of comfort are quite different between the original and the new Ford GT. The original is very uncomfortable to drive; hardly surprising seeing as it was a racing car which required a few of the production run to be sold for road use for homologation purposes.

The new Ford GT has similar looking ventilated seats as were fitted to the original, but the new seats are far more comfortable.

J.W. Automotive customer racing car interior from 1968. Contributor: Adrian Streather

The new Ford GT interior design with the steering wheel on the left. Contributor: Adrian Streather

As a result, the new Ford GT is extremely comfortable to sit in and to drive.

The only issue from inside the new Ford GT which is not perfect is the driver's rearward view. This will be described in more detail in Chapter 6.

The first step toward production

Hand-building the concept version of the Ford GT was the first step towards producing a new design for the sportscar market. The concept car proved the design and featured all the essential elements that Camilo Pardo wanted to make the Ford GT what it is. In a relatively short time the Ford GT concept was ready.

Holman Moody Ford GT MkIIB interior design from 1967 with the steering wheel on the right. Contributor: Adrian Streather

New Ford GT gearstick located in the centre of the cockpit. Contributor: Adrian Streather

The new Ford GT seats being tested for comfort. The verdict was a thumbs up. Contributor: Adrian Streather

Cows to the left of us, cows to the right of us and a new Dodge Viper behind us. Contributor: Matt Malone

Chris Jackson from Roush UK driving the Ford MkIII road car. This is not a comfortable car to drive. Contributor: Richard Truesdell

The author driving the new Ford GT on an English road.
Contributor: Gail Streather

No worries, mate

The test to ensure the Ford GT supercar reached the next phase of production hinged on the concept version passing the test of public opinion. The response to the Ford GT concept was simply overwhelming. As a result of the public response, the official Ford GT program was launched by Ford Division President Mr. Jim O'Connor on the nineteenth of February 2002.

Even in clay the Ford GT looks a convincing supercar.
Contributor: Ford Motor Company

The Ford GT concept car in the flesh alongside an original Ford GT MkI from the 1960s. Contributor: Ford Motor Company

Prototype time

Acceptance of the concept version of the Ford GT was followed by the first handbuilt Ford GT prototype. Ford enlisted the brilliance of the Roush Industries team to help build the prototype.

Note: Roush Industries was originally formed as Jack Roush Performance Engineering in 1976. Roush has become a leading supplier of automotive engineering, development and manufacturing services. Roush is the world's largest supplier of integrated motorsports marketing services, and it manufactures and markets performance vehicles, crate motors, and vehicle components. Roush has its headquarters in Livonia, Michigan, USA, and employs more than 2000 people in over 50 locations throughout North America, Mexico, Germany and the UK.

The sequence of images on the following pages shows what the engineers had to work with, and how they proceeded to hand-build the first Ford GT prototype.

The first Ford GT prototype was revealed to the Ford factory workers and then to the public in November 2002, just nine short months after Mr. O'Connor made the announcement launching this part of the program.

Into production

The final phase for the Ford GT project was to create a production line and build it. There were many anxious customers worldwide who had pre-ordered their new Ford GT supercar and were awaiting the news that their would be pride and joy was actually on the production line.

The Ford GT concept car at its public launch at the Detroit motorshow in 2002. Contributor: Richard Truesdell

The official Ford GT launch by Mr Jim O'Connor, with the concept car 'smiling' in the background. Contributor: Ford Motor Company

Working out engine installation details. Contributor: Ford Motor Company

The chassis (tub) assembly is next. Contributor: Ford Motor Company

Where do all these parts go, boss? There is no assembly manual when constructing concept cars and prototypes. This makes the work even more challenging, but much more rewarding. Contributor: Ford Motor Company

Opposite: Luckily, the SVT-developed engine was delivered assembled, and the Roush lead prototype team just had to install it. Contributor: Ford Motor Company

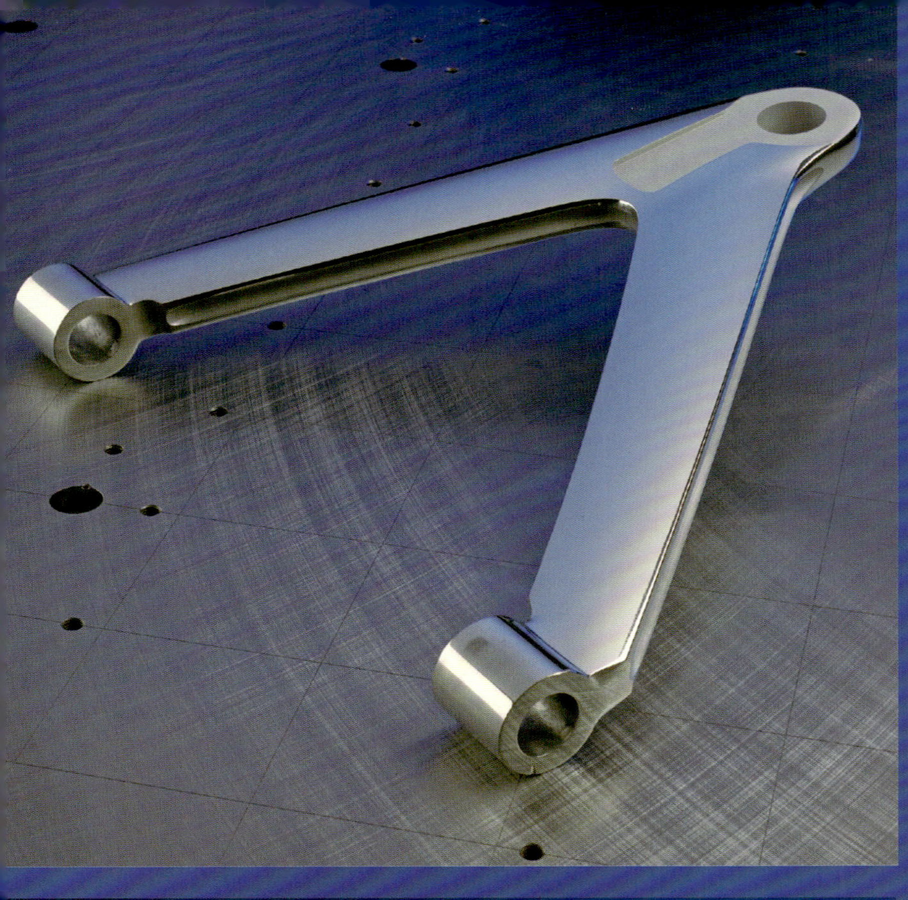

These are just some of the components for the new Ford GT concept and prototype versions that were designed in-house and hand-crafted. A lot of little pieces have to be manufactured to make the complete car. Contributor: Ford Motor Company

The first Ford GT prototype was named Workhorse Number 1.
Contributor: Ford Motor Company

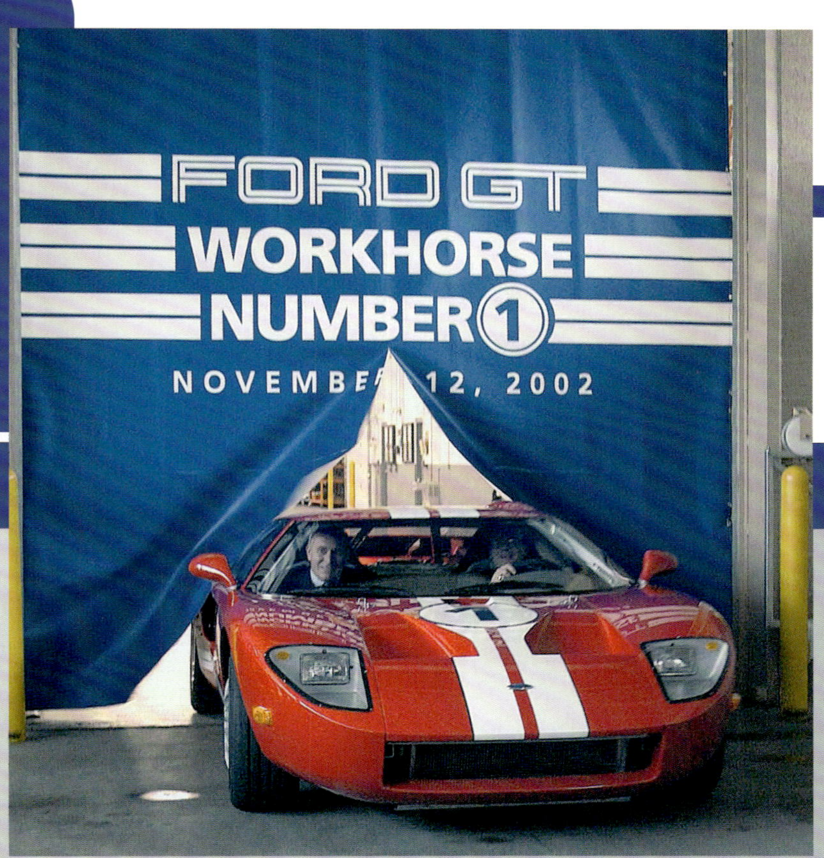

Workhorse Number 1 gets its first real workout on the Dearborn test track in November 2002.
Contributor: Ford Motor Company

However, Ford was going to try something new with the Ford GT. It adopted the same manufacturing process as Ford Advanced Vehicles did for the first Ford GT road cars in 1966. Instead of building the whole car in one place, Ford out-sourced production. This resulted in various stages of the Ford GT being completed at several vendor locations.

The spaceframe chassis assembly is manufactured by TK Budd-Milfab (Detroit, MI). The chassis assembly then transported to Mayflower Vehicle Systems (Norwalk, Ohio) for e-coating. Mayflower also assembles the body-in-white panels using adhesives and fasteners.

On the right of this image can be seen the bare Ford GT chassis assemblies at the beginning of the SSV assembly line. Contributor: Paul Allen; photographer David Wendt

Running gear installation under way. Contributor: Paul Allen; photographer David Wendt

The chassis assembly and body in white panels are then transported from Mayflower to Saleen Specialty Vehicles (SSV: Troy, MI) for painting, external trimming, body panel fitting and running gear installation.

Next the now almost complete car is transported from SSV to Ford's Wixom (MI) Final Assembly Plant for powertrain (engine and gearbox) and interior installation. Wixom staff also carries out the final quality checks prior to delivery.

The hood/bonnet is fitted to Ford GT chassis/serial no. 813 at the Saleen plant in Troy, Michigan. Contributor: Paul Allen; photographer David Wendt

Running gear installation continues for Ford GT chassis/serial no. 813. Contributor: Paul Allen; photographer David Wendt

One of the last pieces to be added is the rear end. Contributor: Paul Allen; photographer David Wendt

The last step is homologation

Due to different regulations between countries, cars manufactured in the USA and exported to other nations must undergo some changes to comply with local regulations. The new Ford GT is no exception. These changes are known in Europe as the homologation procedure.

Made road legal for Europe

As with any vehicle officially imported by Ford into Europe, the Ford GT is converted to meet European regulations. Using the special facility located near the famous Nürburgring circuit in Germany, each of the 101 cars arriving in Europe undergoes a thorough process of conversion, quality checking, and road testing before delivery to customers.

There are a number of detail changes that have been developed and engineered specially for the 101 European Ford GTs to make them road legal. Although these changes will be imperceptible to most people, they do mean that these European cars will have a special cachet that sets them apart from the rest of the vehicles being built in the US.

Mechanically there is little changed, apart from a modification to the car's exhaust system to meet European drive-by noise regulations. There are also a number of exterior (lights) and interior (switches, instruments) changes to ensure legal homologation is fully met. There are four basic homologated versions:

- American.
- European (excluding UK and Switzerland).
- Swiss.
- United Kingdom.

Before the Swiss registration plates can be fitted each imported Ford GT has to be homologated. Contributor: Adrian Streather

Note: The original Ford GT did not have homologation issues, they could be imported into the USA as complete road cars without any changes required. The same rules did not apply to the racing cars. The Shelby American Inc. or Holman Moody assembled racing cars were regarded as American made and could stay. However, if a racing car was imported completed it had to be exported again when the importer had finished with it. Ford GT racing cars were not always granted permanent residence in those days. Chassis no. 110, the MkIIA-X1 Roadster stayed, fell under the gas axe, and was buried to comply with American import regulations of the time.

Note: There may also be other national variants of the new GT. The general Asian market requires an overspeed warning system installed. The Japanese market requires catalytic converter temperature monitoring systems to be installed. Taiwan also has some special requirements, but if and how they impact the new Ford GT is not known at this time.

The American version is the basic build standard and need not be described further. However, the American specifications are not always acceptable to other nations.

Ford GT – Conversion for Europe

Roush Technologies Ltd. was selected by Ford to convert the official 101 Ford GTs for Europe from USA specification to TÜV and SVA approved specifications.

USA market version of the new Ford GT. Contributor: Matt Malone

Roush is now able to offer a conversion service to customers importing cars directly from the USA (known as grey market imports). The conversion comprises:

- New white front marker lights.
- New side turn indicators in the front wings (fenders).
- Change of rear side markers to amber colour.
- New rear fog lamp.
- New reverse (back-up) lamp.
- New fog lamp switch in place of original to add rear fog function, with LED tell-tales added for both front and rear fog.
- New speedometer with illuminated kph scale.
- Category 1 Cobra Thatcham approved alarm installation with new key fob to operate central locking and immobiliser.
- Category 5 Cobra tracker security system (this requires an additional annual subscription of £150 to activate the system).
- Reconfigured software in the central control module of the car to activate all new electrical functions.
- New deep cycle battery to improve starting capability after prolonged storage.
- Battery charger with plug in point on vehicle to maintain optimum battery condition during extended storage.

New Ford GT delivered to Germany undergoing its homologation modifications for the nation it has been sold into. Not all countries have the same rules and regulations. Notice it is fitted with the optional lightweight forged BBS wheels. In Switzerland these wheels would also have to be homologated and approved. Contributor: Wolfgang Kohm

- Stainless steel front registration plate mounting bracket.
- Headlight wash system.
- New exhaust system to comply with European noise regulations, including pneumatic valves and electronic control system.

As a company, Roush has been involved from the very beginning of the Ford GT program as one of the three Tier One suppliers who engineered the vehicle. Roush on the powertrain, Mayflower for the body, and Lear for the interior. Having been part of the project from its inception, it was a logical step that when the car came to Europe it was engineered by Roush in Europe.

Note: The homologation conversion process can be carried at Roush UK or the Capricorn facilities at the Nürburgring.

Switzerland has an additional requirement for all vehicle specifications to be initially approved and then distributed across the country to all the vehicle inspection stations located in the twenty-six Kantons. Each Kanton has its own set of vehicle homologation rules and different ways of applying them. This data will be used every three years when the not so new Ford GT undergoes its mandatory road-worthiness tests.

The UK homologation requirements are essentially the same as for the European version, except that the headlight lenses have to be changed, and the headlights adjusted so they operate correctly for vehicles driven on the left side of the road.

Delivery and homologation centres

Delivery preparation for all USA market customers is carried out at the Ford GT final assembly plant at Wixom, Michigan, USA.

Officially imported Ford GTs for the European market are

The special exhaust system that must be fitted before the new Ford GT can be delivered to customers. Contributor: Wolfgang Kohm

This blue Ford GT is destined for Switzerland. Contributor: Wolfgang Kohm

shipped from the production plant at Wixom, Michigan, USA, to Bremerhaven in Germany. From there they are transported by road to the Capricorn homologation centre established by Ford and engineering partner Roush at the Nürburgring in Germany.

The homologation process for officially imported and now customer imported Ford GTs for the UK is carried out at the Roush UK facility in Brentwood, Essex, England.

First European homologated delivery

Cologne, Germany, 25 May, 2005: The first fully-homologated production Ford GT supercar to be officially imported by Ford Motor Company into Europe is to remain in the Company's ownership and has become part of the Ford Heritage Collection of historically significant vehicles in the UK. The new Ford GT will join two original Ford GT40s in the Essex-based Heritage Collection, both of which have been owned by Ford since they were built in 1964 and 1969.

To provide the perfect partner to the Company's 1969 GT40 MkIII model, which is white with blue striping, the new heritage GT has been finished in Centennial White with blue painted racing stripes on the bonnet roof and clamshell engine cover.

UK market homologated Ford GT, Ford Europe's Press car. Contributor: Adrian Streather

This black Ford GT is homologated for Switzerland but will still be inspected for roadworthiness and continued compliance every three years. Contributor: Adrian Streather

The first deliveries from the Wixom delivery centre, American style, led by Ford President Nick Scheele in command of the white Ford GT. Contributor: Glen Smale – Automotive Research

Capricorn delivery and homologation centre at the Nürburgring. Contributor: Wolfgang Kohm

A new Ford GT arrives for the homologation process from the German port of Bremerhaven. Contributor: Wolfgang Kohm

A close-up of work in progress during the homologation process. Contributor: Wolfgang Kohm

Roush UK. Contributors: Matt Malone (top image) and Roush UK (left image)

The original Ford GT MkIII road car (right) is joined by its grandson the new Ford GT in the Ford/Roush UK Heritage collection at the Brentwood facility in Essex, England. Contributor: Richard Truesdell

Ford GT production version specifications & color schemes

FORD GT

2005 SPECIFICATIONS

EXTERIOR DIMENSIONS

Wheelbase (in) 106.7
Overall Length (in) 182.8
Overall Height at curb (in) 44.3
Overall Width (in) 76.9
Front Track (in) 63.0
Rear Track (in) 63.7
Weight Distribution (ft/rear) 43/57
Overall Shadow (sq ft) 96.8
Approach Angle (deg) 9.2
Departure Angle (deg) 14.0

INTERIOR DIMENSIONS

Leg Room (in) 44.6
Head Room (in) 35.4
Shoulder Room (in) 57.7
Hip Room (in) 57.8

CAPACITIES

Seating Capacity 2
Passenger Volume (cu ft) 52.8
Interior Volume Index (cu ft) 54.4

POWERTRAIN

Engine Type DOHC, 4 valves per cylinder, supercharged V-8
Engine Displacement (L) 5.4
Displacement (cu in/cc) 330/5409
Horsepower @ RPM 550@6,500
Torque @ RPM (lb ft) 500@3,750
Horsepower Specific Output (hp/liter) 101.9
Torque Specific Output (lb ft/liter) 92.6
Compression Ratio (in/mm) 8.4:1
Bore/Stroke (mm) 90.2x105.8
Material Aluminum block
Recommended Fuel 91 octane (premium)
Fuel System Sequential multi-port electronic fuel injection (SEFI) with dual injectors per cylinder
Oil Capacity with Filter (quarts) 12
Usable Fuel Capacity (gal) 17.5

TRANSAXLE

Type 6-speed manual
Gear Ratios 1 - 2.61, 2 - 1.71, 3 - 1.23, 4 - 0.94, 5 - 0.77, 6 - 0.63, Reverse - 3.135
Final Drive Ratio 3.36
Gear Synchronization 1 - Triple, 2 - Triple, 3 - Triple, 4 - Triple, 5 - Double, 6 - Double

CHASSIS

Drivetrain Layout Mid-engine, Rear-wheel drive
Front Suspension Double Wishbone
Rear Suspension Double Wishbone
Steering Type Rack-and-Pinion
Steering Ratio 17 to 1
Turns (Lock-to-Lock) 2.7
Turning Circle (Curb-to-Curb) 40 ft.
Brake System Vacuum Power Assist
Front Brakes (in) 14.0
Rear Brakes (in) 13.2

WHEELS

Standard: 18" Front /19" Rear BBS™ Painted Cast Aluminum Wheels
Optional: 18" Front /19" Rear BBS™ Painted Forged Lightweight Aluminum Wheels

FORD GT

KEY FEATURES

A. A mid-mounted, all-alunminum 5.4L DOHC supercharged V-8 engine that produces 550 horsepower. **B.** A six-speed Ricardo transaxle with twin-disc clutch and limited-slip differential. **C.** A race-inspired, double-wishbone front and rear suspension that contributes to Ford GT's exceptional handling and ride quality. **D.** A computer-modeled interior design that recalls the original Ford GT40. **E.** Massive 14-inch front and 13-inch rear disc brakes that feature four-piston aluminum calipers and cross-drilled and vented rotors to provide maximum braking performance. **F.** An aluminum space frame combined with Super Plastic Formed (SPF) aluminum body panels and extensive use of carbon fiber for strength and lighter weight.

Ford

FORD GT

MIDNIGHT BLUE CLEARCOAT METALLIC

PAINTED RACING STRIPES – WHITE
Painted over hood, roof, rear hatch and painted bodyside "FORD GT" Logo Stripes (Optional)

BODYSIDE VINYL STRIPES – WHITE
Bodyside "FORD GT" Logo Vinyl Tape Stripes (Standard)

NO STRIPES
Delete bodyside "FORD GT" Logo Vinyl Tape Stripes (Optional at no cost)

FORD GT

MARK IV RED CLEARCOAT

PAINTED RACING STRIPES – WHITE
Painted over hood, roof, rear hatch and painted bodyside "FORD GT" Logo Stripes (Optional)

BODYSIDE VINYL STRIPES – WHITE
Bodyside "FORD GT" Logo Vinyl Tape Stripes (Standard)

NO STRIPES
Delete bodyside "FORD GT" Logo Vinyl Tape Stripes (Optional at no cost)

FORD GT

CENTENNIAL WHITE CLEARCOAT

PAINTED RACING STRIPES – BLUE
Painted over hood, roof, rear hatch and painted bodyside "FORD GT" Logo Stripes (Optional)

BODYSIDE VINYL STRIPES – BLUE
Bodyside "FORD GT" Logo Vinyl Tape Stripes (Standard)

NO STRIPES
Delete bodyside "FORD GT" Logo Vinyl Tape Stripes (Optional at no cost)

FORD GT

MARK II BLACK CLEARCOAT

PAINTED RACING STRIPES – SILVER
Painted over hood, roof, rear hatch and painted bodyside "FORD GT" Logo Stripes (Optional)

BODYSIDE VINYL STRIPES – SILVER
Bodyside "FORD GT" Logo Vinyl Tape Stripes (Standard)

NO STRIPES
Delete bodyside "FORD GT" Logo Vinyl Tape Stripes (Optional at no cost)

FORD GT

QUICK SILVER CLEARCOAT METALLIC

PAINTED RACING STRIPES – BLACK
Painted over hood, roof, rear hatch and painted bodyside "FORD GT" Logo Stripes (Optional)

BODYSIDE VINYL STRIPES – BLACK
Bodyside "FORD GT" Logo Vinyl Tape Stripes (Standard)

NO STRIPES
Delete bodyside "FORD GT" Logo Vinyl Tape Stripes (Optional at no cost)

FORD GT

SPEED YELLOW CLEARCOAT

PAINTED RACING STRIPES – BLACK
Painted over hood, roof, rear hatch and painted bodyside "FORD GT" Logo Stripes (Optional)

BODYSIDE VINYL STRIPES – BLACK
Bodyside "FORD GT" Logo Vinyl Tape Stripes (Standard)

NO STRIPES
Delete bodyside "FORD GT" Logo Vinyl Tape Stripes (Optional at no cost)

What does a Ford GT cost?

The base price in the USA for the Ford GT is $139,995. The dealer invoice price is $128,506 and the delivery charge is $1250. Owners in the USA also have to add $2100 in gas-guzzler taxes.

Note: Retail prices are set by the vehicle's manufacturer. These figures appear on each car's federally mandated window sticker. Most price lists also include dealer-invoice prices. Dealer-invoice prices are what the dealer pays the manufacturer for the car and its factory-installed options. The destination charge is not included in the suggested retail or dealer-invoice price and must be added to the cost of the vehicle. Car companies change prices frequently throughout the year. If the prices published do not match those on the vehicle's window sticker, the manufacturer has probably altered the price recently.

Note: It is known that some prospective purchasers have been willing to pay premiums of US$50,000 or more over the base price.

The base price in the USA includes: 5.4 litre supercharged V8 engine, 6-speed manual transmission, limited-slip differential, dual front airbags, anti-lock 4-wheel brakes, air conditioning, power steering, tilt/telescoping leather-wrapped steering wheel, leather upholstery, bucket seats, centre console, power mirrors, power windows, power door locks, remote keyless entry, AM/FM/CD/MP3 player, digital clock, tachometer, map lights, variable-intermittent wipers, visor mirrors, rear defogger, floor mats, rear 'ducktail' spoiler, xenon headlights, fog lights, tyre-inflation kit, 235/45ZR18 front tyres, 315/40ZR19 rear tyres, alloy wheels.

Optional equipment prices (retail) for the USA market version are:

- McIntosh sound system $4000.
- Racing stripes $5350.
- Painted brake callipers $750.
- Forged alloy wheels $3500.

The retail prices for the Ford GT in Europe have been calculated in the currencies of the three markets distributing these vehicles and the figures include sales taxes, import duties and homologation costs for these countries: Britain, £120,900; Germany 177,000 Euros, and Switzerland SFr.269, 700.

Note: The amounts and the types of taxes levied are different between the three nations.

The base price for the European market includes the same items as the USA market version, plus the homologation requirements, such as a new exhaust system.

Hot off the press

Sometimes one gets lucky. As the deadline for this book drew near Ford released a new version of the Ford GT. The timing was perfect for inclusion.

Using the 1966 Sebring 12hr winning Ford GT MkIIA-X1 Roadster (see Chapters 1 and 2 for more descriptions of the racing car) as his inspiration, engineering supervisor for Ford's SVT Kip Ewing, penned a sketch of his vision of a Roadster Ford GT on a place mat. See how important place mats are to car designers! Never leave home without one.

However, getting his idea accepted as a show car project required some creative thinking on Ewing's part, but he did it. Using a 1:18 die-cast model of the Ford GT Coupé, he cut the roof off and then remodelled the body using typical auto body materials like Bondo. Then he repainted it. Kip's efforts brought their justified reward. In June, Hau Thai-Tang, director of Ford SVT and Advanced Product Creation, gave Ewing the stamp of approval he needed to bring his dream to life as a functional show car.

An amazing aspect of Kip Ewing's Ford GTX1 is its multi-adaptable roof. The roof system consists of four individual hard panels. The panels can be configured as a Coupé, T-top, or a full Convertible/Roadster. Ford GTX1 drivers won't get caught in the rain for too long because all four panels of the roof can be stored internally for quick and easy access.

The basic technical specifications of the Ford GTX1 remain identical to the Ford GT Coupé version except for the fact that you cannot drive as fast with the roof off.

The original Coupé version of the Ford GT can be converted to the new X1 configuration. These conversions will be carried out at the Ford GT final assembly plant at Wixom for USA owners. European customers/owners have to contact the Genaddi Design Group for more information. New European deliveries will most likely be converted at the Capricorn homologation facility in Germany or at Roush UK.

Kim Ewing's inspiration was the Ford GT MkIIA-X1 Roadster, seen here at Sebring in 1966. Contributor: C. Nahum Collection; photograph by Gérard Crombac

The Ford GTX1 show car in full Convertible/Roadster configuration. Contributor: Ford Motor Company

The new Ford GTX1 show car at the SEMA 2005 show in Boston, USA. Contributor: Richard Truesdell

Studio images of the new Ford GTX1.
Contributor: Richard Truesdel

The new Ford GTX1 interior. Notice the centre roof section stored behind the seats. Contributor: Richard Truesdell

Six
The real world

The Ford GT moves from picture poster fantasy to being real when:

- It's handed over to its owner.
- People like book authors get to road test one.
- It's seen by ordinary people on ordinary roads.
- It's stuck in Brentwood traffic.
- It's parked outside an English pub, and the driver and his wife are inside having a pleasant afternoon sampling of the local fare.

The Ford GT in the real world, parked outside an English pub on a normal Friday somewhere north of London. Yes, this is the same Ford GT tested by Jeremy Clarkson and the Stig of Top Gear *TV show fame. Contributor: Adrian Streather*

Delivery

Before a Ford GT is handed over to its new owner, the standard pre-delivery and hand over process must be completed. The standard pre-delivery is where the dealer, in co-operation with Ford, carries out a full systems check, followed by a short test drive. If everything passes, a pre-delivery report is written and signed.

Once the car has passed its formal pre-delivery checks, the dealer then signs the official documentation. The dealer then hands over the documents and keys to the excited customer.

After a short lesson on the do's and don'ts, the customer should then carry out their own system function checks and a test drive.

When everyone is happy, the customer drives off into the sunset with a huge grin on his or her face.

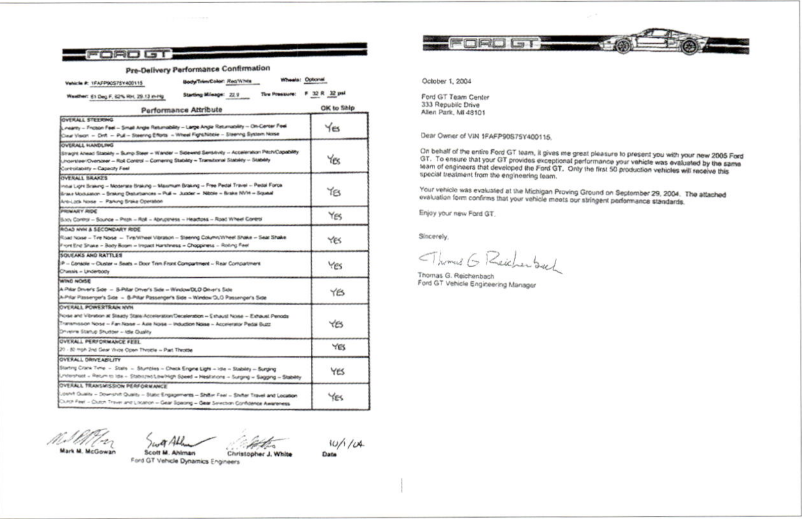

FORD GT

Pre-Delivery Performance Confirmation

Vehicle #: 1FAFP90S75Y400115 Body/Trim/Color: Red/White Wheels: Optional

Weather: 61 Deg F, 62% RH, 29.13 in-Hg Starting Mileage: 22.9 Tire Pressure: F 32 R 32 psi

Performance Attribute	OK to Ship
OVERALL STEERING Linearity – Friction Feel – Small Angle Returnability – Large Angle Returnability – On-Center Feel Clear Vision – Drift – Pull – Steering Efforts – Wheel Fight/Nibble – Steering System Noise	Yes
OVERALL HANDLING Straight Ahead Stability – Bump Steer – Wander – Sidewind Sensitivity – Acceleration Pitch/Capability Understeer/Oversteer – Roll Control – Cornering Stability – Transitional Stability – Stability Controllability – Capacity Feel	Yes
OVERALL BRAKES Initial Light Braking – Moderate Braking – Maximum Braking – Free Pedal Travel – Pedal Force Brake Modulation – Braking Disturbances – Pull – Judder – Nibble – Brake NVH – Squeal Anti-Lock Noise – Parking Brake Operation	Yes
PRIMARY RIDE Body Control – Bounce – Pitch – Roll – Abruptness – Headtoss – Road Wheel Control	Yes
ROAD NVH & SECONDARY RIDE Road Noise – Tire Noise – Tire/Wheel Vibration – Steering Column/Wheel Shake – Seat Shake Front End Shake – Body Boom – Impact Harshness – Choppiness – Rolling Feel	Yes
SQUEAKS AND RATTLES IP – Console – Cluster – Seats – Door Trim Front Compartment – Rear Compartment Chassis – Underbody	Yes
WIND NOISE A-Pillar Driver's Side – B-Pillar Driver's Side – Window/DLO Driver's Side A-Pillar Passenger's Side – B-Pillar Passenger's Side – Window/DLO Passenger's Side	Yes
OVERALL POWERTRAIN NVH Noise and Vibration at Steady State/Acceleration/Deceleration – Exhaust Noise – Exhaust Periods Transmission Noise – Fan Noise – Axle Noise – Induction Noise – Accelerator Pedal Buzz Driveline Startup Shudder – Idle Quality	Yes
OVERALL PERFORMANCE FEEL 20 - 80 mph 2nd Gear Wide Open Throttle – Part Throttle	Yes
OVERALL DRIVEABILITY Starting Crank Time – Stalls – Stumbles – Check Engine Light – Idle – Stability – Surging Undershoot – Return to Idle – Stabilized Low/High Speed – Hesitations – Surging – Sagging – Stability	Yes
OVERALL TRANSMISSION PERFORMANCE Upshift Quality – Downshift Quality – Static Engagements – Shifter Feel – Shifter Travel and Location Clutch Feel – Clutch Travel and Location – Gear Spacing – Gear Selection Confidence Awareness	Yes

Mark M. McGowan Scott M. Ahlman Christopher J. White 10/1/04 Date

Ford GT Vehicle Dynamics Engineers

FORD GT

October 1, 2004

Ford GT Team Center
333 Republic Drive
Allen Park, MI 48101

Dear Owner of VIN 1FAFP90S75Y400115,

On behalf of the entire Ford GT team, it gives me great pleasure to present you with your new 2005 Ford GT. To ensure that your GT provides exceptional performance your vehicle was evaluated by the same team of engineers that developed the Ford GT. Only the first 50 production vehicles will receive this special treatment from the engineering team.

Your vehicle was evaluated at the Michigan Proving Ground on September 29, 2004. The attached evaluation form confirms that your vehicle meets our stringent performance standards.

Enjoy your new Ford GT.

Sincerely,

Thomas G. Reichenbach
Ford GT Vehicle Engineering Manager

An example of an American delivery report handed to the customer before he/she accepts delivery. Contributor: Matt Malone

The average time for the delivery process to be completed is around ten minutes. In Switzerland, an additional part of the delivery process is to confirm that the Swiss homologation paperwork is in order and that the insurance company has delivered the Swiss registration plates. One cannot drive home without them.

For the majority of Ford GT customers this is enough, but not for Swiss-based businessman and car collector Claude Nahum. He felt that this kind of delivery was not quite his style. Claude decided that, after going through the official delivery process at the Grimm-Sud Ford dealer in Geneva, he would do his own unofficial acceptance test drive on the race track.

Claude felt that, as the Ford GT is based on a racing car and he wanted to race it himself, he would have to see how it really performed on the race track. Claude's idea was that under race track conditions he could see all the systems working under load. If anything was going to fail quickly, it would do so more quickly under racing conditions than under normal puttering around driving conditions. Claude wanted to see how tough and resilient his new, and rather expensive, supercar was going to be.

Motor racing was banned in Switzerland in 1956, after the horrendous accident at Le Mans in 1955 so, in order for Claude to carry out his unofficial acceptance test drive, he would have to travel down to the south of France, to the famed Paul Ricard circuit.

And Claude is off on the most fun, unofficial acceptance test drive ever. Contributor: Claude Nahum

Ready for the unofficial Claude Nahum acceptance test. Contributor: Claude Nahum

A little understeer. Contributor: Claude Nahum

Giving it gas. Contributor: Claude Nahum

After the unofficial and somewhat unusual test driving session at the Paul Ricard circuit was completed, Claude gave his new Ford GT a clean bill of health. A job well done and everyone was happy, because nothing fell off or broke which was good because it meant the warranty agreement was not tested.

Note: Using the Ford GT on a race track leads to both the brake pads and rotors (discs) being consumed very quickly. There is nothing wrong with the Ford GT's braking system, this is quite normal. The braking system fitted is designed for a road car, not a racing car. Brake rotors and pads should be considered consumable items when racing; they are not usually covered by warranty either.

Claude (smiling, and why wouldn't he be?) and his Ford GT are joined by an older family member at the Paul Ricard circuit. Contributor: Claude Nahum

Claude's Ford GT at home after its rigorous and successful test drive. Contributor: Adrian Streather

The Ford GTX1 Roadster on the road

As described in Chapter 5, the Ford GTX1 Roadster concept was launched as this book was almost finished. A short extension to the deadline was allowed to ensure that some road and location images of the X1 could be included in this chapter.

Unfortunately, the Ford GTX1 has not made it to European shores just yet (at the time of writing), but very recently some select American journalists were given the opportunity to drive the X1 in California.

Richard Truesdell a major contributor to this book was one of those select journalists. I asked Richard to ensure he took full advantage of the situation when he drove the X1 Roadster to provide some new images so readers of this book would have the opportunity to share in the excitement. Ford USA and Richard did not let us down. Here are his impressions:

"On the GTX1, with its roof conversion, one would expect lots of turbulence in the cockpit. If this is the case, you'll be disappointed. Chalk it up to the angle of the windshield combined with the intended aerodynamic effects of the two flying buttresses behind each seat contributing to the unexpected near silence in the cockpit. Visibility to the rear is marginally improved but that's certainly not the point.

"The pragmatic advantage of the open configuration, beyond the obvious of difference of a limited amount of wind through the hair, is that the $38,000 Genaddi Design modifications add practicality to the GT, especially with regard to ingress and egress. It's no longer necessary to open the doors wide to enter or exit the cockpit, not that you'll park your GT at the mall, it's just good to know you can if need be.

"Driving the GTX1 is a singular experience, taking the

On location with the Ford GTX1 Roadster. Contributor: Richard Truesdell

A very cool looking supercar. Contributor: Richard Truesdell

already fine GT coupé a few notches closer to perfection. There's something magical about having no roof over your head when 550 horsepower is at your disposal, with just your right foot serving to modulate the experience. The melody from the engine compartment provides a Grammy Award-winning soundtrack second to none, at least as far as any auto enthusiast is concerned, and a combination of the mechanical elements and a slight wind whistle that mixes up an aural cocktail that will bring unparalleled joy to anyone lucky enough to be positioned in the driver's seat."

Chapter 2 contains the photographs of Ken Miles and Lloyd Ruby in the pits with their car's lights blazing during the evening and night stages of the Sebring 12hr race in 1966. Richard took the following photos in memory of the great Ken Miles.

On the move.
Contributor: Richard Truesdell

These evening images evoke memories of the original Ford GT MkIIA-X1 Roadster at the Sebring 12hr in 1966.
Contributor: Richard Truesdell

Driving the Ford GT in the real world

Reading test drive reports can often lead to confusion because of the radically different points of view expressed by the authors. How many have asked, "What's behind this report?" or "What experience does the test driver really have?" A key item often missing in such reports is an explanation from the reviewer of their experience and their personal perspective. For example, what type of car does the reviewer usually drive?

The author of this book, for instance, is a Porsche driver. The cars I used in comparison to the Ford GT for my personal review in this book are: Porsche 911 (996) GT2, Sportec SP 700R (extensively tuned GT-2), RUF RTurbo (highly modified Porsche 911 (996) Coupé) and the Porsche Carrera GT.

All these Porsche models meet my personal requirements of power, acceleration, handling, drive and raw feeling. Like myself, the other contributors to this section provide details of the types of cars they were basing their comparisons on.

One of the author's comparisons with the Ford GT, the Sportec SP 700R with 700bhp and lots of torque. Contributor: Adrian Streather

Matt Malone

The Ford GT will always hold a very special place in my heart. Why? Not because it actually beat Ferrari at Le Mans, I wasn't old enough to see that, but because of the great experiences I've been fortunate enough to have behind the wheel of this spectacular car.

How did it start? Well, a friend of mine was lucky enough to have taken delivery of one of the first 50 cars in the USA.

I'll never forget my first drive – awe-inspiring. Point the car straight, put the hammer down, and this car doesn't just accelerate, but rather lunges with a jet aircraft-like thrust that pins you to the back of the seat all the way to the redline – 1st, 2nd, 3rd, 4th gear and still pulling.

The Ford GT made the Ferrari 360 Modena which I drove earlier that morning feel like it was towing a trailer. This car is fast and easily handles the corners. Come into a roundabout at such speeds that your brain is saying "NO!", but the child in you is screaming even louder, "faster, make it go faster". The Ford GT will make you feel very good. It's so balanced and pliable; you'd have to send a Dodge Viper to finishing school in Switzerland for a couple of years to get anywhere close to the Ford GT. Could this experience get any better? Oh yes!

Matt with the Ford GT he drove in the USA. Contributor: Matt Malone

All the reviewers agreed that the Dodge Viper was a rough diamond and needed several years at a Swiss finishing school to even get close to supercar status.
Contributor: Adrian Streather

About a month after my first drive, I was showing the car to a policeman friend who happened to stop by after seeing the car whilst on his patrol. When I asked him if he wanted a ride, he said "yes", so we jumped in. The next thing I know is he says "Hit it as hard as you can and don't worry about getting a ticket". "Okay", I said out loud, and thought to myself, "relax, play it cool, this is too good to be true. I'm in a 550hp, 205mph Ford GT with 37 miles on the clock, with a uniformed police officer riding shotgun ordering me to hit it hard."

Instinct must have kicked in because, without even thinking about it, I seized the moment. We found a straight road with no traffic and I nailed it. 1st, 2nd, 3rd, before he says "that's good, no wait, nail it again" then we ran out of road topping out at 127mph. I was hoping for 150mph plus, but I'll take what I can get. That was a great time, but little did I know the Ford GT had more adventures for me.

A good friend, Rich Truesdell, an automotive journalist from the US, invited me on a road trip. Ten days, 3000 miles, across eight European countries, in a Dodge Viper and a Ford GT on the Autobahn, Autostrada, the Alps, Italy, Le Mans, Nürburgring. I didn't need any time to think about it. "Yes, I think I can make time for that."

The response to the car in Europe was great. Everywhere we went people wanted to see that car and talk to us. I lost track of how many rides we gave. With a car like this language is universal. Part of our trip brought us to the famed Nürburging in Germany, a holy spot for some.

For those who don't know about "the ring", imagine a road course thirteen miles long with one hundred and forty seven curves. The elevation changes by a thousand feet, and the best

The Ford GT at the Nürburgring in July 2005.
Contributor: Richard Truesdell

The entrance to a great adventure.
Contributor: Matt Malone

Team boss Richard gives Armin's next victim a pep talk before they head out onto the Nürburgring. Contributor: Matt Malone

part is; it's open to anyone who is prepared to pay fifteen Euros a lap.

At the Nürburgring we met up with Armin Hahne, considered by some to be one of the best touring car drivers of all time. He was sent there by Ford to show us what the Ford GT could do on the track. While Armin was giving rides around the ring I was enjoying laps in the Viper.

Pulling into the pits, I parked the Viper and walked over to the Ford GT to talk to the group. Armin told me he had one more pass, and asked if I wanted to go? Seeing people stumble out of the car looking somewhat green, I actually had to think about it for a couple of seconds.

The ride I took with Armin around the Nürburgring is tough to describe. The smell of the brakes, the amazing G forces pulling in all directions, the motor pulling and pulling and pulling, the incredible precision with which Armin placed the car on the track, at no time did it feel out of control.

Once I ignored my brain screaming "this isn't possible", an incredible feeling came over me; what a high! When we returned to the pits I felt like a changed man. I have a whole new perspective of the car, the efforts of the Ford design team, and what the Ford GT could do in the hands of a professional driver. The whole experience was very humbling.

The Ford GT is truly an incredible car. Performing right up there with cars costing many more times the price. Today, tomorrow, and forever, this car will always hold a special place in my heart.

Richard Truesdell

Note: Richard is a freelance motoring journalist and enthusiast whose actions are partially responsible for this book. His experience as a petrol head goes back to the early 1960s. Richard has driven almost every American muscle car and European sports car ever made in the past twenty years. However, Richard's true passion is his 1964 Rambler American 440 convertible.

The Ford GT is a magical machine, a contemporary supercar unlike any other. The shape, evokes the famed GT40, and this impression is reinforced the moment you open the door and get seated. The deeply bolstered seats, with their stylistic ventilation grommets, the dashboard switches and the unusually positioned speedometer, seemingly in another county, all strengthen the illusion. For all its allure, the Ferrari 430 doesn't present the illusion that you're behind the wheel of a 250LM.

Turn the key, push the red start button above the radio and the 550hp supercharged V8 ignites, and in the US version at least (the European cars feature a more restrictive and quieter exhaust system) the murmur at idle is something between that found in a contemporary V8 Ferrari and a classic American muscle car.

Pulling out, the clutch engagement takes a bit getting used to. In spite of all the torque available, it's necessary and desirable to rev up to about 2500rpm, then let the clutch out; but once you get rolling, the GT is as easy to drive as a Focus, with excellent feedback coming from the perfectly weighted steering.

Richard on top of the world. The horses grazing around the car roam the mountain border between Austria and Italy. They don't have to pay the toll. Contributor: Adrian Streather

The smoothness of the power delivery encourages one to run through the gears at every opportunity. At speed, and by this I mean over 130mph, you have to be impressed by the quiet in the cabin; tire noise is the main issue here as there's virtually no wind noise generated by the substantial A-pillars. The big surprise has to be the absence of whine from the supercharger, especially given that the engine is scant inches behind your ear.

When driving in Germany, one naturally seeks out unrestricted sections of the Autobahn to explore the GT's top end, and my favourite technique is to get settled in at around 150mph in fifth gear, tuck in behind a big BMW or Benz, then downshift to fourth and put my foot to the floor. If they know what's good for them, any cars ahead move to the right as the speedometer hits 155, 160, 165, 170, 175 and finally 180mph.

At this point each 5mph increment up-tick takes a while and, as we were approaching Stuttgart at around four in the afternoon, an attempt at 200mph was out of the question (too much traffic to attempt safely), so we had to be content to settle in at 170mph and continued to be impressed by the utter lack of drama as the GT found its natural sweet spot.

All this accelerative ability would be wasted without comparable brakes, and here the GT shines, with excellent pedal feel combined with exceptional stability, even in panic stop situations. On the mountain roads of the Austrian and Italian Alps there was a total absence of any fade. Even when ratcheting up the aggressiveness quotient, the GT exhibited world class braking capabilities, easily on the par with the finest competitors from the UK and Germany.

On long runs on the Autobahn and Autostrada, especially late at night when traffic thins out a bit, it's easy to become one with the car, the GT feeling as if it's an extension of each of your senses. This is testimony to the success with which Ford's engineering team was able to properly calibrate all the variables, resulting in a refined supercar that communicates exceptionally well with the driver in all circumstances, providing a superlative driving experience.

Adrian Streather

My first drive of the new Ford GT started just outside Ulm, Germany, in a service station. Whilst the Ford GT was being refuelled I was handed the keys, with the comment "your turn".

The first time I slid into the driver's seat of the Ford GT it was like taking a step back in time. The interior layout takes some time to absorb. The speedometer is located on the far right of the dash, angled towards the driver. This was somewhat unique, but not of great concern to myself because what do you need the speedometer for in a supercar anyway?

The speedometer never lies. Contributor: Richard Truesdell

Dash layout of the Ford GT, with the large dash-mounted switches clearly visible. Contributor: Adrian Streather

Guillotine canopy door. Contributor: Adrian Streather

Low speed driveability check. This is a very common activity when you need to please the expedition team leader and photographer. Contributor: Adrian Streather

Car park practice, but not in Ulm this time. Contributor: Adrian Streather

The large switches on the leading edge of the dash were also unique to my experience. I'm used to switches being hidden all over the place, but never in practical reach. The new Ford GT uses a similarly designed dash to the original, and it shows just how practical thinking still works forty years later.

One doesn't sit in a Ford GT, one is absorbed by it. I loved the seats, but then I would; I'm tall and I like to be hugged. The daunting part of the Ford GT first time around is looking at the top of the canopy door. It does give you the impression that it's going to cut off your head as it's shut. Of course, it doesn't, but the first time I pulled the door closed I did duck.

The centre console is a little high for my liking, but the gearstick is nicely positioned and easy to operate. Long arms do lead to a little elbow bashing around the centre area until you develop a little technique.

Starting the Ford GT is a two-step procedure. Turn the ignition on, and then press the starter button. All things being equal, and as long as you've mastered the alarm system, the Ford GT's supercharged 5.4 litre V8 engine bursts into life. The sound of the engine, which is parked only a short distance from the back of ones head, immediately provides a sense of what's to come. There's nothing quite like the sound of a gurgling, rumbling American V8.

Having driven very powerful monster supercars before I was interested to see how the Ford GT would be in the low speed driveability area. During a test drive with Alois RUF in one of his new creations some years ago Alois said, "The key to a successful supercar is its driveability. If you cannot drive it through a village easily, what's the point of it all?" Alois was totally correct. If you cannot drive your supercar through the thousands of villages that dot the entire European landscape, then you're stuck with the boring Autobahns, or embarrassing yourself every time you stall at a level crossing or at traffic lights. Driving fast is fun, but there's more to driving than just sitting in a very expensive guided missile.

Austria, and the Ford GT was playing camera car for this segment. Contributor: Matt Malone

Autobahn is also occupied by drivers from many nations. Certain drivers, from certain nations, do not respect the unwritten laws of the Autobahn, "get out of the way of faster moving traffic" so the brakes and steering were given a work out on more than one occasion.

One area that really impressed me was the even application of power when it's requested by the driver. The supercars I'm used to driving are not that user friendly. Not once did the rear end of the Ford GT step out when I gave it gas by stomping on the accelerator. On the supercar confidence scale the Ford

The team leader gets all the good jobs, and even gets to pay! Contributor: Matt Malone

I was pleasantly surprised by the Ford GT. The clutch is easy and light compared to what I am used to. I just eased off the clutch pedal, lightly pressed the accelerator pedal and off we went, nice and easy. Very different to the Porsche Carrera GT or the Sportec SP 700R which give you a feeling of. "Just get on with it, I don't like driving slow, oops stalled, that'll teach you".

It was only a short trip through the car park until we reached the Autobahn entry ramp. Somehow, I had come to grips with the Ford GT in a very short distance. It was as I prepared to hit the accelerator to enter the Autobahn that I became aware of a slightly annoying problem: I was unable to adjust the outside mirrors to suit my line of vision. This lack of rearview vision would be my only complaint about the Ford GT from this drive, and all other drives since. I don't mind looking at the engine in the rearview mirror, but the outside mirrors are simply not good enough. A lot of head turning is required.

Once I had convinced myself that all was clear, by actually turning my head and looking, I launched the Ford GT onto the Autobahn in the direction of Kempten, heading for Austria.

My time on the Autobahn was spent testing the Ford GT in guided missile mode. Numerous times, speeds in excess of 160mph (257kph) were reached. I found that while taking curves at these speeds did require an above normal concentration level, I was never in doubt that it would get around. Unfortunately, the

Things are starting to get narrow ... Contributor: Matt Malone

GT rated ten out of ten. Ten out of ten means "I am not going to try and kill you today".

Another item about the Ford GT that really impressed was the ride comfort. I am used to a bone crunching ride but, whilst the Ford GT is stiff, it certainly did not crunch my bones. It definitely made me feel I could easily do the annual pilgrimage to Le Mans with some level of comfort and wellbeing which would last the nine hour trip from home. Pity about the luggage capacity of the Ford GT, though (there isn't any). The fuel consumption would also make the trip somewhat expensive, but the Ford GT is a supercar after all, and nothing is perfect.

Sadly, the Autobahn eventually ran out and it was time to do some village driving. This is when one realises another unique fact about the Ford GT. It's so wide! It was not uncommon to have both the rear wheels running on white lines. The one on the inside and the one on the outside of the lane. However, in Germany and Austria, other drivers are so not used to seeing supercars running through their villages that they actually get out of the way, whilst wrestling with their mobile phone cameras to record the passing of a legend through their village.

Mountain climbing in the Ford GT was effortless and fun. The massive amount of available power makes overtaking even on the steepest and windiest of roads effortless and safe.

The Brembo-designed braking system is superb, especially for an American made car. The air conditioning system works very well and even the noise level inside is well within my own comfort level. The installed sound system was never tested because I like to listen to the engine.

Going up. Contributor: Matt Malone

Few other drivers attempted to chase or challenge the Ford GT until we reached an Italian Autostrada. A Porsche 911 (996) GT-2 driver attempted to race the Ford GT. The cars were quite evenly matched at the lower speeds, but the torque of the American supercharged V8 engine eventually won the day.

In summary, the Ford GT surprised me. It was extremely easy to drive, it delivered power when asked, but in an even manner. The braking system was superb, and even Porsche drivers turned and looked as the Ford GT roared past. However, driving on European roads is one thing. What about taking the Ford GT on a trip to England, with its narrow lumpy B-roads and serious traffic congestion. Thanks to Paul Harrison of Ford Europe and David Jones of Roush UK, I was about to find out, and so was my wife. Gail was not with me on the European test drive, but she was keen to join me on the English adventure.

Roush UK is located north east of London, on an industrial estate in Brentwood. As Gail and I headed towards our meeting with the Ford GT, closely following behind my cousin Brian who

This guy turned up in Maranello spoiling for a fight, but the team went for pizza instead. Contributor: Matt Malone

The Ford GT is the car for girls who just want to have fun. Contributor: Adrian Streather

English B roads from the perspective of the passenger (right) side. Contributor: Gail Streather

was guiding us to the facility, I remember thinking "there are no wide roads, this is going to be fun". On these roads there was going to be a huge difference between the Audi A3 we were driving and a Ford GT.

Once we arrived at Roush, we were introduced to David Jones, who then proceeded to give us the once-over of the facility on our way to the car. The Ford GT had been parked outside for us, right alongside a long queue of Roush workers purchasing their morning tea from the visiting snack van. I was quickly overcome by the dread of stalling the car in front of all these people ...

David handed me the keys and left us to it. One small explanation which was not given involved the passenger side door: it takes two clicks on the remote to unlock it from the outside. This is something I learned when we returned the car, having spent the whole day opening the passenger door from the inside.

I cranked the machine up and off we went, without stalling. The purpose of this test drive was not to test the speed or the power, but the driveability on probably the worst congested roads in Europe. The condition of the English B roads would also test the ride comfort. I already knew what the Ford GT could do, but I did not know how it handled everyday use.

The entire day was spent cavorting around the counties of England north of London. I am not sure if we managed to find every bad road in the area, but we certainly gave it a good go. By the end of the day I was convinced that the Ford GT would not make a good daily driver if one lived in a rural area and needed to commute. The fear of somebody hitting the car on these narrow bumpy roads would ensure it stayed parked in the garage. English B roads are inhabited by many creatures, not just cars. The amount of heavy industrial traffic using them is astonishing, and then there are the buses!

The problem of the lack of rear vision really played a significant rôle on this trip. The car being left-hand drive, and driving on the left side of the road creates a few viewing issues for the driver. On these roads the lack of rear vision could be considered hazardous for the inexperienced. I've driven many left-hand drive Porsches in England, and I am used to driving left-hand drive cars anyway, so I managed to deal with the problem. However, it is something which is not ideal.

The highlight of the day, apart from the pleasure of a country drive, was the attention that the Ford GT attracted wherever it went. At one point an urgent pit stop was required, and anyone familiar with English roads knows that strategically-placed off-road parking for calls of nature are few and far between. Eventually, I found a suitable place to stop, and set off in search of a tree. While doing so, an entire college of young men poured out of nowhere to inspect the Ford GT. After nature had its way, I returned to the car, opened it up, and Gail and I just stepped back and let them look.

Then we took the Ford GT back to my cousin's house in Brentwood. Margaret and Brian Streather had put us up for the night and had asked if they could see the car. When we turned up they had called their friends; a great time was had by all examining

Pit stop with the first of the Ford GT fan club arriving. There were more to come. Contributor: Gail Streather

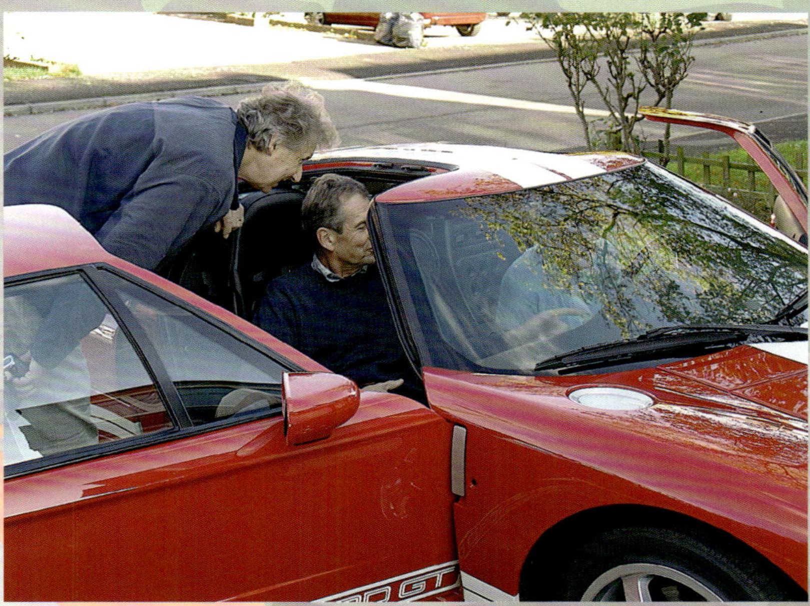

Family and friends inspect the supercar. Contributor: Adrian Streather

something they would normally only ever see on the TV.

Whilst we were stuck in heavy traffic heading back to Roush, a man walked past the car. He looked like one of those archetypal English gangsters from the East End of London: very smooth and very dangerous. He leaned through the driver's side window and, with a huge smile on his face, just said, "Very nice car", and then he stood up and just walked on.

The other surprising reaction came on the roads. In the Porsche community we encourage all Porsche drivers to flash their lights at each other and wave, as a form of recognition. Motorcyclists do this too. As were driving along a number of Porsches went past us going the other way. Every one of them flashed their lights and waved. There is no way they could have mistaken the Ford GT for a Porsche, so I took this as a measure of respect for the car itself.

Driving the Ford GT on this test drive was certainly an experience, and it was fun. The narrow B road conditions are not conducive to comfortable driving in the Ford GT, but it handled them with great ease, a nice ride and, when required, with an earth shattering turn of speed and an equally wicked noise from the exhaust.

Pan European Ford GT road trip highlights

This section just covers the death defying feats and other highlights of my three day involvement in the great adventure of the first Pan European Ford GT road trip. The Ford GT road trip team members for my part of the trip were:

- Organiser and team leader, Richard Truesdell from California, USA.
- Test driver, Matt Malone from Boston, USA.
- Ford support team leader and test driver, Chris Johnson from Roush UK.
- Ford support vehicle driver, Zoran Hriberski from Roush UK.

The whole team together for breakfast in the Hotel Stern in Austria. From left to right: Adrian (author of this book), Matt, Chris, Zoran and Richard. Contributor: Richard Truesdell

One of the interesting aspects of my part of the trip was that Richard loved to take photographs. We were put into some very interesting circumstances, like holding up traffic, doing run after run to get the shot, and missing dinner because we got to the hotel very late. Mind you, it was fun, especially when I was doing my stint as the camera car driver.

However, when everything lined up and all the dots were joined the result was spectacular and worth the effort.

Camera car driver duties were shared around, except for Zoran who had to drive the Roush/Ford support van. He carried all the spares for the Ford GT, including the spare wheels and our luggage.

Navigation was often fun too. Whilst Richard had originally mapped out the whole route, situations often called for these plans to be changed. Whilst we tried hard to avoid paying Autobahn charges and tolls, when driving through the mountain passes we had no choice. It was a good job somebody was carrying Euros. Unfortunately, it was me.

Going up the mountains was great fun. Going down into enemy territory would be a challenge. It was decided by the group that seeing as I had the most mountain driving experience I would lead. Thanks guys.

Next we had to survive the trip behind enemy lines to Maranello, Italy, the home of Ferrari S.P.A.

Chris had to drive past us many times to get the shot Richard was looking for at this location. The locals and the traffic didn't help. Contributor: Adrian Streather

As the team climbed further into the Austrian Alps, Richard spotted this location for his first Alpine photoshoot. The view was spectacular. Contributor: Adrian Streather

These images were taken in a tunnel in the Austrian Alps. Positioning the cars for the photographs was determined by the traffic light operation at the roadworks just up the road from where we were shooting. Some time was required for the camera car to be on the wrong side of the road, but it all came together in the end. Contributor: Richard Truesdell

Just to prove I was driving the Dodge Viper camera car at this time, Richard climbed aboard the Ford GT with Chris and began photographing the Viper. This time they were on the wrong side of the road. Zoran and the support can be seen in the top image behind the Viper. Zoran received some serious abuse from one of the Austrians behind him a short time later. Contributor: Richard Truesdell

Okay guys, which way are we supposed to be heading? Contributor: Richard Truesdell

It cost ten euros per car to get to this point, but the photograph was worth it. The team's next stop was behind the lines in enemy territory: Maranello, Italy. Would we escape with our lives? Contributor: Richard Truesdell

The Ford GT did strike some minor difficulties going down the mountain. Some of the corners were so tight that the car couldn't get around first time. Secondly, the Ford GT was so wide that Chris had to hang his head out the window to ensure the outside mirror did not make contact with nature's obstacles. However, we all got down safely in the end. Contributor: Matt Malone

The team slowly infiltrates enemy lines and starts to approach the Ferrari factory main entrance. Okay, we got lost the first time and found the wrong gate, but a quick check of the battle maps and we eventually made it to the factory main entrance unscathed. Contributor: Adrian Streather

Our command centre was set up right outside Enzo Ferrari's favourite restaurant. Contributor: Adrian Streather

Chris opened the engine bay for the Ferrari people to admire an American engine. Contributor: Adrian Streather

American V8 engine power. Remember that Ferrari has traditionally built V12 engines, and supercharging is not on the the menu either. In these photographs, you'll notice that the Ford GT was fitted with the optional, forged BBS lightweight wheels. When I drove the same Ford GT in England, these wheels had been changed to the standard cast BBS versions. Contributor: Adrian Streather

The famous Ferrari shop. I did venture in, but didn't buy anything. Contributor: Adrian Streather

The team made a safe departure from enemy territory and headed for Monte Carlo. Well almost; the Viper took a different route as I had to return to Geneva and then home to Walzenhausen. I had another book to finish. Contributor: Richard Truesdell

Sarthe and the Ford GT reunited

Le Mans. Two words that carry tremendous historical significance for all auto enthusiasts. Epic battles between cars and drivers that transcend the ages: Bugatti, Mercedes, Aston Martin, Jaguar, Ferrari, Ford, Porsche and, most recently, Audi. But no matter what your perspective, Le Mans, often means one thing (at least for most Americans), Ford versus Ferrari: cars, drivers and two proud manufacturers locked in mortal combat for sports car supremacy in the sixties.

On a sunny, cloudless day in June 2005, I found myself driving under the famed Dunlop Bridge in Ford's modern day recreation of the famed GT40, the 2005 Ford GT.

With its styling that clearly evokes and emulates the greatest Ford race cars of all time, for ten memorable minutes I felt as if I

Richard, Chris and Matt hook up with Christophe Schwartz and his Ford Mustang at Le Mans before reaching the main entrance. Contributor: Richard Truesdell

First stop is the Sarthe museum. Contributor: Richard Truesdell

was Phil Hill, and that I was behind the wheel of chassis number 102, his car when Ford first mounted its assault on Le Sarthe on June 20, 1964. Circulating the course, my heart virtually beating out of my chest, I had reached the automotive Promised Land.

The opportunity to act out one of my fondest childhood fantasies had come about through the generosity of Mr. Hérve Guyomard, the Bugatti circuit director at Le Mans, who once owned and drove chassis no. 1020, the Ford GT MkI on display at the Sarthe museum that I had photographed just moments before.

Note: Chassis no. 1020 was originally painted midnight blue and delivered to Shelby American Inc. as a display car. It was sold to Ford France in 1967, repainted in the Ford France white colour scheme and raced at Le Mans and many other events by drivers such as Jo Schlesser and Henri Greder. After it was retired, chassis no. 1020 was sold to Pierre Bardinon and then to Franco Sbarro, and eventually found its way to the Sarthe museum.

Walking through the pits, the weight of history was palpable to me; I would soon be driving on hallowed ground that over the years has hosted some of motorsports most memorable events.

As I walked towards the Ford GT one image was dominating my thoughts, the sight of three Ford GT MkIIAs crossing the finish line together in 1966, ending Ferrari's domination of Le Mans and the start of an uninterrupted four year run of Le Mans victories.

Driving around the Bugatti Circuit is best enjoyed behind the wheel of the Ford GT. From the cockpit, everything was in

Next stop is Mario Andretti's favourite part of the Sarthe circuit, the Dunlop Bridge. Contributor: Richard Truesdell

the right place, with the exception of the steering wheel (GT40 race cars had their steering wheels on the right, British-style. That small issue aside, navigating the course for several laps went a long way towards giving me a full appreciation of the enormity and significance of the experience as, just a week before, this same circuit had been host to the 2005 running of Le Mans. This was a lifelong dream fulfilled.

Pulling into the pits, I thought my day was finished but I was greeted by Mr. Guyomard who simply said to me "Go out and take a last hot lap, you deserve it". Quite frankly, nothing more needs to be said.

The Ford GT parked in the famous pits at Le Mans. It should be remembered, however, that the pits didn't look like this in 1966. Contributor: Richard Truesdell

Richard receives permission to drive the track. This section is part of the Le Mans Bugatti circuit. Contributor: Richard Truesdell

Christophe gets himself and his Ford Mustang into the photograph with the Ford GT trackside.
Contributor: Richard Truesdell

One last hot lap at the Sarthe circuit then it was time to leave.
Contributor: Richard Truesdell

Time for a quick stop for refreshments at the famous Hotel De France before heading north, and home to England.
Contributor: Richard Truesdell

Seven

The replicator's showroom

Replicas came into being because the total number of Ford GTs manufactured between 1963 and 1969 was too small to support the depth of love and dedication which developed out of the core Ford GT fanbase. The number of fans continued to rise long after the GT's racing days were over.

Low production numbers opened the door for dedicated Ford GT lovers to take control and, ultimately, responsibility for keeping the Ford GT legend alive. The people and companies behind this are affectionately described here as the 'replicators'.

A racing car version of the C.A.V. GT manufactured replica, owned by Roy Sales, where it was designed to be, on the race track. Contributor: John Spence

It could be argued that the replicator movement began with Alan Mann Racing (P40), Bruce McLaren (MkIIA-X1) and Ford France (Roadster) during the heady early days of 1965. These teams all wanted to create their own highly competitive versions of the Ford GT and they did. For Ford GT historians and fans alike this process created mass confusion with the chassis numbers later, but these things happen.

Many years after the original Ford GT went out of production the Safir Company in England built a number of new-build, or continuation, Ford GT MkIs. A new continuation model of the MkII is also being offered by Holman Moody in the USA. The new Ford GT and Ford GTX1 could also be considered as continuation models, albeit modified for the demands of the modern customer.

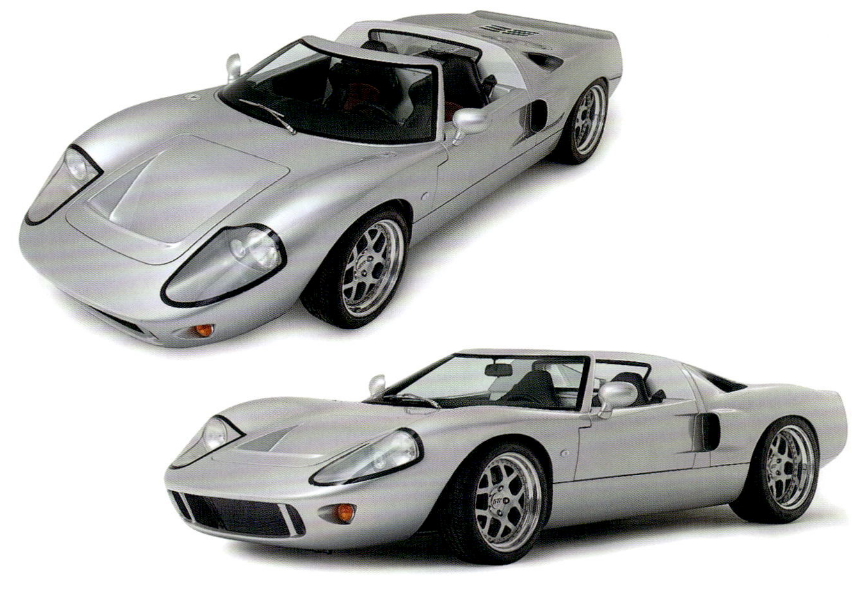

GTr460 by Gloster Cars. Contributor: Gloster Car Company – Simon Farrell

The new Ford GT inspired products like the GTr460, under development by the Gloster Car Company in England, and the really new kid on the block, the superb-looking Barchetta from GT40NZ Ltd. in New Zealand. This was once a straight Ford GT40 replica, but the previous owner had some rather novel ideas of how it should look.

Ford GT replicas are available from numerous companies around the world, but those who contributed to this book are: Auto Futura (C.A.V. GT) in South Africa; GT40NZ in New Zealand; M.D.A. in England; and E.R.A. in the USA.

The Barchetta under development by GT40NZ Ltd. Contributor: David Harvey

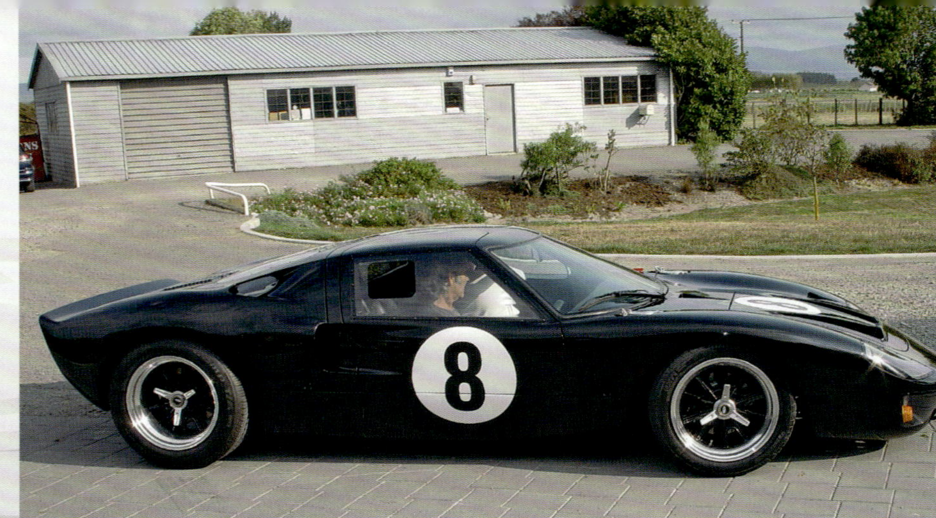

The GT40NZ replica, affectionately known as "8-ball". Contributor: David Harvey

E.R.A. Ford GT replica road version. Contributor: Bob Putnam – E.R.A. Replica Automobiles

There are the enthusiast replicators who build their own cars at home. They can purchase kits from the companies in this chapter, or they can create their own personal version from scratch. Most start with a basic kit.

Regardless of whether the replica is commercially or privately produced, the dedication and passion that goes into these Ford GT-inspired replicas never ceases to amaze the petrol head community. There is absolutely no question that the replicators filled the gap between the end of the original Ford GT production run, all the way until 2002 when those amazing words of the great visionary Lee Iacocca, first spoken in 1963: "We need a flagship model", reverberated around the Halls of Dearborn, Michigan, USA.

Without the dedication of the Ford GT replicator movement it's doubtful that the Ford GT legend would have endured this long. The replicators ensured that the Ford GT was not consigned to pictures in history books and posters sold on the internet, but instead lived on, on road and track, alongside the few remaining originals.

This chapter is dedicated to those enthusiastic companies and individuals who continue to play their significant role in keeping the Ford GT legend alive.

Note: Replicas are still needed because the new Ford GT has only been built in small numbers, with production ending in the last quarter of 2006. Also a good replica can be built for much less than the price of the limited edition Ford GT. The motto of the replicator industry should be: "Keep the legend on the street".

Ford GT based continuation models

When the original Ford GT production program, both race and road car ceased in 1969, J.W. Automotive (J.W.A.) retained the GT manufacturing rights from Ford. The manufacturing rights package included:

- All the original engineering drawings and blue prints.
- All tools, moulds and jigs.
- A significant quantity of spare parts which were handed over to the company P. & M. Racing Preparations in Chiswick, England which acted as spares agents for J.W.A.

In 1980, John Willment signed a manufacturing agreement with Safir Engineering Ltd. of Byfleet, Surrey, England, owned by Peter Thorpe. In the deal was included the exclusive right to use the name Ford GT. The agreement allowed Safir to build a limited run of GTs, manufactured to the automotive standards and regulations of the 1980s. The new version would be known as the Ford GT MkV.

Two Safir Ford GT MkV continuation models. In the foreground is chassis no. 1136, and in the background, car no. 57, is chassis no. 1124. Both are in the USA. Contributor: Wolfgang Kohm

The original Holman Moody MkIIA/MkIIB, chassis no. 1016, is still racing in 2005. It last raced under the official Holman Moody works team banner at the 1967 Daytona 24hr race. Contributor: Claude Nahum

The chassis for the MkV was updated from the original design by Len Bailey, part of the original Ford GT design team. The modernised chassis utilised a fabricated steel monocoque instead of pressed steel panels.

New body panels were constructed using original moulds, and so the Ford GT MkV bore a striking resemblance to the original Ford GT MkI. The chassis numbers followed the originally registered production sequence.

Another example of the Safir version is Ford GT MkV chassis number no. 1115. It was the twelfth off the line manufactured in 1986. The engine installed is a Ford 302in^3 (5-litre) V8 fitted with four Weber carburettors. The engine is mated to a five-speed ZF gearbox. The exterior is painted in Cirrus white and the interior is all black.

Australian racing driver Vern Schuppan owned a Safir MkV. When I asked him about it this is what he said: "Yes I once owned a Safir Engineering GT40, a new one that was built for me to order. I probably only did one run of maybe 50 to 100 miles in the English countryside in it."

Note: Safir registered the number GT40 as a trademark in 1985. The identification code GT40 was never officially used by Ford or any of the teams to identify their cars. Officially, they were all Ford GTs. However, the identification code GT40 became a legend along with the actual car. Safir, realising that the code had not been trademarked, did so. Safir GT40 Spares Ltd. of Cincinnati, USA purchased the GT40 trademark in 1999 when the original company, Safir Engineering shut down.

Holman GT-40P MkII

Holman Moody was one of the Ford works racing teams. It joined the Ford GT program for racing seasons 1966 and 1967. The company, once headed by John Holman and now headed by Lee Holman, announced that it was going to build a new but original version of the Ford MkII GT40 called the GT-40P MkII.

Lee Holman introduces the new car: "These cars are for the serious car collector and/or vintage racer. They are built to the same quality and performance used to win Le Mans in 1966. These MkIIs are authentic, new team cars with most of the parts interchangeable with the original cars raced by Holman Moody, Shelby American Inc. and Alan Mann. Our policy is to build the best GT-40 MkIIs possible, these cars are not copies of any one original team car, but combine the best, most serviceable options from the original Ford effort. Changes have been made for safety and other reasons."

The company press release said that Lee Holman, the President of Holman Automotive, Inc. and Holman Moody Inc., is producing new 1966 specification GT MkII Le Mans race cars. These cars are to be built at the Holman shops in Charlotte, North Carolina, USA, using the original Ford GT40 MkII blueprints, specifications, and base chassis that Holman Moody used to build its original GT40 MkIIs.

Ever since the Ford GT40 MkII won Le Mans, Holman Moody has been asked if an original MkII could be remanufactured. Due to high tooling costs for such a small number of cars, Holman Moody only repaired or restored the few existing MkIIs. Now, with the interest in vintage racing at an all time high and the number of inquires growing substantially, Lee Holman and a number of the original Ford Le Mans team members decided to build a limited production of authentic racing Le Mans MkIIs.

These cars will have the advantage of the Holman Moody team's vast racing experience, blueprints, race reports, and paperwork from the Ford Le Mans program. The Holman cars will be built just as the originals were raced, using original MkII body

Holman Moody MkII replica, no. 201. Contributor: Holman Automotive via Greg Kolasa the SAAC GT40 registrar

moulds, chassis from original tooling, Kar-Kraft style transaxles, new 427 Ford dry sump engines, and a number of the original spare parts.

One of the most important aspects of this project is the people that Mr. Holman has pulled together to build these new MkII race cars. These are the workers who helped Ford build and race the original Le Mans GT40s, MkIIs, and MkIVs. They will assure that these new MkIIs will be true to original design and as great as the MkIIs that made history. The Holman GT40 Mark II is not intended for road use.

Reports received from the USA say that Holman Moody built one replica GT40 MkII in 1992 and another was partially built in 2000. Both appeared at the annual gathering of the Shelby American Automobile Club at Connecticut's Lime Rock Park circuit, USA, in June/July 2000, which was also the SAAC's twenty-fifth anniversary.

Ford GT inspired replicas

The E.R.A. GT

World renowned replica building company, E.R.A. Replica Automobiles, of New Britain, Connecticut, USA, run by Bob Putnam, says of its GT40 replica that it's a classic race car, carefully adapted to the street.

E.R.A. has two versions available; the MkI, and the MkII with a 427 (7 litre) engine fitted. One customer has even installed a 680hp (507kW) engine.

The E.R.A. GT has been designed to standards far beyond what is expected of a kit car. The body, chassis, suspension, and interior duplicate the original car closer than any other car selling for less than $250,000, but race-car-quality alone was not enough. E.R.A. claims its body is much straighter than the original, with all-weather sealing – and that its chassis is designed for the street as much as the track. Even air conditioning is available.

The E.R.A. GT kit was designed to be put together like a production car. No fabrication is necessary, so your garage simply becomes the final assembly line. Carefully chosen components are thoroughly integrated into the overall design. All the holes, caged nuts, receptacles, brackets, adapters, etc. necessary to mount these components were designed into E.R.A.'s kit from the beginning.

Except for the drivetrain, wheels and some standard comp-

Above: E.R.A. MkI replicas. Contributor: Bob Putnam–E.R.A. Replica Automobiles

E.R.A. MkII replica. Contributor: Bob Putnam–E.R.A. Replica Automobiles

E.R.A. Ford GT replica racing version. Contributor: Bob Putnam–E.R.A. Replica Automobiles

onents of the suspension, everything necessary to complete a finished automobile is included. From a custom aluminium radiator to wiring harness clips. Furthermore, the standard pieces are of the highest quality.

E.R.A. recommendations for the parts it does not supply with the kit are:

- Any small-block Ford V8 engine (260, 289, 302 or 351in^3).
- Alternator mounting brackets are supplied to suit the engine selection.
- The original GT40 ZF-5DS-25/1, 4-bolt transaxle is available in the stronger ZF-5DS-25/2, 7-bolt version as used in BMW M1s and De Tomaso Panteras of the mid to late 1970s. The ZF-5DS-25/2 transaxle does require modification to fit the Ford small block engines even though it has to be turned upside down.
- A custom bellhousing is available to adapt the transaxle to the engine.
- Standard Ford clutch parts and a custom throw-out (thrust or pilot) bearing are used. The pilot bushing is supplied with the custom bellhousing.

Note: New transaxle transmissions manufactured from the original tooling are available from RBT Transmissions.

The E.R.A. optional exhaust system is a duplicate of the original, with a true 180 degree design. Available for 289, 302 and 351in^3 Ford V8 engines with Windsor-style heads. This exhaust is ceramic coated: the finish is very durable and very attractive. It also decreases the heat radiated from the exhaust, reducing under-hood temperatures.

M.D.A. Ford GT replicas

M.D.A. Cars is owned and run by Mark Sibley in England. Mark has been building and supplying parts for the GT40 for almost two decades.

The M.D.A. MkI GT40

The MkI replica is built upon the M.D.A. steel space frame chassis with integral structural rigidity, and developed on a jig built system supplied by an ex-formula racing company.

This concept chassis was proven, drawn and reverse engineered to produce the first M.D.A. MkI, which is different from other Ford GT replicas. The M.D.A. replicas have a fixed bracket suspension with adjustable arms, lower engine cradle position, front suspension pick ups and substantially more leg room.

M.D.A. Ford GT MkI replica. Contributor: Mark Sibley

The M.D.A. chassis has other features, such as a centre spine gearshift mount for left-hand drive customers. Mounting plates for a roll cage as standard eliminate the need for welding or drilling. The rear engine area is radically different. The engine and gearbox mounting position is lower so the car's centre of gravity is greatly improved. There is more clearance around the front end of the engine (a particular problem with originals). Because the suspension is fully adjustable, setting up the ride handling for all personal requirements is easily carried out. The M.D.A. chassis is configured to accept the Renault UN1 transaxle.

The M.D.A. MkII GT40

The M.D.A. Ford GT40 MkII replica is an awesome machine. The appearance of the car from any angle sets it apart from other contenders. With the extra air intakes and the business-like rear end culminating with an adjustable air spoiler, it just looks the part. With a floor-mounted, bias adjustable, pedal assembly, deep vent nose panel, authentic lighting, original style cam locks, chrome bonnet hinges, fuel caps, and a window air scoop over the exhaust at the rear, it all looks correct in every detail.

M.D.A. Ford GT MkII replica. Contributor: Mark Sibley

James Bond 007 – *Die Another Day*

M.D.A. supplied a MkI GT40 replica for the James Bond 007 movie, *Die Another Day*. The producer wanted a Gulf Racing coloured Ford GT as part of the dramatic opening scene.

The car was especially prepared to look just like the Ford GT chassis no. 1075 that won both the 1968 and 1969 editions of the Le Mans 24hr race.

This GT40 replica did not live to tell the tale. Contributor: Mark Sibley

The GT40NZ Endurance

David Harvey owns and runs his own Ford GT replica and a Ford GT-inspired new product business in New Zealand. His company is called GT40NZ Ltd. His Ford GT replica is called the Endurance (nicknamed "8-ball").

GT40NZ Endurance Ford GT replica. Contributor: David Harvey

*GT40NZ Endurance Ford GT replica.
Contributor: David Harvey*

The GT40NZ Endurance has the classic lines of the original Ford GT MkIB (Gulf team look) with the feel and comfort expected in a modern car. This is a car designed for those who require modern day refinement in this most classic of Ford designs. Any purchaser of this sports car can expect luxury and comfort, daily drivability, and extraordinary performance.

This Ford GT replica model is for those who will enjoy the adrenaline rush of the GT40, but expect a light clutch pedal, power steering, and a modern feel to the brake pedal, while seeing cockpit appointments of the finest carpets and hand stitched leathers as essential. The noise levels have been tuned to moderate the howl of the Ford V8 red lining at 6500rpm, should one wish to have a conversation.

David's superb replica is designed for road use so the performance is important for prospective customers. His machine is speed-limited to 150mph (250kph) and it can do 0-62mph (0-100kph) in 4.9 seconds.

The C.A.V. GT by Auto Futura

Drive a GT40 anywhere and people will tell you their long held desire to sit behind the wheel of this iconic sportscar. Whether it's an original or a recreation of the original, the response is always the same: one of awe.

With this kind of reaction in mind, the C.A.V. GT had to do justice to the legend, and a painstaking process of development began to perfect the building of this Ford GT MkI recreation.

As with the original car, the C.A.V. GT started with a dream. The original founder of the C.A.V. had been planning for years to build a GT40 recreation in South Africa. In 1999, with two partners, his dream became a reality and C.A.V. (Cape Town Motor Vehicle Corporation trading as Cape Advanced Vehicles) was formed.

At the outset, the idea was to build components under licence for a manufacturer in the UK, but just making the parts was, somehow, not very satisfying. The mystique of the GT40 was itching to find a more concrete form in the Cape Town-based

The C.A.V. GT on the Kilarney race track in South Africa. The scene of many epic Ford GT battles during the Springbok series from 1966 to 1969. Contributor: John Spence

C.A.V. GT in San Diego, California, USA.
Contributor: John Spence

company. It was not long before complete cars were being rolled out the factory door in 2000.

Unfortunately, business and passion are often not very comfortable partners and the original company did not stand the test of time. A combination of volatile exchange rates, growing too quickly, and misdirected diversification, saw the demise of the Cape Town Motor Vehicle Corporation in late 2003. By this time around 80 cars had been built and exported, mainly to the USA, with a handful going to various other countries. When it came time to divide up the spoils there was no-one fighting to get their hands on the GT project and it seemed as if the C.A.V. GT was destined to die with the company.

By this stage the C.A.V. GT had evolved from a modest space frame kit car to a sophisticated stainless steel monocoque chassis sports car. To any petrol head it was hard to believe that no more were going to be produced.

In late 2003, the GT was offered in component form to Carcraft (owned by Jean Fourie), a specialist car assembling and tuning company, on a build to order basis. Jean had spent the previous year successfully developing a GT40 race car for an individual client. C.A.V., in a last ditch effort to keep its GT alive, hoped to market the car in component form through an independent company like Carcraft. John Spence joined Jean in this venture, and three component programs were sold before C.A.V. stopped production completely in late 2003.

In a decision, once again fuelled by a passion for cars and a love for the Ford GT era, an investor stepped forward in early 2004 and all the tooling and rights to build the C.A.V. GT were purchased by Auto Futura.

The initial concept in this rebirth of the C.A.V. GT program was to downscale the production and, instead, to build just two top quality cars a month, with the help of a few carefully selected production staff.

The new stainless steel chassis.
Contributor: John Spence

Instead of trying to do most or all the work in-house, a lot of work was outsourced and managed by Auto Futura, with the final assembly of the cars subcontracted to Jean at Carcraft.

Anyone who has been involved with car manufacture will understand what a mammoth task it is to get a finished car through the factory door. After sorting through the stock and finding out what needed to be manufactured in order to complete the first few cars, it became obvious that the project needed the full-time dedication of people who could build the cars and run a business.

In April of 2004 Jean and John purchased Auto Futura from the investor, and the transformation of the C.A.V. GT began.

From the beginning, it was obvious that whilst the C.A.V. GT had been favourably received around the world, there was significant room for improvement. With both Jean and John being perfectionists, an ambitious redevelopment program was initiated during 2004 and 2005. This program resulted in the refined stainless steel monocoque chassis, revised suspension geometry, new front and rear uprights, new braking systems, new structural and body materials, improved body panel fit, and a host of other under-the-skin changes.

Drawing on their artistic backgrounds, John and Jean decided that each component not only had to be functional, but had to look the part as well. Both are the kind of fanatical car owners who appreciate attention to detail, and this shows in the cars they produce. They admit that sometimes it's been hard to know where to draw the line between commercial requirements and the passion they share for the car, as they're still running a business.

C.A.V. GT belonging to Buzz Clark of South Africa, a happy customer willing to pass on his positive experiences.
Contributor: John Spence

What they were both sure about, and would not compromise on, was chassis design, suspension geometry, new suspension parts, and braking systems: all the key elements of any thoroughbred sportscar.

Whilst their cars are nice to look at, there has never been any doubt in John and Jeans' minds as to what the C.A.V. GT was intended for – driving very fast and very hard. This philosophy

The new C.A.V. GT assembly line. Contributor: John Spence

is attested to by the comments of owners who have had the fortunate opportunity to really push their C.A.V. GTs on road and track with a permanent grin from ear to ear saying it all.

The one hundredth C.A.V. GT off the line was the first of the new generation C.A.V. GTs featuring all of the new upgrades. Orders for cars 118 and 119 have just been placed, and Auto Futura looks set to be producing, perhaps, the world's best Ford GT MkI replica, in terms of build quality, performance, road manners and engineering design, for some time to come. The C.A.V. GT is now available in the USA, Canada, UK, Germany and South Africa, with Australia coming on line in the near future.

Technically, the C.A.V. GT draws heavily on the original for inspiration in form and function. The C.A.V. GT chassis is a monocoque rather than the more common space frame construction used in other replicas. The original F.A.V. produced chassis assemblies were made of mild steel and many have needed extensive rebuilds to combat rust. One of the major advantages for C.A.V. GT owners is that they don't have to worry about rust.

The C.A.V. chassis consists of approximately sixty-seven stainless steel panels (sixty-six of which were redesigned or upgraded during the redevelopment program), that are CNC punched and bent before being TIG welded together.

One problem with the original Ford GT was that tall drivers had serious problems trying to fit into the car. Just ask Jeremy Clarkson of the BBC motoring show, *Top Gear*. Surveys carried out by Auto Futura in the USA showed that around 30% of potential sales were lost because customers were too tall to fit into a C.A.V. GT.

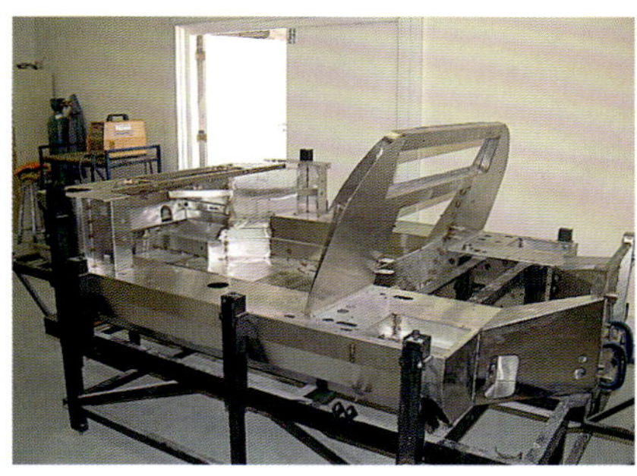

New stainless steel C.A.V. GT chassis (tub) assembly. Contributor: John Spence

A bold decision was taken at that point to totally revise the chassis by dropping the floor pan revising the interior panels, installing a fully adjustable race style pedal box, and completely redesigning the seats. The net result allows drivers over 6ft (183cm) to sit comfortably in the C.A.V. GT without the need for a Crabbe or Gurney bubble. All this has been achieved without the need to compromise the extremely faithful adherence to the original MkI profile.

The stainless steel chassis is constructed in a specially designed jig and TIG welded. Contributor: John Spence

The new revised version of the chassis is considerably stiffer and stronger than the original design, and features a dropped floorpan, increasing the C.A.V. GT's interior cabin space and headroom. The chassis design features integrated rollover/side impact protection bars, and accepts a full roll cage for those who want to race their cars.

The suspension layout is pure GT40. At the front there are unequal length offset A-frame wishbones with anti-roll bar linkages and billet aluminium uprights with bump steer adjustment. The front uprights, which are machined from billet

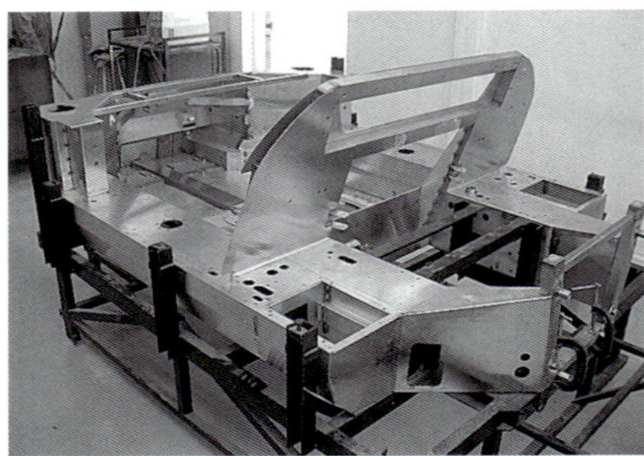
The C.A.V. GT chassis (tub) is also built for tall people. Contributor: John Spence

aluminium, even have the company logo engraved into them.

The rear suspension consists of independent double trailing links with an inverted lower A-frame wishbone and upper transverse link with anti-roll bar linkage, coupled to new design, cast aluminium uprights.

The new Wilwood braking system was chosen for its racing pedigree and the fact that it allows for the perfect set up for road and track.

The original GT40 fibreglass bodies were quite agricultural in build quality. They were not symmetrical and, as they were designed for the track, fit, finish and durability were not top

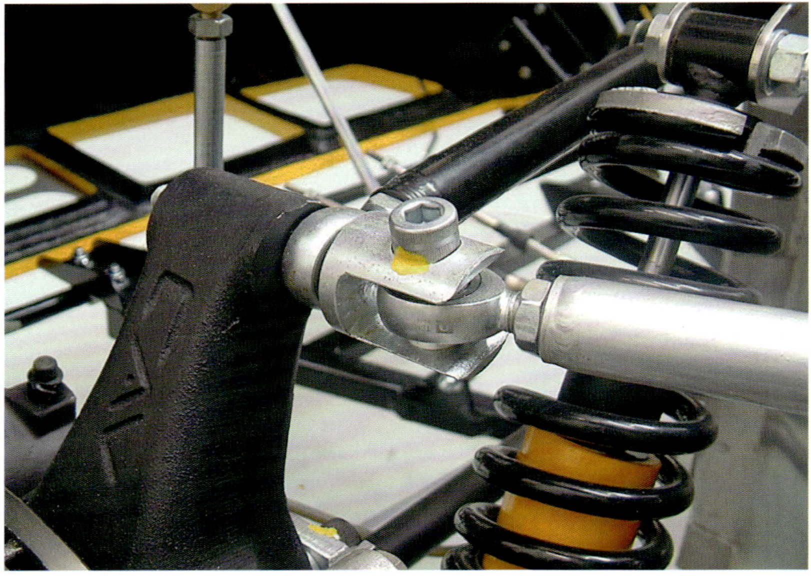
The new suspension yoke assembly. Contributor: John Spence

priorities. However, the modern customer is used to high quality cars, and the fit and finish on a sports car of this nature is now all important.

Auto Futura uses a vinyl ester resin in preference to the older style polyester resin, the former being stronger and more stable, giving the car a quality of shape and finish that will last for years to come. The body of the C.A.V. GT is meticulously hand shaped

The finish of the C.A.V. GT belonging to Canadian Joseph Feinburg is testament to the quality offered in the Auto Futura product line. Contributor: John Spence

in a process that takes more than two hundred man hours.

Once a body is custom fitted to a chassis, they stay together. This is old fashioned craftsmanship and there's simply no way to short cut this process. The C.A.V. GTs have a sheet metal look to them which is very rare in fibreglass cars.

Recently, the company decided to offer its car in component form to those who wanted the joy of assembling their car themselves. The self assembly program uses exactly the same components that are used in the factory to build a rolling chassis. There is a comprehensive build manual to guide the customer through the assembly, as well as real time e-mail support from the factory. The C.A.V. GT can be purchased in stages or as a complete component assembly project, with various factory options being available.

The C.A.V. GT is undoubtedly something special. It combines the spirit of the golden era of sports prototype racing with the new advances in technical components and design, whilst not losing any of the nostalgia of the 1960s. It is true in spirit to the original but has been updated for the modern sports car enthusiast. The really good news is that the edge, that gut wrenching acceleration, ferocious grip and cacophony of V8 sound are all very much still in evidence as the C.A.V. GT is not a tamed version of the original GT40, it is built with passion for the driver who wants to really feel something, and occasionally scare the living daylights out himself.

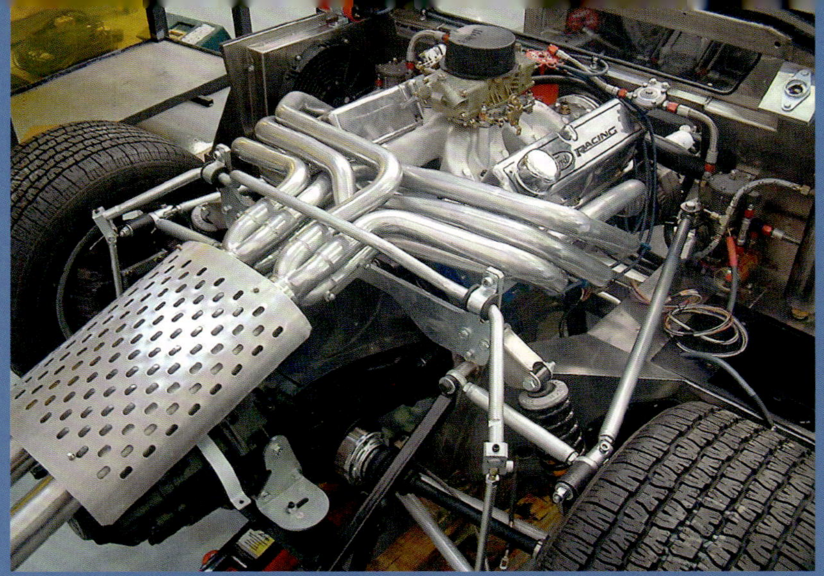

The engine is the beating heart of the C.A.V. GT. Contributor: John Spence

Paul Roos and Geoff Hurrell built their own C.A.V. GTs. Contributor: John Spence

This C.A.V. GT is on show at the Toronto, Canada motorshow in some esteemed company. Contributor: John Spence

This C.A.V. GT belongs to American Tom Hughes. Contributor: John Spence

Ford GT inspired new products

Gloster Car Company GTr460 Roadster

The Gloster Car Company has taken the legend of the Ford GT40 a step further by producing the GTr460. By retaining the spirit of the original, and combining modern engineering and the latest drivetrain components, Gloster has produced simply the most stunning roadster.

The GTr460 is a hand-crafted sports car which fuses tradition with the highest calibre of automotive technology and offers electrifying performance and outstanding agility.

Power for the GTr460 comes from Ford's latest 4.6 litre V8 engine. It features a lightweight aluminium block and heads, quad cams, 32 valves, fuel injection, full engine management and diagnostic system. The V8 produces an effortless 320hp and 315lbft of torque.

Two further engine packages are available: these are the GTr460S and the GTr500C. The 460S is a supercharged version of the 460. The 500C is a 5.0-litre high-performance, normally-aspirated engine. Both produce in excess of 400hp.

The transmission is a Getrag (Audi) 6-speed manual transaxle: automatic transmission is also available.

Other features which will appear on the production model include:

- Removable hard top.
- Electric windows.
- Power assisted steering.
- Air conditioning.
- A.P. Racing brakes.
- Gloster suspension uprights in cast aluminium.
- Stainless steel exhaust and catalytic converters.
- Emerald M3D ECU (which permits live mapping).
- Traction control.

The GTr460 Roadster prototype in real life.
Contributor: Gloster Car Company – Simon Farrell

What lies beneath? Contributor: Gloster Car Company – Simon Farrell

GT40NZ Barchetta, here with original BMW engine. Contributor: David Harvey

GT40NZ Barchetta

The GT40NZ Barchetta came about purely by accident. David was offered a very interesting project. It was an abandoned chopped up GT40 kit. The car's complete centre and rear roof sections had been cut off due to fitting problems in the original kit. The project was complete with most major components engineered into the chassis. However, this was no ordinary run of the mill GT40 replica kit.

Shoehorned into the rear was a BMW 5-litre V12 with a custom-built manifold to hold the 46mm triple Weber carburettors. These had come from either a Ferrari or Maserati V12 engine. Whilst the idea of using a BMW engine was intriguing, it had to go and was replaced by a more suitable and authentic Ford V8 engine.

The whole front end had been reworked to provide a low windscreen profile. In jest the suggestion was that the car was the marriage of a GT40 and Italian flair, so it has been affectionately dubbed the GT40NZ Barchetta.

From this starting point David developed a fully drivable concept car due for completion the first quarter of 2006.

Dedication personified

When a commercial company invests in creating a Ford GT-inspired product, it's doing so basically for business reasons. It hopes to pass its passion onto others who do not have the time nor experience to realise their dreams of Ford GT ownership themselves.

There is a group of private individuals whose dream is also to own a Ford GT, but who simply cannot afford to purchase the genuine article nor a purpose-built Ford GT replica. Few of us mere mortals can. So these dedicated and passionate Ford GT fans build their own. Their investment is their own blood, sweat and tears. Oh yes, it also takes money and space, and often upsets the wife ...

One of these dedicated Ford GT fans is Graham Endeacott. This is his story, the story of his passion coming to fruition with a few bumps along the road.

"I don't know what started my interest in the GT40. It was just one of those things that I grew up with. I do know where my interest in building a GT40 stems from, a man called Ken Attwell. The motoring magazines were full of articles about his first replica, a MkIII which was quickly followed by the MkI. Although I couldn't afford one at that time, I followed all the write-ups.

"I decided to visit Ken Attwell in Swansea and look at his cars. The MkIII was nice, but it had to be a MkI for me as I preferred its looks. The GT40 has been described as the most beautiful racing car ever, a mixture of beauty and aggression. To me, the big thing about the GT40 was the fact that it was a racing car which could be used on the public roads.

"I placed my order and a few months later, returned to Swansea with a friend to collect my kit. I actually collected the kit from a boat yard as it was a boat manufacturer who did all the fibreglass for Ken.

"I already had a list of parts I'd need, including the ubiquitous Ford Zephyr dashboard grille. On the way home we spotted a scrapyard on a Welsh hillside. A detour was made and this scrapyard turned out to be a gold mine of old cars, including a Ford Zephyr complete with dashboard grille. Alas, no amount of persuasion or money would make the owner sell any parts. We left the scrapyard and its contents slowly but surely turning to rust!

"The kit I purchased from Ken Attwell (KVA) was designed to accept suspension components from the Ford Granada/Scorpio (UK version). There were two problems that I could see with this:

- The front hubs have quite a large offset which would lead to very heavy steering.
- I didn't think the brakes would be up to the job of stopping a car that would ultimately be capable of 165mph.

"There wasn't much I could do about the steering, unless I changed the front uprights. As for the brakes, the biggest that I could fit would be 11in vented discs with 4-piston callipers at the front, and 10.75in vented discs from the Cosworth Scorpio at the rear. The rear calliper had a large single piston and incorporated the handbrake mechanism.

"I decided that my car should have the proper engine fitted which means a small-block Ford V8. I purchased a 302in^3. (5.0-litre) Mustang engine from a breakers (wreckers) yard. When I mounted the engine onto my engine stand, it sagged alarmingly. As a precaution I roped the engine to the rafters of my garage to give it some additional support.

"What amazed me about the Mustang engine was the amount of emissions equipment it had on it. I seemed to throw away miles of vacuum tube! In the end, I threw everything away except the block assembly and the cylinder heads!

"As regards the transmission, most Ford GT replica builders were using Renault transaxles, the original ZF transaxle, although still available, cost £6500 which was seriously expensive.

"I decided to try the Renault transaxle. I soon found out that the major problem with the Renault transaxle was that due to the configuration of its input and output shafts, the engine would sit about 4in too high.

Sometimes the original dream car is beyond the realms of possibility, but a replica is feasible.
Contributor: Graham Endeacott

The original engine and transmission. Contributor: Graham Endeacott

An inside view. Contributor: Graham Endeacott

"My next option was to try a Porsche 911 transaxle which could be used upside-down and would be able to handle the torque of the 5.0-litre engine. The only downside would be fabricating a shift-linkage which would have to go all the way to the back of the transaxle. I was very lucky at this stage to make contact with three people who gave me enormous amounts of help, advice and encouragement. They were John Allen, Bryan Wingfield and Ronnie Spain.

"John pointed out some of the many differences between the replica kit I had and the real GT40s. I discovered that my MkI had MkIII doors, as had all the kits. The MkIII had a different nose section to the MkI, it was slightly wider and the front edge of the doors flare out to accept this extra width. The spare wheel cover was also from a MkIII. Although I never wanted my car to pass for the real thing, I did want it to look like one.

"The look I was after was that of the MkI road car complete with wire wheels and Ford badges. I had a set of wire wheels made, 6 x 15in at the front and 8 x 15in at the rear. These wheels were to cause me problems later on. The original Ford oval badges were still available for the sills, but I never did find the origin of the F.O.R.D. lettering on the nose and had to have some made based on drawings I did after looking at as many photographs as possible.

"As I was using wire wheels, the ultra-wide rear wheelarches would have to go. Bryan Wingfield was good enough to supply me with new rear arches taken from the original moulds. These were then grafted on to my own bodywork. Bryan also supplied me with a set of sills and a windscreen and provided technical help and information for which I shall always be grateful.

"Slowly but surely the car was coming together. For cost reasons I opted for a 4-barrel Holley carburettor fitted to a specially machined Shelby Hi-Riser manifold. Bryan loaned me an original, unused exhaust system to use as a pattern, together with a set of tail-pipes which were fitted with race silencers.

"Finally the engine start up time was upon me. Everything was wired up and connected and ready to go. The engine turned over, but was very tight having been completely rebuilt. After numerous tries the battery went flat. I then connected jumper leads to my own car, but by this time the starter motor was overheating and starting to jam. After a cooling down period I tried again. This time the engine caught and quickly died. The fuel tank was empty; I had used nearly three gallons of petrol just trying to start it!

"After I'd added some more fuel I was ready to try again. My neighbour was on hand, filming everything as the engine fired up, or more accurately, backfired. There was an enormous blow-back from the carburettor and a jet of flame about three feet high shot out of the carburettor. I'd been manipulating the carburettor by hand, so my right forearm was without hair for a weeks. Now the engine was running, I let it settle at a fast idle.

Which one is the replica? Contributor: Graham Endeacott

As the Ford GT replica stands today awaiting a new transaxle. Contributor: Graham Endeacott

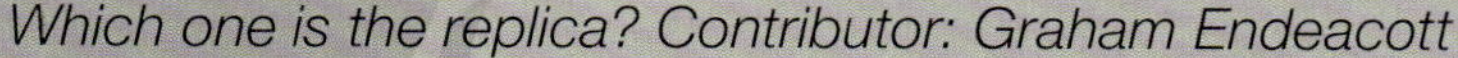

"With the racing silencers fitted I would think that the engine could be heard over a mile away. I couldn't let the engine idle for long as the water temperature was climbing rapidly; this was a sign of things to come!

"I had thought long and hard about how to register the GT40. I specifically wanted my GT40 to have a 1966 registration which has a D suffix. By an incredible stroke of luck I managed to acquire the registration number HOB 111D.

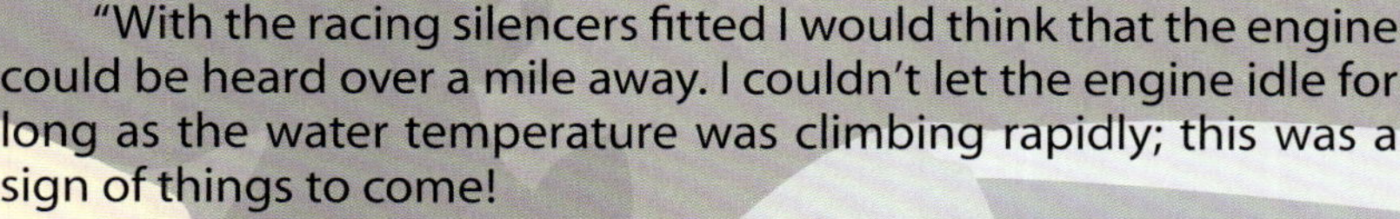

"Now that the car was up and running, I did quite a bit of testing. The first problem I encountered was the gearlever coming away in my hand. Another was that the engine was very tight and, after a couple of starts, the starter motor had a tendency to jam. All that was needed was a gentle push and the car would restart.

"I'd imposed myself a rev limit of 3500rpm for the first 1000 miles. My first major run in the car was down to Essex, a distance of about 180 miles. The journey revealed some problems, whilst moving the engine ran at a steady 75° C, but once in traffic, the temperature gauge would climb very rapidly. The cooling system couldn't cope.

"It was during this trip that a close examination of my car was carried out by John Willment of J.W. Automotive fame. I also had the opportunity to photograph my car alongside Ford's own GT40s, chassis no. 1008 and MkIII chassis no. 1107.

"On the way home I passed my self-imposed 1000 mile mark and, therefore, had the opportunity that I was waiting for. I was grinning from ear to ear. At each and every roundabout that I came up to, I would slow down and then boot the throttle on exiting the roundabout.

"Further testing confirmed that the brakes weren't really up to scratch. I did some calculations and added another calliper to each rear wheel. This gave a much better balance, but they could never be described as awe-inspiring.

"Then a new problem manifested itself, broken spokes in the rear wheels. I am not a hard driver. It turned out that the spokes were incorrectly manufactured and were repaired without charge.

"After driving 6000 miles in 6 months, I'd come to know the car very well, but there were still some problems. The lack of braking efficiency, overheating, heavy steering, poor gear change, and the inaccurate bodywork. I wasn't happy either with the Holley carburettor. It always idled on the rich side, and the idle jets on a Holley aren't adjustable, plus, every time the main jets were changed the fuel bowls had to come off and this always ruined the gasket.

"I decided to rectify all these points. I totally rebuilt the chassis with new suspension front and rear and new brakes, which were now 12in discs with 4-piston calipers front and rear. I fitted four Weber 48 I.D.A. carburettors on an original GT40 manifold. Similarly, out went the wire wheels, to be replaced with a set of

GT40 Borrani wire wheels which should be stronger than my custom-built set. The rebuilt chassis has bigger pipes, a bigger radiator, and will now carry a spare wheel. I have most of the glassfibre parts and moulds that I need to rectify the bodywork, and I am awaiting delivery of a ZF gearbox.

"A lot of this work should have been done when I first built the car but we live and learn by our mistakes. As for me I just can't wait to be back in the driving seat."

Replicas in the park

These images are all of replica Ford GTs, and they're all impressive looking machines. Hard to tell them apart from the original.

Ford GT replica family reunion at Le Mans in 2004. Contributor: les Coyotes

Commissioned replica

For the Goodwood festival of speed in 2003, Ford commissioned a member of the GT40 enthusiasts club in the UK to create a replica of chassis no. 1016 as it looked when it was the Holman Moody team Ford GT MkIIA, car no. 5, at Le Mans in 1966. The resulting replica is very smart and looks quite accurate from the outside.

The real version of chassis no. 1016 was a resident of the USA at the time of the Goodwood show. It is now a resident of Switzerland. See Chapter 8.

Ford-commissioned replica of Ford GT MkIIA, chassis no. 1016. It carries the same race number as the real car which came third at Le Mans in 1966. Is the other Ford GT MkIIA, car no. 2, representing chassis no. 1046, also a replica? Contributor: Wolfgang Kohm

New kid on the block

Richard Truesdell discovered this brand new Ford GT replica whilst visiting the Essen, Germany, motorshow in November 2005. The banner on the wall behind the cars says all that needs to be said. The replica is known as the SPF GT.

When the surviving world's population of original Ford GTs described in the next chapter is added to the production of the new Ford GTs and the ever growing numbers of professionally manufactured Ford GT replicas, there is a guaranteed, long, healthy and vibrant future for this Ford supercar legend.

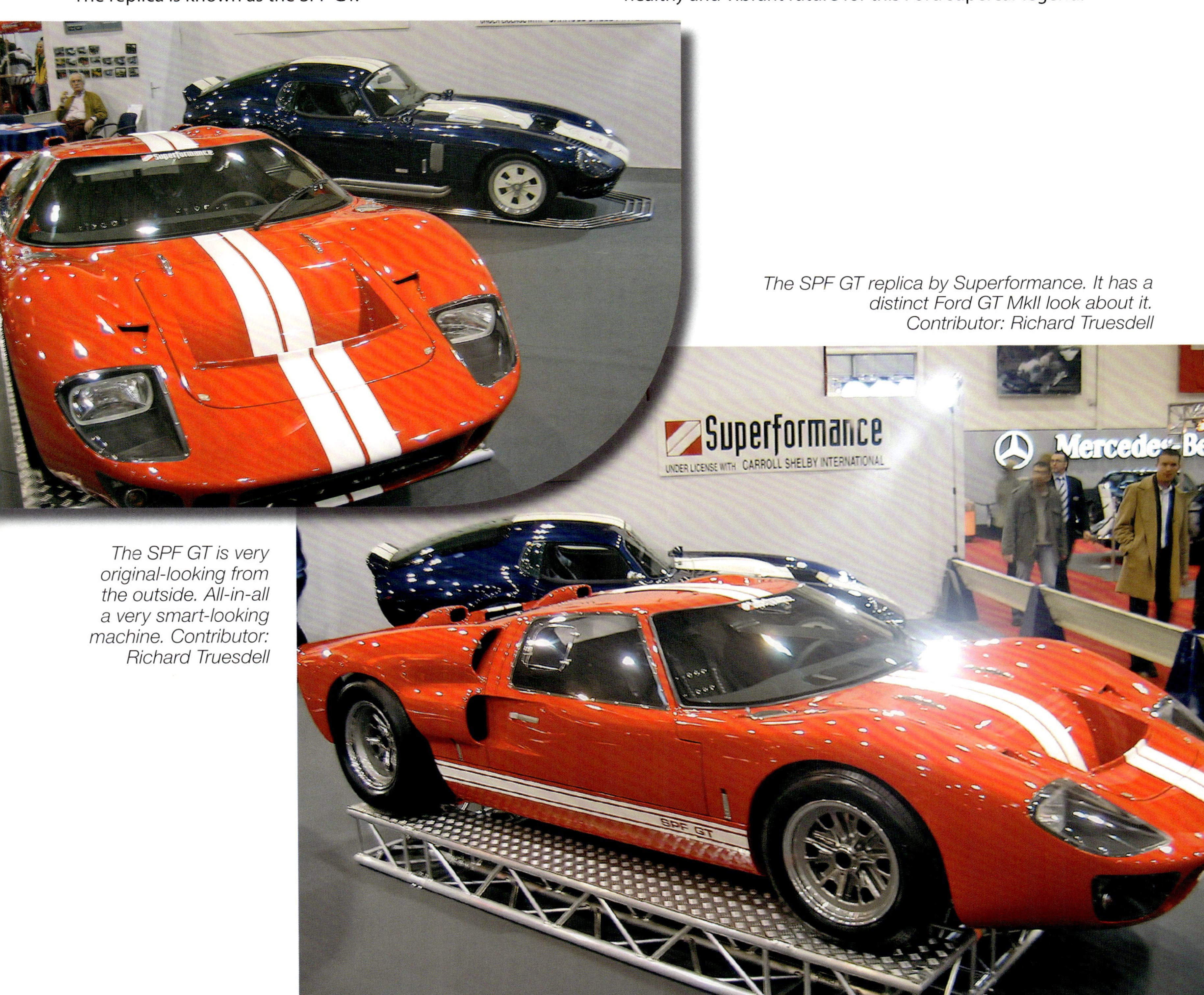

The SPF GT replica by Superformance. It has a distinct Ford GT MkII look about it. Contributor: Richard Truesdell

The SPF GT is very original-looking from the outside. All-in-all a very smart-looking machine. Contributor: Richard Truesdell

Eight

Life after forty

As history shows, the major racing teams abandoned the Ford GT after Le Mans in 1969. However, it was not until 1975 that the Ford GT was completely phased out of non-classic racing use. A Ford GT MkI (believed to be chassis no. 1022). owned in 1973 by Carlos Gaspar, had found its way to Angola in Africa to be campaigned by Emilio Marta. Emilio's last race with a Ford GT was recorded in late 1975 at the Angolan Moçamedes racing circuit.

Ford GT MkI, chassis no. 1045, at the Brighton Speed Trials in the mid-1970s. Owner/driver, Adrian Hamilton, won on this day. Contributor: Adrian Hamilton

These days, there's a healthy number of forty-something year old Ford GTs around the world. They can be found in museums, private collections, and even stored away in quiet, private places. Some are kept just as reminders of those glorious victorious years of 1964 to 1969, and others are raced in organised historic racing events to show the next generation of racing fans what the Ford GT was capable of in relation to its peers.

The first known historic race involving the Ford GT was the Ford Sports day at the Croft racing circuit in England in late 1973. The race was called the GT40s and Ford V8 Powered Saloon Race, and was held over 10 laps. The two Ford GT MkI entries were driven by Christopher J. Carver-Long and Steven H. Smith. The first major American historic racing event was established at the Laguna Seca circuit in California in August 1974. This event became the Monterey Historic Festival. The Goodwood Festival of Speed in England was inaugurated in 1992, followed in 2002

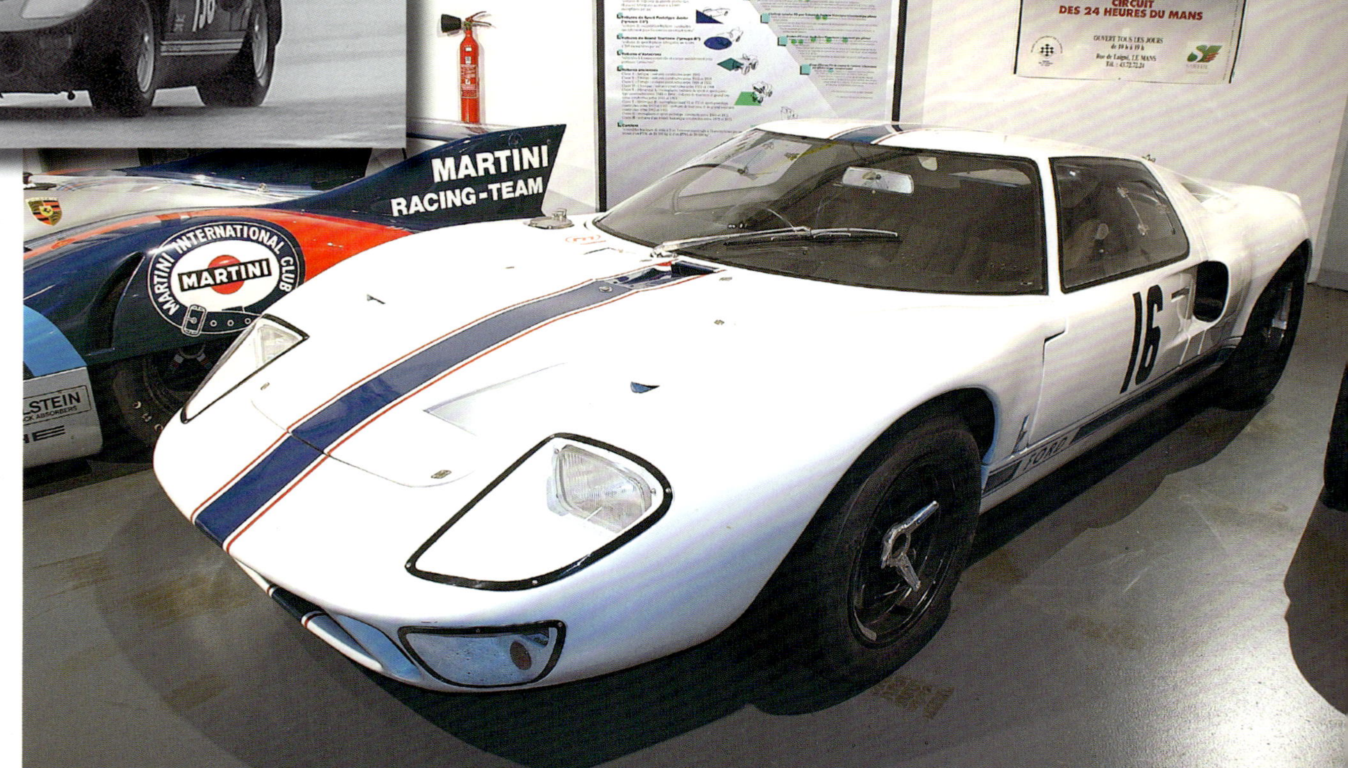

Ford GT MkI, chassis no. 1020, at the Le Mans museum. It retains the same colour scheme and race number as when it appeared as part of the Ford France team at Le Mans in 1967. The drivers were Pierre Dumay and Henry Greder. Contributor: Richard Truesdell

Bernard Thuner off and running in chassis no. 1016 at the Le Mans classic of 2004. Contributor: Claude Nahum

Ford GT MkI, chassis no. 1078, now owned by Claude Nahum of Switzerland, racing at the Spa circuit in Belgium in 2005. It has to be Spa, it's raining. Contributor: Claude Nahum

by the Le Mans Classic 24hr in France and, in 2002, the latest major historic event was held in Turkey at the new Formula One circuit in Istanbul.

More entrants, please

As the popularity of the historic motor racing events spread around the world, so did the need for more historic racing cars to participate in them. As the number of entrants increased, so did the number of times two Ford GTs with the same chassis number were discovered. Were these 'twin sets' made up of one genuine and one fake Ford GT? Or was there something else behind this?

As the business of rebuilding and restoration expanded to feed the demand for Ford GTs, not all the rebuilds and restorations were totally perfect. As the value of the historic Ford GT on the open market started to climb, many people began to realise just how lucrative the business could be.

Original, authentic, or something else?

I have personally been involved in a number of aircraft restoration projects. I have built rally and race cars, and have expertise in the Porsche world. I have conducted a number of historic Porsche related pre-purchase inspections (PPI) for buyers around the world. As a result, I had to develop my own set of guidelines when doing these historic PPIs. I've applied the same set of guidelines when discussing the Ford GT's provenance. These guidelines and inspection criteria are mine. They only reflect my own opinion, but have served me and my clients well. They will not work for everyone. My PPI authenticity categories are:

- Unrestored original.
- Authorised rebuild.
- Authentic restoration.
- Authentic DIY rebuild or restoration.
- Non-authentic rebuild or restoration.
- Replica.

Unrestored original

If the Ford GT remains in the same condition as it was when originally purchased, and retains all its original parts, then it's an unrestored original. Its racing history and authenticity of documentation of are great value before attempting a physical inspection.

Note: The paint scheme carried by the Ford GT at the time of inspection may not be considered particularly relevant to the actual status or condition of the vehicle. A car with a new paint scheme, but with original components, could still be considered as an unrestored original. However, any paint scheme issues should be declared to a potential purchaser, who may then try to negotiate the price down or dig deeper into the paperwork.

Authorised rebuild

During the racing life of the Ford GT, many chassis numbers were destroyed. Racing teams would resurrect these cars using a new (spare) numbered chassis (tub) purchased from Ford Advanced Vehicles, J.W. Automotive or P & M Racing Preparations in Chiswick, England (after 1969).

Note: P & M Racing Preparations in Chiswick, England, was appointed sole agent for the remaining Ford GT spares by J.W.A. after the GT40 programme ended in 1969. P & M took possession of all remaining spare chassis assemblies and other major components.

Some resurrections used a numbered chassis (tub) from another Ford GT which had served its time and was of no further use. The caveat that I use for this category is that the organisation that did the rebuild must have been authorised and/or licensed to carry out the work by the Ford Motor Company, USA, or its works organisations/teams. The authorisation paperwork is therefore limited to the letterheads of Ford Advanced Vehicles, Kar-Kraft, J.W. Automotive, Shelby American Inc., Holman Moody, Alan Mann Racing and Ford France.

Any of these organisations could licence a third party to carry out the work. An example would be the restoration facilities operated by former J.W.A. company employee and Ford GT genius John Etheridge. Another would be Bryan Wingfield, who worked with John Etheridge and then built up his own racing car restoration business.

John Wyer required any rebuild/restoration facility or private home rebuilder requesting to purchase a new or used numbered chassis (tub), to provide proof that the original had been scrapped and put beyond any further use.

John Wyer may have foreseen the potential problems of the emergence of too many twin set Ford GTs, especially with many of them being restored to road registrable configuration in the early days, after the Ford GT's racing career came to an end.

Authentic restoration

Some of the Ford GTs wrecked during their racing careers ended up burnt out, crushed and rusted hulks. These wrecks were usually sold by the racing teams to people who saw their restoration potential and, more often than not, could actually afford to carry out the challenging job of a full restoration.

Again, the documentation would be my starting point. It's generally regarded that an authentic restoration as being a complete and functioning Ford GT which contains at least 30% of its original major components, including the original numbered chassis (tub).

Note: The original data plate is not necessarily a requirement as long as the chassis (tub) can be proven to be the original. Data

The fibreglass front end is a consumable part, and having a spare is a requirement of any professional racing team. Use of the spare does not affect authenticity. Contributor: Adrian Streather

Modern fluid system components do not affect authenticity either. Many are legal requirements that must be met for historic racing events. Contributor: Adrian Streather

plates were often replaced during the racing days because they were damaged, lost or destroyed usually by fire and sometimes for the purpose of cheating, but that is another story ...

The major structural replacement parts must be original, and from the same model or version. Apart from the chassis (tub), the engine, transmission, suspension structure and the core body parts must comply with the original manufacturers specifications.

There are some acceptable exceptions, however. Many components decay with age, such as rubber gaskets, rubber mounts, and hoses. Rubber components have a shelf life, so can't be expected to be replaced with original parts. Many removable parts are also considered as consumables, such as the front and rear fibreglass body sections, radiators, oil coolers, brake rotors and pads. All these parts can be replaced with accurately manufactured modern equivalents.

Safety is a prime concern with any car used on the road or race track, so some flexibility has to be applied when reviewing the origin of parts used in oil, coolant, fuel and hydraulic systems.

Knowledge of current national, international and series racing regulations also helps. Many of these regulations require modern standard safety equipment and fuel systems be fitted.

Another key element in this category is that the restoration was carried out by a recognised restoration facility with proven Ford GT expertise. Most of the original restoration companies employed former Ford GT project personnel. This only requires a little research to determine the restoration company's expertise and manufacturing processes.

Authentic DIY rebuild or restoration

Some people purchased Ford GT remains with the intention of carrying out the rebuild and/or restoration themselves. Many such rebuilds and or restorations have been accomplished to the highest quality and may be considered for classification in the authentic category.

There are many highly skilled and competent DIY mechanics with the correct tooling and access to factory drawings, along with capability and competence required for such work. However, these criteria must be established first, and then coupled with all the other requirements of the authentic rebuild and or restoration category to grant a DIY rebuild full authentic status during the PPI.

Non-authentic rebuild or restoration

This category is used when none of the requirements for authenticity have been satisfied, or there is sufficient suspicion about the true origin of the car being inspected. Examples would include a Ford GT that has been built up around a data plate using a non-OEM or approved manufactured chassis (tub), or one that has been restored around a single original piece of bodywork, structural component or single part retrieved from a wreck, such as a fuel pump.

Summary

There are two types of pre-purchase (PPI) inspection:

- Authenticity confirmation and verification.
- Condition report.

An authenticity PPI is very serious, because the purchase price has an historical element built into it. A condition report PPI, whilst being equally serious, usually involves a Ford GT which is not necessarily being presented as completely authentic or historically significant.

An interesting collection of data plates, all photographed in France. Chassis no. J11 is the older J-car sibling to twins J9 and J10. Contributor: les Coyotes

Unused J-car chassis no. J10 was used as the basis for the 1969 Ford G7A Spyder CanAm racer. Chassis no. J10 has since been rebuilt into a Ford GT MkIV. The twin sister to chassis no. J10 is chassis no. J9. This chassis assembly is currently being used to create a new Ford G7A Spyder. Chassis no. J9 was purchased in 1969 as a spare for the G7A project, but was never used. Contributor: Ford Motor Company

Chassis no. J10 as it looked after being rebuilt as a Ford GT MkIV. Contributor: James Holden Jr.

On the subject of data plates

The first Ford GT twin set

Ford GT MkIIA chassis no. XGT-2 was delivered by Holman Moody to Alan Mann Racing for Graham Hill to drive at Le Mans in 1966. The origins of the actual chassis, no. XGT-2, remain obscure. The number is not standard for a Ford Advanced Vehicles chassis (tub) delivered to the USA. It's possible that the modifications carried out by Holman Moody in the USA to convert the original F.A.V. supplied chassis (tub) into its special version of a Ford GT MkIIA required an experimental classification at the time.

Note: Shelby American Inc. was responsible for the basic works Ford GTs delivered to the USA. It's possible that Holman Moody received two chassis (tub) assemblies direct from F.A.V. because the customer was the Alan Mann Racing team and the deal was outside the Holman Moody contractual obligations to Shelby American Inc. and Ford USA which required a change in chassis identification.

Chassis no. XGT-2, racing as car no. 7, didn't finish Le Mans 1966. Thereafter its history has been difficult to follow. A Holman Moody storage document says it was in storage without its roof in 1967. It has also been discovered that the skeletal remains of chassis no. XGT-2, including the intact chassis (tub) assembly, was in the Alan Mann Racing team workshop in 1968.

Note: The major body parts, including the roof structure and doors, of chassis no. XGT-2 were sent back to Holman Moody in the USA for use as spares.

Alan Mann (left) and Graham Hill. Contributor: Ford Motor Company

Graham Hill leads in chassis no. XGT-2 (car no. 7) after the first lap of Le Mans 1966. Contributor: Ford Motor Company

Ford GT MkI chassis no. 1009 was built by Ford Advanced Vehicles and purchased by Peter Sutcliffe in November 1965. Peter first raced chassis no. 1009 as car no. 6 at the Kyalami 9hr race in late November 1965. He used the car for the rest of what was known as the pre-Springbok series, which ran into January 1966. Chassis no. 1009 was also driven by Peter Sutcliffe at both the Nürburgring 1000km and Le Mans 1966.

According to Ed Nelson, Peter Sutcliffe took chassis no. 1009 to Surfers Paradise, Australia, in August 1966. Ed then purchased chassis no. 1009 from Peter while it was still in Australia.

Using the money from Ed Nelson, Peter Sutcliffe purchased the ex-Ford France Le Mans Ford GT chassis no. 112. Alan Mann Racing carried out some modifications, which included the installation of a 5.3-litre engine, and when the modifications were completed Peter took chassis no. 112 to South Africa for the first official Springbok Sportscar Racing series in November 1966.

Unfortunately for Ed Nelson, chassis no. 1009 did not arrive in England in time for him to prepare it for the 1966 Springbok series. He was forced to purchased Nick Cussons' former road

The original Ford GT MkI, chassis no. 1009, at the Nürburgring when owned by Peter Sutcliffe. Contributor: Veit Arenz

The first chassis no. 1009 driven by Ed Nelson and David Piper at the Sebring 12hr in 1968. Contributor: C. Nahum Collection; photograph by Gérard Crombac

car, chassis no. 1021, in a partnership with Colin Crabbe, for the Springbok series. Ed was contracted to race for Alex Blignaut of SAMRAC so he had no choice. Ed says that he was not a "happy camper" with the turn of events.

Eventually, chassis no. 1009 was made race ready. Both Ed Nelson and Eric Liddell confirm that they both drove in chassis no. 1009, as car no. 36, at the Monza 1000km race in 1967.

Ed Nelson continued to campaign chassis no. 1009 throughout the 1967 and 1968 racing seasons in Europe and in the USA.

When he retired from motor racing Ed sold chassis no. 1009 to Team Malcolm Guthrie for the Springbok series of 1968. The first race for chassis no. 1009 under the Team Malcolm Guthrie banner was the Kyalami 9hr, with Malcolm Guthrie sharing the driving with former motorcycle world champion Mike Hailwood. Things did not quite go to plan.

Malcolm Guthrie recalls what happened next: "I hit the rock face at Kyalami so hard that the car was totally destroyed".

Malcolm Guthrie was now without a car for the rest of the series. As luck would have it, the J.W.A.-Gulf team had entered its 5.7-litre Mirage M1 in the same race, with Jacky Ickx and David Hobbs. Malcolm Guthrie approached John Wyer after the race and the latter agreed to sell him the Mirage M1 (chassis no. M10001).

The luckless and wrecked chassis no. 1009 was shipped back to Alan Mann Racing in England for repair. Alan Mann reported that the car was too seriously damaged, but a replacement could be built. Team Malcolm Guthrie signed a deal with Alan Mann and, with the magic of what racing teams did in the 1960s, Team Malcolm Guthrie received a completely new chassis no. 1009 to replace his wrecked chassis no. 1009.

How was chassis no. 1009 reinvented?

Easy really. The rivets holding on the chassis no. XGT-2 data plate were drilled out, and the data plate removed. The same operation was undertaken for the data plate attached to the wrecked original chassis. The data plate from 1009 was then riveted in place on XGT-2. Viola, chassis no. XGT-2 now became chassis no. 1009.

The rest of the Ford GT was rebuilt to the exclusive Alan Mann Racing Ford GT P40 standards. The brand new Alan Mann Racing version of chassis no. 1009 was delivered to Team Malcolm Guthrie in time to compete at Le Mans in 1969, where it was driven by Malcolm Guthrie and Frank Gardner.

For Le Mans, Team Malcolm Guthrie was actually entered by Alan Mann Racing. Team Malcolm Guthrie stood no chance of receiving an invite to Le Mans based on its own race results because the team's impressive results were in non-FIA championship races. Alan Mann Racing gave Team Malcolm Guthrie its ticket into Le Mans.

Sadly, the new chassis no. 1009 did not finish Le Mans in 1969 due to an overheating rear driveshaft. It was too long for the standard 5-speed ZF transaxle, possibly due to a genuine mistake from Alan Mann Racing which had had long ceased using the ZF transaxle. Alan Mann had been using the DG300 and Hewland transaxles in its cars, and it's possible that the driveshafts from one of these transaxle types had been inadvertently fitted.

Chassis no. 1009 was campaigned for the remainder of the 1969 season, including the Springbok series, under the Team Malcolm Guthrie banner and usually driven by Malcolm Guthrie, who employed others to drive his Mirage M1.

The remains of the original chassis no. 1009 that once raced around Kyalami in 1965 were deemed unrecoverable by Alan Mann Racing, but remained the property of Team Malcolm Guthrie.

These remains were sold to Bryan Wingfield in 1971, who then spent a number of years returning these remains back into their original Ford GT MkI condition. When the work was completed, using as much of the original chassis (tub) as possible and all other salvageable parts, a twin new/original chassis no. 1009 rolled out of the Bryan Wingfield workshop.

The Bryan Wingfield restored version of Ford GT MkI, chassis no. 1009, photographed at Le Mans in 1973. Contributor: les Coyotes

Ford GT MkI, chassis no. 1002, photographed at Montlhéry, France, in 2000. Some claim that chassis no. 1009 was rebuilt using this chassis, rather than XGT-2. Clearly the reported death of chassis no. 1002 has been grossly exaggerated. Contributor: les Coyotes

Note: Bryan Wingfield was one of the original J.W. Automotive team race mechanics, and served with John Wyer right through until the Ford GT went of out service with the Gulf team after Le Mans in 1969.

Bryan Wingfield later sold his version of chassis no. 1009 to Californian resident Wayne Skiles, who then swapped it for the seriously wrecked remains of the more historically significant (at least in America) Ford GT MkIIB chassis no. 1012. It's believed that Walter Cantrell still owns this version of chassis no. 1009.

The former Holman Moody MkIIA chassis no. XGT-2, reconfigured to chassis no. 1009 by Alan Mann Racing, was sold to Gil Jackson in the USA in 1971. It was road registered SBH 87H prior to the sale. Gil Jackson is believed to still own this version of chassis no. 1009.

Gil Jackson and Walter Cantrell own the first legitimate set of twins in Ford GT history.

What about chassis no. XGT-2? Information provided by Sir Malcolm Guthrie identifies the source chassis for his second version of chassis no. 1009 as chassis no. XGT-2. He was told by Alan Mann Racing that the core chassis used for his rebuild was the one driven by Graham Hill at Le Mans (XGT-2). However, it's believed that a Ford GT MkIIA in the USA does carry the chassis (tub) no. XGT-2. Possibly the original data plate of chassis no. XGT-2 was returned to Holman Moody by Alan Mann Racing.

It's a known fact that the major body parts of XGT-2 were shipped back to Holman Moody. It's entirely possible that a new version of XGT-2 may have been created by Holman Moody, or was authorised by Holman Moody. Unfortunately, the available information is too slim and tenuous to draw any clear-cut conclusions.

Note: Sir Malcolm Guthrie recently stated that he'd recently been told that the chassis (tub) used for the initial rebuild of his chassis no. 1009 may not have been chassis no XGT-2, but chassis no. 1002 built in 1965. However, research shows this is not correct. No race records show Graham Hill driving chassis no. 1002; also chassis no. 1002 was sold at auction for £305,000 as completely original in 1999. The auction house confirmed chassis no. 1002 as being original and the authenticity of 1002 was further confirmed in 2000 by a very reliable source.

Note: Some sources claim the chassis from XGT-2 which was used to rebuild a new 1009 for Sir Malcolm Guthrie was actually labelled AMGT-1009. All efforts to obtain a photograph of the data plate from the current owner were unsuccessful. As far as Sir Malcolm could remember, the data plate stated GT40/P1009 as the chassis number when he received it from Alan Mann Racing.

Other known twin sets

Due to the understandable sensitivity of the subject, the other Ford GT twin sets are described in this section of the chapter only to provide information about their existence, along with a bit of history. Discussions on originality, authenticity or any other classification are left to those who wish to dig deeper.

Chassis no. 1012 in its first race at Daytona in 1966.
Contributor: C. Nahum Collection; photograph by Gérard Crombac

Chassis no. 1012

Chassis no. 1012 started life as a Shelby American Inc. team Ford GT MkIIA in 1966. 1012 built up quite a race record, starting at Daytona in 1966 where it finished second.

1012 is the car that Ken Miles crashed during testing at Le Mans in 1966. Holman Moody handed the car over to Alan Mann Racing in April 1966, and it was raced at the Spa 1000km by Sir John Whitmore and Frank Gardner.

For the 1967 racing season, 1012 was converted to MkIIB specifications by Holman Moody, and driven at the Daytona 24hr by Bruce McLaren, Dan Gurney and Lucien Bianchi.

Unfortunately, time ran out for 1012. In March 1967, 1012 was destroyed by Peter Revson during testing at Daytona. It's said that he went off the track at 185mph (298kph), his life being saved by the purpose-built roll cage in the Ford GT MkII.

The burnt and crumpled wreck of 1012 was shipped back to Holman Moody for conversion to components, if any were actually usable. Not only was 1012 burnt and severely crushed, corrosion (rust) from the fire extinguisher chemicals and exposure to the environment had also started to set in.

Note: Information received from various repair and restoration facilities indicates that the chassis (tub) of the GT40 was very prone to rusting once its unprotected steel was exposed to the environment.

The Don Davis version of 1012 photographed in July 2005 in Monte Carlo. Contributor: Richard Truesdell

1012 version one

In 1970, the burnt, crushed and corroded remains of chassis no. 1012 were purchased by Californian resident Don Davis. Don built a replacement around a Ford GT chassis frame (named as shown on the receipt) purchased from J.W. Automotive for £655.22 in 1971. The original Holman Moody data plate for GT40/P1012 was attached to this new frame assembly.

Don completed the rebuild of his version of 1012 in October 1973 when he fitted the body sections from Ford MkIIA chassis no. 1047 and the doors of MkIIA no. XGT-2. These parts were among the components supplied by Holman Moody to Don Davis along with the remains of chassis no. 1012.

Don modified the rear bodywork by widening it, and fitted 13-inch wide Halibrand wheels. He also installed Weber carburettors in place of the original Holley 4-barrel version. Chassis no. 1012 was painted metallic grey, as it was just minutes before Peter Revson crashed it. Le Mans 1967 team stripes were then added as an additional decoration.

1012 version two

In return for his assistance during the mammoth rebuild of chassis no. 1012, Don Davis gave his friend Lyle Digness the remains, which he considered unusable, of the original chassis no. 1012. Later, Lyle Digness sold these remains to Wayne Skiles in California, USA.

Wayne Skiles shipped the remains of 1012 to England in 1978 where a four-year rebuild was carried out by John Etheridge and Bryan Wingfield. It's said that approximately one third of the original chassis assembly was salvaged. The rebuilt chassis (tub)

The Bryan Wingfield version of 1012, photographed in France in 1996. Contributor: les Coyotes

The Bryan Wingfield version of 1012, in new colours, at the Le Mans Classic in 2004. Contributor: les Coyotes

was fitted with a new roof, floor, a rebuilt rear bulkhead, and reconstructed fuel tanks.

During the rebuild process, in 1981, Wayne Skiles sold his version of chassis no. 1012. It has since passed through a number of owners and recent information puts it in Italy.

Chassis no. 1033

Ford GT MkI chassis no. 1033 was once part of the Swiss Scuderia Filipinetti racing team stable. The chassis number indicates it was a racing car version, though it's known that it was used as a road car by team owner Georges Filipinetti. Chassis no. 1033 appears in racing results from late 1968 onwards, which shows that it had been converted from a road car into a racing car.

Chassis no. 1033 was entered for Le Mans 1969 by the Ecurie A.S.A. - E.S.C.A. team, but it did not qualify. Its last recorded race was in April 1970 at Montlhéry, France, with the E.S.C.A. Zitro team. Then, chassis no. 1033 seems to disappear.

There is a claim that the original chassis (tub) of 1033 ended up in the USA, where the car was completely restored. Later, a second version of chassis no. 1033 appeared for sale. It was claimed to be the original converted back into a road car. Written reports from people who have seen the actual car say that, whilst it is close to the appearance of an original Abbey panelled Ford GT, it has many obvious differences.

Chassis no 1048

Chassis no. 1048 was entered into its first race in July 1966. From the racing records it was primarily raced in mainland European events. There is a claim that the car was destroyed in a crash at Le Mans in 1971. This is true, but not at the 24hr race as is often written. Chassis no. 1048 carrying the race no. 76 and driven by its owner Jean-Claude Guérie crashed during the Le Mans 3hr

One of the last pictures of chassis no. 1048 taken whilst it was still racing. This photograph was taken at Montlhéry, France in 1970. Contributor: les Coyotes

race held on the same day as Le Mans testing in April 1971.

The remains of chassis no. 1048 were purchased in 1973. The new owner of the sad remains contracted the full restoration to a company in Switzerland. The restoration of chassis no. 1048 was completed and, for the next twenty years, everything was okay. However, in 1997, an auction for another chassis no. 1048 caught the eye of the owner, who thought he had chassis no. 1048 safely tucked up in his garage.

Cutting a long story short, the whole saga ended up in the Swiss courts. The judge hearing the case found that the original owner of the 1048 remains had not received an authentic restoration, but a very good replica in its place. The other version of what is now claimed as the real original version of chassis no. 1048, appears to have been in the USA for many years, but was recently resold in Europe.

Chassis no. 1040

There also appear to be two versions of chassis no. 1040. This is another former Scuderia Filipinetti Ford GT MkI which, according to the records, was burned in an incident in 1967. One version of chassis no. 1040 is currently located in the USA, and the other version somewhere in Europe.

Chassis no. 112

Chassis no. 112 was built in early 1965 and is considered to be the last of the prototype Ford GTs. What made it special was that it was built as a MkI Roadster by Ford Advanced Vehicles. Chassis no. 112 was the second F.A.V. built Roadster.

The first Roadster was chassis no. 110, which appeared for the first time at Le Mans testing in April 1965, where it was driven by Sir John Whitmore and Innes Ireland.

Ford GT MkI, chassis no. 112, owned by Ken Senior is located in a museum (run by his son Ian Senior) near Weybridge in Surrey, England. Contributor: Richard Truesdell

Chassis no. 112 at Le Mans in 1966.
Contributor: C. Nahum Collection; photograph by Gérard Crombac

Inset, top: Chassis no. 110 at the Nürburgring in 1965.
Contributor: Günther Asshauer-Udo Klinkel collection

The first race for the Ford GT MkI Roadster, chassis no. 110, was at the 1965 Nürburgring 1000km driven by Richard Attwood and Sir John Whitmore.

Unfortunately, in May 1965, chassis no. 110 was wrecked. Chassis no. 112 had been built in Roadster configuration in time for Le Mans, but for a new customer, Ford France.

Note: Sir John Whitmore and Innes Ireland drove chassis no. 1006 at Le Mans in 1965.

Ford France campaigned chassis no. 112 as a Roadster at Le Mans in 1965, and then had it converted back to a Coupé for Le Mans 1966. In both races the Ford France entry wore car no. 15.

In late October 1966, chassis no. 112 was purchased by British privateer Peter Sutcliffe. He had a 5.3-litre engine installed by Alan Mann Racing, along with some other work, then shipped it to South Africa for the first race in the Springbok series of 1966. Richard Bond was often engaged to share the driving of chassis no. 112 with Peter Sutcliffe.

In 1968, the ownership of chassis no. 112 passed to Bob Vincent, but the 5.3-litre engine had been replaced with a more standard 4.7-litre engine. Bob Vincent campaigned chassis no. 112 himself in the British RAC Sportscar Championship. After 1968, chassis no. 112 seemed to disappear.

However, as can clearly be seen from a visit to Ken Senior and his family in Surrey, England, chassis no. 112 was not destroyed or sold off to the USA. It remains stored awaiting restoration.

Ford's own MkIII road car

Not exactly hidden away from view, but certainly only viewed by a very few people, is the Ford owned MkIII road car, chassis no. 1107. The MkIII has always been owned by Ford, and it is currently housed at the Roush facility in Brentwood, Essex, England. The accompanying images of the MkIII were all taken by American motoring journalist Richard Truesdell.

The Ford Heritage Collection's MkIII out in the open for the beginning of its photo shoot with Richard Truesdell. Contributor: Richard Truesdell

It's all original under there. Contributor: Richard Truesdell

Original engine. Contributor: Richard Truesdell

Original interior. Contributor: Richard Truesdell

Out on the road, with Roush's Chris Johnston at the wheel and Matt Malone as the impressed passenger. Contributor: Richard Truesdell

New Ford GT follows the original through the narrow roads of Brentwood, Essex in England. Contributor: Richard Truesdell

The Shelby Museum Collection

The Shelby Museum is located at 5020 Chaparral Court, Boulder, Colorado, USA. Its collection includes:

- Ford GT MkIIA chassis no. 1015, which was shipped to Shelby American Inc. in September 1965. Painted white with blue sill stripes and a black nose, 1015 won the Daytona 24hr in 1966. However, 1015 is most famous for its second place at Le Mans in 1966, for which it was painted light blue with white stripes and day-glo red patches.
- Ford GT MkI chassis no. 1021, which was purchased by Nick Cussons (Imperial Leather soap) after it was completed in November 1965. Nick Cussons was the team owner, but also drove 1021 himself in many races. He engaged other drivers, such as Richard Bond, to partner him or drive for him. Later, Ed Nelson purchased 1021, and its regular drivers were David Hobbs and Colin Crabbe.
- Ford GT MkI. chassis no. 1037, was part of the famous Comstock Canadian racing team. 1037 was driven by the equally famous Canadian racing car driver Eppie Wietzes in 1966.
- Ford GT MkIIA chassis no. 1046, was shipped to Shelby American Inc. in January 1966. This is the Ford GT that won Le Mans in 1966 driven by Bruce McLaren and Chris Amon. Prior to the Daytona 24hr in 1967, 1046 was modified to MkIIB specifications. After Daytona the car was shipped to Holman Moody for storage. It was later sold in Europe and returned to the USA from Belgium in 1983.
- Ford GT MkIV chassis no. J7, was driven by Mario Andretti and Lucien Bianchi at Le Mans in 1967. Mario Andretti crashed it at the Esses after Dunlop.
- Ford GT MkIII road car, chassis no. 1102, UK registration number SPP 604D. This was one of only six MkIII road cars built by J.W. Automotive. This one was given to John Wyer, and was registered in his daughter Pia's name in 1967.

The Shelby Museum is located at 5020 Chaparral Court, Boulder, Colorado, USA. The collection includes Ford GT MkIIA, chassis no. 1015, which was shipped to Shelby American Inc. in September 1965. Painted white, with blue sill stripes and a black nose, 1015 won the Daytona 24hr in 1966. However, 1015 is most famous for its second place at Le Mans in 1966, for which it was painted light blue with white stripes and day-glo red identification patches.

Ford MkIIA, chassis no. 1015, returned to Le Mans in 1996, thirty years after its almost glorious first visit. Contributor: les Coyotes

Mario Andretti driving car no. 1, chassis no. J7, with the famous Dunlop sign in the background. Contributor: Ford Motor Company

The Blackhawk Collection

The Blackhawk Collection can found at 092 Eagles Nest Place, Danville, California 94506, USA. A very special thank you is owed to Chris Clarke who organised for the Mirage M1 to be taken outside and photographed.

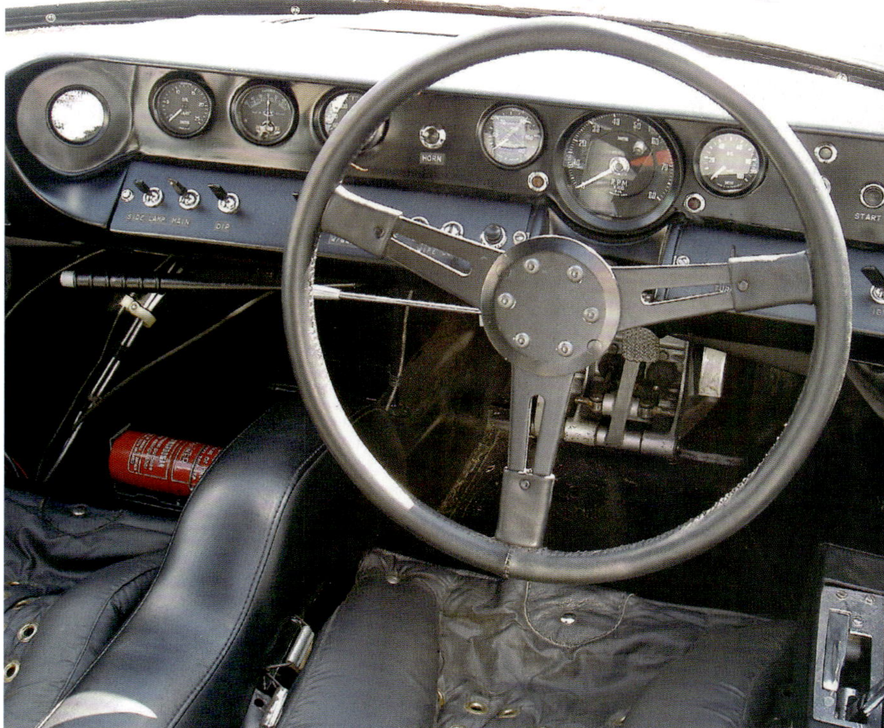

This page & overleaf top: Former J.W.A.-Gulf and Team Malcolm Guthrie Mirage M1, chassis no. M10001. Contributor: Chris Clarke of the Blackhawk Collection

Claude Nahum's Ford GTs

Claude Nahum can best be described as a passionate Ford motor racing fan with a particular passion for the Ford GT. He owns two of them. Claude has an extensive collection of very historic cars located in a special, purpose-built garage near his home in Geneva, Switzerland. The Ford GTs he owns are:

- Ford GT MkI chassis no. 1078.
- Ford GT MkIIB (former MkIIA) chassis no. 1016.

Note: Claude has compiled major dossiers on both the Ford GTs in his collection. The description in this section on chassis nos. 1078 and 1016 provides just a basic overview of the history of these Ford GTs, along with some information that Claude was not aware of until he met me. Hopefully one day Claude will publish his extensive dossiers on the two Ford GTs in his collection.

Chassis no. 1078

Whilst Ford GT MkI chassis no. 1078 does not have a spectacular

Claude Nahum and part of his collection. Contributor: Adrian Streather

Chassis no. 1078, photographed in 2004, when under the stewardship of Claude Nahum. Contributor: Claude Nahum

racing record it certainly has an interesting history. The Le Mans 1968 part of its story can be found in Chapter 4. Chassis no. 1078 was one of the Ford GTs that soldiered on into 1970 as a racing car before it was seriously damaged in a testing accident.

It was purchased new from J.W. Automotive in 1968 by Geoffrey Edwards Esq. of Jersey, the Channel Islands. Mr. Edwards led an interesting life. He appears to have made his fortune running Operation Magic Carpet, which was the codename for the delivery of weapons, including ex-RAF Lightning jet fighters, to the Government of Saudi Arabia in 1966. It's said that he purchased the Strathaven team and chassis no. 1078 for his son.

The J.W. Automotive delivery documents from 1968 state that chassis no. 1078 was painted Borneo green (colour code P031-4390), with a black-trimmed interior. It came with:

- A lightweight roof and lightweight panels.
- An aluminium, fully ducted spare wheel cover.
- Stage II vented discs.
- Orange springs with uprated Koni dampers.
- 1967 engine with Weslake heads brought up to 1968 specifications.
- BRM wheels with Goodyear tyres front and rear.

Chassis no. 1078 was primarily driven during the 1968 season by David Piper and Mike Salmon. It suffered its first major career shortening incident in May 1968 at the Spa 1000km race when Mike Salmon rolled it on the 22nd lap at Eau Rouge. Race conditions were typically Spa, wet, cold and miserable. The car was repaired and made ready for Le Mans in September.

Note: Le Mans in 1968 was held in September (as mentioned

in Chapter 4) which meant it became the last round of the World Championship and, in fact, it was the last race of the what was considered the professional racing season.

Another change took place within the Strathaven team before Le Mans. Eric Liddell was offered the drive with Mike Salmon, to replace David Piper. The ACO had accepted David Piper's own Ferrari 250LM as an entry for the big race. Richard Attwood was the other David Piper team driver.

Note: This situation worked out to David Piper's advantage because he and Richard Attwood finished seventh overall at Le Mans 1968.

Above: The original engine fitted to chassis no. 1078 just before it was replaced at Le Mans in 1968. Contributor: C. Nahum Collection; photograph by Gérard Crombac

Below: Chassis no. 1078, car no. 12, on the starting grid for Le Mans 1968. Contributor: Eric Liddell

Chassis no. 1078 in its new colour scheme as campaigned by Alain De Cadenet and David Weir in 1969 and 1970. Contributor: Manfred Förster

The records clearly show that the Strathaven Ltd. racing team disappeared after Le Mans 1968 (maybe it was just to be a one off effort). Whatever the reason, chassis no. 1078 was sold to Alain De Cadenet, who then sold a share of it to American driver David Weir. Together they campaigned the car under the team banners of Eurie Evergreen and then Team Snake Speed. The original colour scheme of Borneo Green was changed to dark blue, with a wide orange stripe down the middle.

Campaigning of chassis no. 1078 by Alain De Cadenet and David Weir, with backup drivers, Piers Forrester and Michael Ogier continued until the end of the official 1970 racing season. The last race in 1078's short career was the Paris 1000km, in October 1970.

The team had decided that chassis no. 1078 would continue into the 1971 racing season and David Weir had decided to have a go at another major sportscar race. He entered chassis no. 1078 under the Team Snake Speed name for the 1971 edition of the Daytona 24hr race in Florida, USA. However, whilst testing and preparing the car at Silverstone in late 1970, disaster struck, and David Weir crashed. The damage was so severe that the chassis (tub) assembly had to be written-off. The racing career of chassis no. 1078 was ended (or so it was thought at the time, for yet another Ford GT phoenix would soon arise from the ashes).

The crumpled remains of chassis no. 1078 were sold in 1971 to John Etheridge, the former J.W.A.-Gulf team mechanic. John purchased unused left-hand drive (LHD) chassis (tub) no. 1111 from P & M Racing Preparations, after proving to John Wyer that the original had genuinely been scrapped and disposed of.

Chassis (tub) no. 1111 was converted back to right-hand drive configuration, and the original data plate from chassis no. 1078 was transferred to the new chassis. Over the next few years, all the surviving components from the original chassis no. 1078 were also rebuilt and transferred to the chassis (tub) assembly and, eventually, from the ashes of the original came its authorised replacement. As part of the rebuilding process, the new chassis no. 1078 was prepared for road registration.

Chassis no. 1078 was finally road registered in June 1978, resplendent with its new red exterior and gold BRM wheels. This chassis was to move through a number of different owners in its new look. It even featured on the cover of the July 1982 edition of the magazine *Classic and Sportscar*.

Unfortunately, chassis no. 1078 was crashed in London by a friend of the AC/DC band member Phil Rudd, who had purchased it in September 1982. John Etheridge carried out the repairs, whereupon it was sent to New Zealand in 1984 and registered LR7381.

Chassis no. 1078 remained in New Zealand until 1990 when Phil Rudd sold it and the new owner had it shipped back to England.

Chassis no. 1078 retained its red paint until circa 1997 when it was repainted in its original Borneo green colour scheme.

After passing through the hands of Adrian Hamilton, this car was completely restored by Redman Bright Motor Race Engineering in 1998. It was during this restoration that it acquired its current widebody look. The restoration process took twenty-

Chassis no. 1078 photographed in the paddock at Montlhéry, France, in 1991 carrying the UK registration number CGG 943S. Contributor: les Coyotes

Chassis no. 1078 photographed with its new, original colour paint scheme in 1997. Contributor: Adrian Hamilton-Duncan Hamilton Ltd

two months. The test drive, at Silverstone, was undertaken by none other than Richard Attwood, who gave it a clean bill of health, and it's now registered XSU 161.

In October 2001, chassis no. 1078 was purchased by Claude Nahum. It was shipped to Geneva and was stored to wait out the Swiss winter.

In May 2002, this GT once again took to the track, and has been a regular entrant at historic races ever since, including:

- Le Mans Classic 24hr in 2002.
- Le Mans Classic 24hr in 2004.
- Spa 1000km in Belgium in 2005.

One of the other major highlights for Claude Nahum since

Chassis no. 1078 in action, driven by its current owner Claude Nahum. Contributor: Claude Nahum

Reunited. David Piper and his old racing mount from 1968. Contributor: Claude Nahum

Chassis no. 1078 photographed in Geneva, Switzerland in November 2005. Contributor: Adrian Streather

One last look at chassis no. 1078, this time in action at Spa in 2005.
Contributor: Claude Nahum

purchasing chassis no. 1078 was the visit, in 2004, of its former 1968 Strathaven team driver, David Piper.

This chassis has had its share of racing incidents, resulting in numerous minor repairs and a major restoration. However, it's always maintained in pristine condition and ready to race.

Chassis number 1016

Chassis no. 1016 is historically a very significant Ford GT and joins a select few of these top of the line, original Ford GTs in Europe.

The original racing exploits of this chassis are documented in Chapters 2 and 3 of this book. It's the Ford GT which came

Chassis no. 1016 in action at Le Mans in 1966 where it finished third. Contributor: C. Nahum Collection; photograph by Gérard Crombac

Chassis no. 1016 under new ownership doing what it should be doing. Maybe getting its nose cut off by a Chevron was not part of the plan, but it is part of racing. Contributor: Claude Nahum

Ford MkIIB, chassis no. 1016, as it appeared for its last race at the Daytona 24hr in 1967. Contributor: Ford Motor Company

third at Le Mans in 1966, driven by Ron Bucknam and Richard Hutcheson. Earlier in the 1966 racing season Ron Bucknam had been partnered in chassis no. 1016 by Richie Ginther at the Daytona 24hr and A.J. Foyt at the Sebring 12hr.

After Le Mans 1966, this chassis was shipped back to the USA and used for various motorshows and publicity events. Once the shows were over it was shipped to the Holman Moody facility and converted to MkIIB specifications for the upcoming 1967 racing season, in which it only participated in one race.

The last official track time for chassis no. 1016 was at the Le Mans trials in April 1967. After the trials it was shipped back to New York. The car was supposed to have been totally restored by Holman Moody prior to being donated to the Harrah Automobile Collection in Reno, Nevada, USA; but it wasn't. 1016 retained its Le Mans trials colour scheme, was given race number two decals, incorrectly serialised as chassis no. 1015, and, via a roundabout route of motorshows and displays, eventually arrived at Harrah's in 1970. Thirteen years later it was sold into the private sector, still incorrectly labelled as chassis no. 1015. It was not until 1992 that its true identity was discovered.

Chassis no. 1016, along with the real chassis no. 1015 and chassis no. 1046 were shipped to Le Mans in 1996 to celebrate the thirty year anniversary of their historic one-two-three finish. Unfortunately, chassis no. 1016 had been badly damaged in a race at Elkart Lake in the USA just prior to it being shipped to Le Mans. 1016 was hastily repaired and made to look the part, but was only able to crawl around the Le Mans Sarthe circuit.

Chassis no. 1016 on the Sarthe circuit in 1996, albeit going slowly. Contributor: les Coyotes

Chassis no. 1016 in the paddock with its equally famous brethren at Le Mans in 1996. Contributor: les Coyotes

Note: Chassis no. 1046, along with a couple of other very historically significant Ford GTs, was discovered by Adrian Hamilton, disassembled and packed in purpose-built packing crates in Belgium in 1983. Adrian agrees that with 20/20 hindsight he should have kept them.

Chassis no. 1016 was returned to the USA after the 1996 edition of the Goodwood Festival of Speed in England. On its return to the USA it underwent a full crash repair and restoration process. After the repairs and restoration were completed, the car continued to participate at major historic events around the world, including a return visit to the Goodwood Festival of Speed in 2003.

In 2004, chassis no. 1016 was put up for sale and Claude Nahum purchased it. Since this time it has continued to race at historic events all over Europe.

Chassis no. 1016 in action with its new owner at the Paul Ricard circuit in France. Contributor: Claude Nahum

When this section was being written, chassis no. 1016 was racing in Istanbul, Turkey, driven by its current owner Claude Nahum. Claude won his class in the race despite having to make a quick splash and dash pit stop after nearly running out of fuel a few laps earlier.

David Piper told the author during a recent conversation that he was mightily impressed with Claude's driving on the Istanbul F1 circuit. He said that Claude had mastered the new circuit very well and very quickly, despite the fact that it was pouring with rain.

David Piper also said that he was driving his Porsche 917 in the same race and he was not enjoying himself in the rain.

Chassis no. 1016 being prepared for its trip to Istanbul in November 2005. Contributor: Adrian Streather

Ford GT MkIIB (chassis no. 1016, third at Le Mans in 1966 as a MkIIA) on the Istanbul F1 circuit in November 2005. Claude Nahum won his class. Contributor: Claude Nahum

Ford GT survivors in Europe

Historic racing events very often provide perfect opportunities to photograph the Ford GT survivors. Here are just some, photographed over the past 23 years.

J.W.A.-Gulf team Ford MkI, chassis no. 1084, photographed in the Montlhéry circuit paddock in 1982. 1084 was built up around chassis no. 1004. Chassis no. 1004 was raced by the Shelby American Inc. team at Le Mans in 1965. Contributor: les Coyotes

Ford MkI, chassis no. 1082, was once part of the Ecurie Ford France team. This photograph was taken at an event at Montlhéry in 1982. Contributor: les Coyotes

Ford MkI, chassis no. 1071, at the Trocadero Esplanade in 1999. This Ford GT MkI was driven in the 1969 RAC British Sports Car Championship by Piers Forrester and Andrew Hedges. Andrew Hedges passed away in October 2005. He will be sorely missed. Contributor: les Coyotes

Ford MkI, chassis no. 1006, on the Montlhéry race track banking in 1995. This Ford GT was originally driven by Sir John Whitmore and Innes Ireland at Le Mans in 1965. Contributor: les Coyotes

Left: Ford GT MkI, chassis no. 1010, at the Le Mans Classic in 2004. This is the former Essex Wire Corporation, Terry Graham/Peter Sands Ford GT MkI that was driven at the Daytona 24hr and Sebring 12hr by Piers Forrester and Andrew Hedges in 1970. Contributor: les Coyotes

Below: Ford MkI, chassis no. 1023, at the Trocadero Esplanade in 1999. 1023 was purchased new in November 1965 from Ford Advanced Vehicles (F.A.V.) by Alan Mann Racing. It was later sold to Malcolm Gartlan who then campaigned it in the 1967 British RAC Sportscar Championship. It was often driven by either John Harris or David Prophet. Contributor: les Coyotes

Above: Ford GT MkI, chassis no. 1077 (purchased by Yamaha) at the 2004 Le Mans Classic. Contributor: les Coyotes

Ford GT MkI, chassis no. 1062, at the 2004 Le Mans Classic. This Ford GT was owned by the Ford Motor Company from 1966 until 1980. It has been in private hands ever since. Contributor: les Coyotes

Ford GT MkI, chassis no. 1042, in Scuderia Filipinetti colours at the Le Mans Classic in 2004. The body of this car is made from carbon fibre as the original was burnt out in 1967. Contributor: les Coyotes

Ford GT MkI, chassis no. 1018, at the 2004 Le Mans Classic. This was a Shelby American Inc. team car and was driven by David Piper and Australian Laurie O'Neill. Contributor: les Coyotes

Ford GT MkI, chassis no. 1014, at the 2004 Le Mans Classic. This was once part of the Neil Corner team and was sometimes driven by John Blades. It appears to have spent most of its time on the English racing circuits. Contributor: les Coyotes

Ford MkI, chassis no. 1051, at the Trocadero Esplanade in 1999. No racing history available. Contributor: les Coyotes

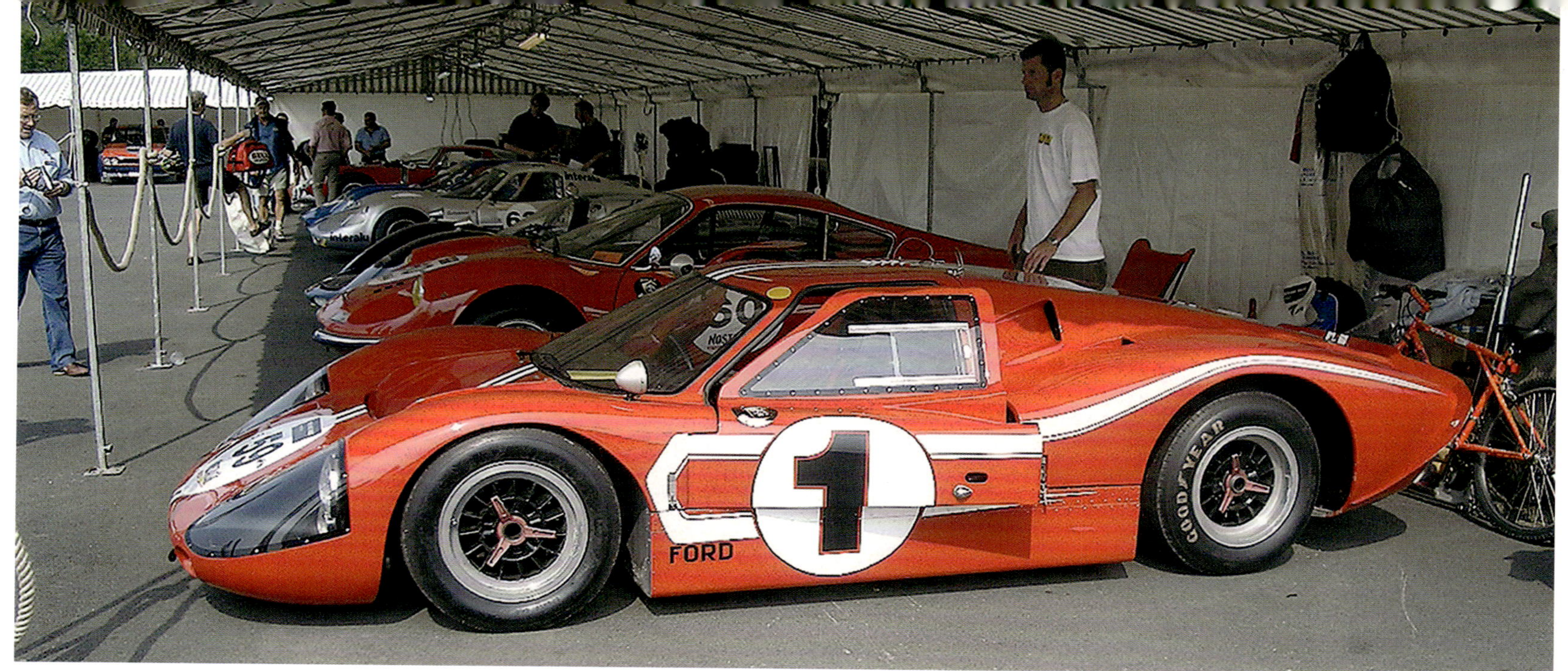

Ford GT MkIV, chassis no. J11, at the 2004 Le Mans Classic. This MkIV has no racing history from 1967. It was built by Brian Angliss in the UK from spare parts around an unstamped (manufactured in 1967) spare J-series chassis (tub) assembly. Contributor: les Coyotes

Ford GT MkIV, chassis no. J11, with its engine and more modern sub systems exposed. Contributor: les Coyotes

Roll of Honour

This Roll of Honour contains a comprehensive list of all the drivers (and their country of origin) who have driven or owned either the original Ford GT MkI/MkII/MkIIA/MkIIB/MkIV racing or the MkI or MkIII road cars.

A.J. Foyt (USA).
A. Bamford (UK).
A. Harmon (USA).
Adrian Hamilton (GB).
Al Virzi (USA).
Al Whatley (USA).
Alain De Cadenet (GB).
Alan Harvey (GB).
Alan Rees (GB).
André Bungener (CH).
Andrew Fletcher (GB).
Andrew Hedges (GB).
Anthony Hutton (UK).
Arthur Blank (CH).
Arthur Urciuoli (USA).
Augie Pabst (USA).
Bob Bondurant (USA).
Bob Brown (USA).
Bob Grossman (USA).
Bob Johnson (USA).
Bob McLean (CDN).
Bob Smith (GB).
Bob Vincent (GB).
Brian Auger (GB).
Brian Jordan (GB).
Brian Muir (AUS).
Brian Redman (GB).
Bruce Jennings (USA).
Bruce McLaren (NZ).
Bruce Spicer (AUS).
Bruno Thuner (CH).
Carlos Gaspar (P).
Carlos Pace (BR).
Carlos Santos (P).
Charles Lucas (GB).
Chris Amon (NZ).
Christopher J. Carver-Long (GB).
Claude Ballot-Léna (CH).
Claude Dubois (B).
Claude Nahum (CH)
Clive Baker (GB).
Colin Crabbe (GB).
Craig Fisher (CDN).
D.Brown (USA).
D. Schulz (USA).
Dan Gurney (USA).
David Bowden (AUS).
David Charlton (ZA).
David Davies (UK).
David Hobbs (GB).
David Piper (GB).
David Prophet (GB).
David Weir (USA).
Denis Borel (CH).
Denis Hulme (NZ).
Dennis Leech (GB).
Derek Bell (GB).
Dieter Spörry (CH).
Dominique Martin (CH).
Dr W. Arterberry (USA).
Duncan Hamilton (GB).
Edmond Meert (B).
E. Mather (UK).
Edsel Ford II (USA).
Edward Lowther (USA).
Edward Nelson (GB).
Emerson Fittipaldi (BR).
Emílio Marta (ANG).
Eppie Wietzes (CDN).
Eric Liddell (GB).
Eric Samon (F).
Félix Serra (E).
Firmin Dauwe (B).
Francis C. Grant (USA).
Francisco Godia-Sales (E).
François Mazet (F).
Frank Gardner (AUS).
Franz Albert (A).
Fred Lorenzen (USA).
Georges Crenier (B).
Georges Hacquin (B).
George Humble (GB).
George Lassum (AUS).
George Parlby (AUS).
Gordon Spice (GB).
George Stauffer (USA).
Graham Hill (GB).
Gustave Gosselin (B).
Guy Ligier (F).
Harley Cluxton (USA).
Henry Greder (F).
Helmut Kelleners (D).
Herbert Müller (CH).
Herbert von Karajan (A).
Herbert Wetanson (USA).
Hervé Bayard (F).
Howard Brown (USA).
Hughes de Fierlant (B).
Ian T. Richardson (GB).

Roll of Honour

Ian Williams (GB).
Innes Ireland (GB).
Jack Sears (GB).
Jackie Epstein (GB).
Jackie Oliver (GB).
Jackie Stewart (GB).
Jacky Ickx (B).
James Fielding (UK).
Jean "Beurlys" Blaton (B).
Jean Todt (F).
Jean-Claude Depret (F).
Jean-Claude Guérie (F).
Jean-Claude Ogier (F).
Jean-Daniel Grandjean (CH).
Jean-François Piot (F).
Jean-Michel Giorgi (CH).
Jean-Pierre Hanrioud (F).
Jean-Pierre Jabouille (F).
Jean-Pierre Rouget (F).
Jean Oulette (CDN).
Jeff Lewis (USA).
Jerry Grant (USA).
Jim George (USA).
Jo Schlesser (F).
Joakim Bonnier (S).
Jochen Neerpasch (D).
Jochen Rindt (A).
Joe Marcus (USA).
John Blades (GB).
John Cooper (GB).
John Cussins (GB).
John Davenport (GB).
John Harris (GB).
John Jordan (GB).
John Love (RSR).
John Macklin (GB).
John Mecom Jr. (USA).
John Miles (GB).
John Raeburn (AUS).
John M. Taylor (GB).
John Whitmore (GB).
José Juncadella (E).
Joseph Chandler (USA).
Juan Fernandez (E).
Julian Gerard (GB).
Julian Sutton (GB).
Keith Holland (GB).
Ken Miles (GB).
Kevin Bartlett AUS).
Lloyd Ruby (USA).
L. N. (Nick) Cussons (GB).
Laurie O'Neill (AUS).
Len Cheney (USA).
Lucien Bianchi (I).
Luís Fernandes (P).
M.Finburgh (GB).
M.R.J. Wyllie (GB).
Mac Daghorn (GB).
Malcolm Guthrie (GB).
Mario Andretti (USA).
Mario Cabral (P) Mario Casoni (I).
Mark Donohue (USA).
Martin Colvill (UK).
Martin Johnson (UK).
Masten Gregory (USA).
Maurice Charles (GB).
Maurice Henry (USA).
Maurice Trintignant (F).
Michel Martin (F).
Mike Hailwood (GB).
Mike Salmon (GB).
Mike Spence (GB).
Nicholas Granville-Smith (GB).
Neil Corner (GB).
Nino Vaccarella (I).
Noel Edmunds (GB).
Oscar Koveleski (USA).
P.Hess (USA).
Pablo Bréa (RA).
Paddy Driver (ZA).
Patrick McNally (AUS).
Paul Hawkins (AUS).
Paul Sands (GB).
Paul Vestey (GB).
Paul Weldon (UK).
Paulo Gomes (BR).
Pedro Rodriguez (MEX).
Peter Arundell (GB).
Peter de Klerk (ZA).
Peter Gaydon (GB).
Peter Gethin (GB).
Peter Lawson (GB).
Peter Procter (GB).
Peter Revson (USA).
Peter Rossler (D).
Peter Sadler (GB).
Peter Sutcliffe (GB).
Phil Hill (USA).
Phil Rudd (NZ).
Pierre Dumay (F).
Pierre Maublanc (F).
Piers Forrester (GB).
R.Clarke (GB).
R. Gronelli (NL).
R. L. Stafford (USA).
Raymond Caldwell (USA).
Ray Cuomo (USA).
Ray Heppenstall (USA).
Reinhold Jöst (D).
Richard Attwood (GB).
Richard Bond (GB).
Richard Holquist (USA).
Richard Hutcherson (USA).
Richard Thompson (USA).
Richie Ginther (USA).
Robert Danny (GB).
Robert Grossman (USA).
Robin Darlington (GB).
Robin Widdows (GB).
Ron Fry (GB).
Ronnie Bucknam (USA).
Roy Pierpoint (GB).
Roy Pike (USA).
Roy Salvadori (GB).
Sam Walton (USA).
Sid Taylor (GB).
Sidney Cardoso (BR).
Sir Max Aitken (GB).
Skip Scott (USA).
Steven H. Smith (GB).
T.C. Harrison (GB).
Terry J. Drury (GB).
Terry Sanger (GB).
Tim Schenken (AUS).
Tom Malloy (USA).
Tom Payne (USA).
Tony Bancroft (GB).
Tony Lanfranchi (GB).
Trevor Graham (GB).
Umberto Maglioli (I).
Vern Schuppan (AUS).
Vic Damone (USA).
Viscount Downe (GB).
W.Hill (USA).
William McNamara (USA).
William Wonder (USA).
Willie Green (GB).
Willy König (D).
Willy Mairesse (B).
Wilson Fittipaldi (BR).

References

Period documentation

Weekend Telegraph, May 1965, written by Courtney Edwards.

Autosport magazine, Vol. 33, No. 5, 1966.

Classic and Sportscar magazine, July 1966 issue.

Ford Advanced Vehicles delivery documentation for various chassis numbers.

Ford Advanced Vehicles (Ford of Britain) press releases:

- January 1966.
- April 1967.

J. W. Automotive delivery documentation for various chassis numbers.

J. W. Automotive spare parts purchase receipts.

Official racing program for the Daytona 24 hour Continental, at the Daytona International Speedway, February 2nd 1966.

Official racing program for the Sebring 12 hours of Endurance, Alitalia trophy at the Sebring raceway on March 26th 1966.

Official racing program for the Croft Autodrome on March 27th 1966.

Official racing program for the BRSCC International at Snetterton on April 8th 1966.

Official racing program for the 1000km Spa-Francorchamps on May 22nd 1966.

Official racing program for the Grovewood Trophy Car Races at Mallory Park on Whit Sunday, May 29th 1966.

Official racing program for the R.A.C. British Grand Prix at Brands Hatch on July 16th 1966.

Official racing program for the Guards International Trophy at Brands Hatch on August 29th 1966.

Official racing program for the Martini International at Silverstone on May 20th 1967.

Official racing program for the BUA International Trophy Meeting at Crystal Palace on the Spring Bank Holiday, May 29th 1967.

Official racing program for the R.A.C. British Grand Prix at Silverstone on July 15th 1967.

Official racing program for the Tourist Trophy Meeting at Oulton Park on June 3rd 1968.

Period articles written by:

- Patrick McNally, Sebring 12hr 1967.
- Gregor Grant, Sebring 12hr 1967.
- John Bolster, Le Mans testing 1967.
- Patrick McNally, Monza 1000km 1967.
- Patrick McNally, Spa-Francorchamps 1000km 1967.
- Alan Phillips, Targa Florio 1967.
- Patrick McNally, Nürburgring 1000km 1967.
- Gregor Grant, Le Mans 24hr 1967.
- John Bolster, Le Mans 24hr 1967.
- Bruce McLaren, Le Mans 1967.
- Patrick McNally, rule change investigative reports 1967.
- Patrick McNally, BOAC 500 at Brands Hatch 1967.
- Simon Taylor, Rheims 12hr 1967.
- Chris Nixon, Surfers Paradise 12hr 1967.
- Gregor Grant, Paris 1000km 1967.

Current documentation:

Cars for the Connoisseur (Editor Charles Harbord) editions:

- June 2001.
- February 2002.
- August 2003.
- September 2004.
- July 2005.
- November 2005.

Ford GT Mk.I chassis no. 1078 by Claude Nahum.

Ford GT Mk.IIA/B chassis no. 1016 by Claude Nahum.

Faszinierende Rennwagen - Hightech auf Rädern by John Tipler, published by Bechtermünz (Weltbild Verlag GmbH). Originally published as *Racing Cars - Masterpieces of Engineering* by Amber Books Ltd.

Ford Europe press releases:

- March 2003.
- July 2003.
- March 2004.
- November 2004.
- May 2005.

Technical:

Ford GT owner's manual by Ford Motor Co.

Ford GT specifications data by Ford Motor Co.

Note: Extensive use was made of the internet. It's not possible to list all the websites visited or what was found during each visit. However, I would like to thank the worldwide Ford GT enthusiast and motor racing communities for keeping all the racing legends alive.

Just some of the great motorsport & sports car books from Veloce Publishing –

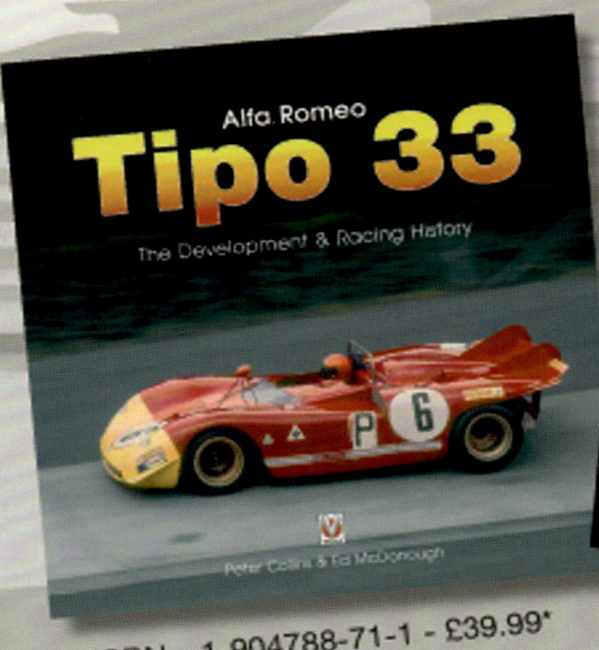

ISBN – 1-904788-71-1 - £39.99*

ISBN – 1-904788-31-9 - £34.99*

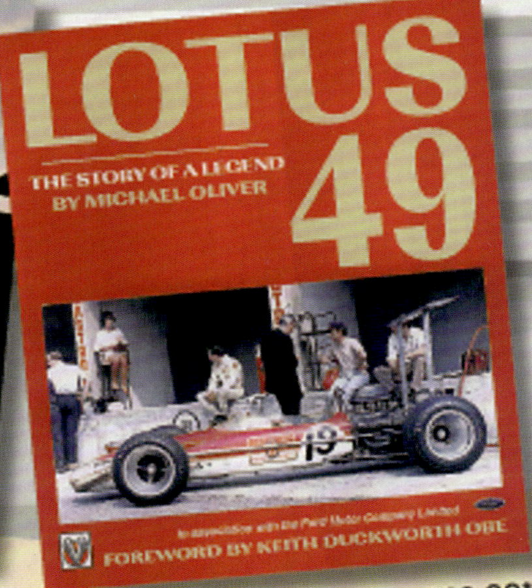

ISBN – 1-904788-01-7 - £50.00*

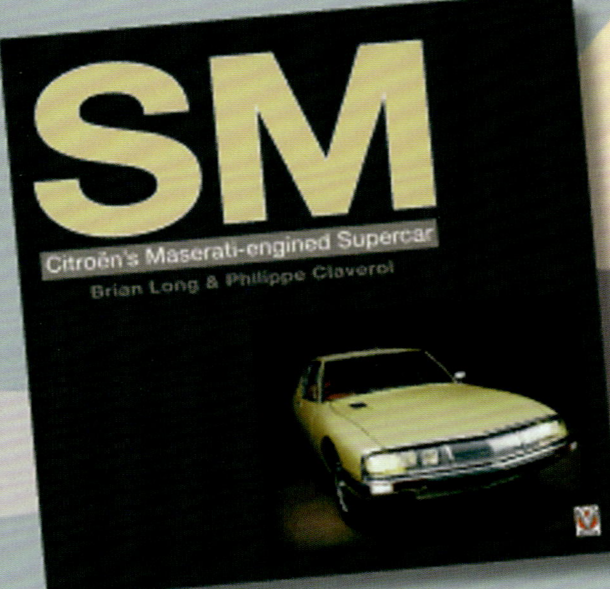

ISBN – 1-904788-60-2 - £39.99*

ISBN – 1-84584-052-6 - £17.99*

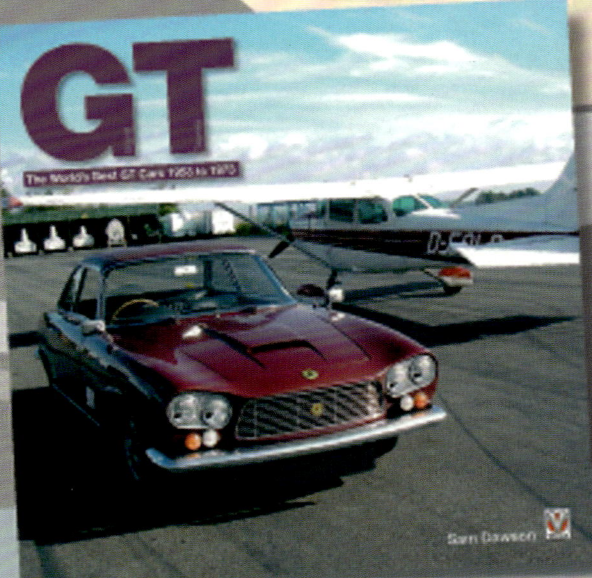

ISBN – 1-84584-060-7 - £25.00*

Index